PITTSBURGH AND THE APPALACHIANS

PITTSBURGH and the APPALACHIANS

Cultural and Natural Resources in a Postindustrial Age

Edited by

Joseph L. Scarpaci WITH Kevin J. Patrick

UNIVERSITY OF PITTSBURGH PRESS

Photographs and illustrations, unless otherwise noted, are by the editors or contributors.

Published by the University of Pittsburgh Press, Pittsburgh, Pa., 15260

Manufactured in the United States of America
Printed on acid-free paper
10 9 8 7 6 5 4 3 2 1

Library of Congress Cataloging-in-Publication Data

Pittsburgh and the Appalachians : cultural and natural resources in a postindustrial age / edited by Joseph L. Scarpaci with Kevin J. Patrick.

p. cm.

Includes bibliographical references and index.

ISBN 0-8229-4282-8 (cloth : alk. paper)

1. Pittsburgh (Pa.)—Economic conditions. I. Scarpaci, Joseph L. II. Patrick, Kevin Joseph.

HC108.P53P58 2006

330.9748'86—dc22 2006008631

In memory of Sam and Anthony Cicero
"Cultural Ambassadors" for Pittsburgh and the Region
Inspirations to their Children and Grandchildren
—JLS

In memory of James Youhon, Pittsburgher
—KJP

CONTENTS

ILLUSTRATIONS

PITTSBURGH AND THE APPALACHIANS

INTRODUCTION

Pittsburgh and the Appalachians in the New Millennium

Joseph L. Scarpaci

Few American cities reflect the challenges and promises of a new global economy more clearly than does Pittsburgh. America's economy is no longer premised on industrial prowess, and Pittsburgh and the Appalachians have had to use their cultural and natural resources to make the transition from a smokestack economy to one based on services. Hints of this metamorphosis were evident when the "steel city" ranked in the top five most livable cities in the 1983, 1985, and 1989 compilations of the *Places Rated Almanac*. This transition is nothing less than remarkable.

As a titan of the industrial age, Pittsburgh had one foot in the East (including the Appalachians) and the other in the Midwest. Located at the edge of the Allegheny Mountains, Pittsburgh was the doorway to the East. It provided access into the trans-Appalachian routes that led to Baltimore and Washington via the Potomac Valley and to Philadelphia, New York, and New England across southern Pennsylvania. Seated at the forks of the Allegheny and Monongahela rivers, Pittsburgh also prospered as the gateway to the West for traffic headed either down the Ohio Valley, or through the Beaver, Mahoning, and Cuyahoga valleys to the Great Lakes. In the catbird seat of the North American manufacturing belt, the city and region are endowed with essential industrial resources. Central to these were local metallic ores (enough to spark an early iron industry), lots of salt, sand for glassmaking, natural gas, oil, and plenty of bituminous coal from the Pittsburgh seam, arguably the world's richest mineral deposit. The city fulfilled its destiny as an industrial powerhouse in the twentieth century. Today, it struggles to position itself in a postindustrial age. Its historical legacy is laced with European immigrants and African Americans who came up from the Deep South in search of better-paying jobs. These workers gave the barons of nineteenth and twentieth American capitalism—Andrew Carnegie, George Westinghouse, Andrew Mellon, and others—their dedication, sweat, and sacrifice to forge great industrial empires.

I can still recall the bitter smells emanating from the Jones and Laughlin (J&L) steel plant on the banks of the Monongahela River as I was whisked along the Parkway as a young child. That same mill gave me a chance to earn $7.25 per hour as nonunion laborer way back in 1972. That rate is significantly higher than the 2005 minimum wage of $5.15. These wage levels—separated by thirty-three years of urban history—lend themselves to facile interpretations of the city's fate: deindustrialization cut Pittsburgh's ties to Appalachia, eliminated well-paying jobs, and ushered in too many low-paying jobs, such as burger flipping at fast-food restaurants.

This explanation is much too simplistic. In the place where J&L once stood there now stands a high-tech research and development complex that grew out of a public-private partnership (something that Pittsburgh is particularly good at). Carnegie Mellon University and several high-tech firms grace that spot on the river's floodplain. Next to the complex is the 2.5-mile Eliza Furnace Trail; a rails-to-trails path wedged between the inbound and outbound lanes of Interstate 376 (the Parkway). It is crammed with joggers, cyclists, walkers, and skaters and affords a view of the glass- and-steel-clad research and development park as well as the large-faced clock and stacked houses of the city's South Side. This riverbank transformation speaks volumes about Pittsburgh and the Appalachians in the postindustrial age and mirrors broader trends in America at large.

I recall my parents and grandparents telling us how schoolchildren in the 1930s and 1940s would bathe and change their clothes in the middle of the day because of the heavy ash fallout from the city's furnaces. The bulky steelworks along the rivers made us believe that the smelly gases were a natural by-product of the iron and steel industry. As high school and college students, we took pride in knowing that the newly formed Environmental Protection Agency (1970) borrowed heavily from Pittsburgh and Allegheny County's air and water quality codes. It became clear, even on the eve of Pittsburgh's slide into deindustrialization, that the city and region had much to teach the rest of the nation.

Native Pittsburghers who have lived through the region's transformation have heard more than their fair share of disparaging remarks about the city's dirty air. Many people still believe falsely that the air quality remains at World War II levels. We enjoy telling those critics about the Golden Triangle, the funicular railways (inclines), Oakland's Pitt and Carnegie Mellon campuses, Schenley Park, the Strip District, Schenley Farms, the South Side, Chatham Village, Mt. Washington, and the city's close proximity to hiking, skiing, and whitewater sports in the Laurel Highlands, the Alleghenies, and the entire Appalachian range.

The city and region discussed in these pages are markedly different from the city of my youth. Unionized workers formed almost a third of the workforce when we were kids, but today union numbers have been cut to less than half that number. Health care and specialized services have replaced steel and manufacturing as the leading source of jobs. Pittsburgh's suburbs have sprawled in all directions and have cost the city a growing population base. The old football and baseball stadiums fell to the bulldozers, and Pittsburgh, like most US cities, has built new stadiums to attract a broader fan base and strengthen its economy. And the Appalachians are no longer idle lands that need to be developed with roads and mined for coal; there, recreation and niche services have created new paths to economic development. In terms of deindustrialization, decline in blue-collar unionization, greater suburbanization, and downtown revitalization, Pittsburgh and the Appalachians resemble much of the manufacturing belt (that elusive region found loosely in the triangle consisting of points between Boston, Duluth, and St. Louis). The chapters here will enhance the reader's understanding of these broad processes that have transformed America during the past half century. While profiles of Pittsburgh and the Appalachians dominate these pages, they also tell a story about America at large.

I

TWENTY-FIRST-CENTURY PITTSBURGH

Cities and regions are dynamic spaces that reflect changes on different geographic scales. Each scale offers a particular vantage point through which the forces driving those changes—economics, technology, politics, and culture—can be understood. Here, geographers Kevin Patrick and Ted Muller provide a sweeping portrayal of Pittsburgh from its heroic plans for downtown revitalization, through the urban morphology of its neighborhoods, to the dynamic evolution of its Monongahela Valley mill towns.

First, Muller shows how the various downtown renewal programs executed since the end of World War II have been essential in ensuring that Pittsburgh stays ahead of the industrial and economic forces nipping away at its allure. Efforts to revive retailing on Firstside, Fifth Avenue, and the adjacent North Side–North Shore complex are also key in getting locals to shop in, work in, and visit the city center. Muller's articulation of Pittsburgh's recent past reveals the triumphs and challenges experienced by one American city in an era of progressive modernism, decentralization, and economic restructuring.

In chapter 2 Kevin Patrick borrows what is perhaps the most recognizable land-use figure in urban sociology and urban geography: Burgess's concentric zone model, as modified by Homer Hoyt's sector model. Originally conceptualized on the Chicago experience of the 1920s, the concentric zone model aims to explain how the early twentieth century American city accommodated industrialization and population growth fueled by national and international immigration. In the case of Chicago, topography was relatively flat and the eastern edge of Lake Michigan enabled Burgess to identify a fairly uniform geometry that radiated out from the city's central business district at the waterfront. But what about hilly Pittsburgh with its three rivers and dissected plateau, hills, and hollows? Patrick grafts the city onto the Burgess model and shows how aspects of the city's past conforms to key features of Burgess's model. Underlying this chapter is the idea that the shape of a city and its various sectors and zones of land use reflect broader economic processes that drive industrial capitalism.

In "The Steel Valley," Ted Muller carefully documents the industrial restructuring of the Monongahela Valley, Pittsburgh's steep-walled bastion of heavy manufacturing, primary metals, and metal fabrication. He details how public-private partnerships characterize the evolution of the city's steel industry. These alliances have moved from big political and economic stakeholders to smaller, more complex and civic-based organizations. The chapter shows how some community and business groups, whether arguing for more rail-to-trail conversions along the rivers, or niche firms carving out a toehold in specialized manufacturing or high-tech production, make up the renaissance of the twenty-first century.

ONE

Downtown Pittsburgh

RENAISSANCE AND RENEWAL

Edward K. Muller

Despite a metropolitan population in decline since 1960, steady suburbanization, and the loss of several major corporate headquarters in the past two decades, downtown Pittsburgh remains a vigorous and vital central business district, in marked contrast to the downtowns of many older mid-level cities. Office occupancy rates remain stable, and the rehabilitation of older buildings indicates a steady demand for office space. Cultural attractions and tourism are increasing; hotel space is being expanded. Although retailers struggle to compete with suburban malls, they remain an integral part of the downtown business mix. Parking is tight, traffic congestion is a constant annoyance, loft housing is growing in popularity, and the boundaries of downtown are expanding, albeit slowly, to the east and north across the Allegheny River. Several factors particular to Pittsburgh helped to sustain the Golden Triangle, as downtown is frequently called, during the post–World War II era when the downtowns of other cities were rapidly deteriorating. But, most notably, active involvement of the civic leadership—both public and private—through programs of urban renaissance, renewal, and redevelopment has played a major role in maintaining the downtown's viability.

Postwar Renaissance

In 1943 when Pittsburgh's leaders turned their attention, however briefly, away from the war and toward the future of their city, they despaired over what they saw. Despite the concentration of powerful industrial corporations in the region, a severely degraded environment so diminished the quality of life that corporations not only found it increasingly difficult to recruit and retain topflight personnel but some even considered moving their headquarters out of Pittsburgh to New York City. Dense smoke lay over the city many days like a dirty blanket, defying earlier attempts at control. Downtown was merely a small triangle of land formed by the convergence of the Monongahela and Allegheny rivers to form the Ohio. Vehicular traffic, streetcars, and railroads that ran on both riverfronts consumed portions of the historic Point and severely congested downtown. Although a federally sponsored flood control program was finally underway, the memory of the devastating 1936 St. Patrick's Day flood added to the dismal image. Assessment values of downtown real estate had not recovered from Depression lows, and no new office buildings had been completed for more than a decade (Alberts 1980, 57–58). Although the first major highway improvements were under construction after years of squabbling among governmental agencies, many projects remained on the planner's shelves, mired in local politics. The private, nonprofit Pittsburgh Regional Planning Association had scored some successes since its rejuvenation in 1936, but the slow pace of progress left its leaders despairing at the scale of the task that confronted them (Lubove 1969, 87–105).

Under the leadership of chairman Howard Heinz, who died unexpectedly in 1941, and executive director Wallace Richards, the Pittsburgh Regional Planning Association had taken the lead role in promoting and shepherding projects through the labyrinth of politics and bureaucratic agencies. Nevertheless, frustrated at the limited progress, civic leaders organized the Allegheny Conference on Community Development in 1943 as a means to develop a postwar plan, elicit broad community support, and focus the energies of the city's powerful corporate leaders. One hundred and fifty community leaders constituted the Allegheny Conference (as it is usually called), but Richard K. Mellon, heir to the powerful Mellon family financial interests, dominated the organization. Under Mellon, the Allegheny Conference engaged able planning consultants, established an agenda for renewal of the city, and lined up private sector consensus behind it. Significantly, the Republican, Protestant, and blue-blooded Mellon, of Ulster descent, recognized the necessity of working closely with the city's Democratic Party boss, Irish Catholic David L. Lawrence, who came from distinctly humbler origins. Communicating through aides (for reportedly the two men rarely met), Mellon and Lawrence formed a public-private partnership of considerable clout, which engineered twenty years of redevelopment and bowled over opposition to specific projects (Stewman and Tarr 1982).

Plans for improving Pittsburgh after the war addressed four concerns: an overspecialized economy, degraded environment, inadequate infrastructure, and deteriorating downtown. The city's planners and civic leaders had participated in national discussions on solving urban problems, which had taken place for years before and during the war. Generally, proposals for Pittsburgh reflected the accepted wisdom of the day, similar to those under discussion for many other cities. What set Pittsburgh apart, however, was its ability to get the renewal process underway before the federal acts of 1949 and 1954 jump-started urban renewal in most cities (Teaford 1990). State legislation passed between 1945 and 1947 allowed Allegheny County and Pittsburgh to undertake redevelopment and set up authorities that could raise revenue, operate beyond the jurisdiction of a single municipality, and avoid local political embroilments (Lubove 1969, 106–41).

Leaders used traditional industrial development methods with some success to attract new companies that would help to diversify the economy and keep local industries from moving out of the region. Bolder strategies were needed, however, to tackle the environmental and infrastructural issues critical to encouraging new investment, especially downtown. With flood control largely a federal responsibility and dam and reservoir construction underway, air pollution loomed large among local environmental issues. Enforcement of the smoke abatement ordinance that was passed in 1941 but held in abeyance until after the war tested the public-private partnership. Mellon employed heavy-handed tactics to obtain compliance by local companies and the railroads, while Democratic Mayor Lawrence risked the support of both coal miners opposed to reducing coal consumption and his working-class electorate facing costs of conversion from coal to gas heating fuels. Enforcement began in October 1946, and Pittsburgh's skies brightened during the ensuing decade. The creation of a multicommunity sewer authority and construction of a new sewage treatment plant began the long process of cleaning up the rivers. The construction of the area's first two expressways to the east and west from downtown and the opening of a state-of-the-art airport in 1951 addressed important transportation needs. The stage was being set for downtown redevelopment (Stewman and Tarr 1982).

The tip of the Golden Triangle, known as the Point, held the key for redeveloping downtown. Railroad warehouses and tracks, highways, an unused exposition building serving as a pound for towed cars, vacant lots, run-down shops and houses, and tons of litter sullied the historic Point area. Traffic to and from the two bridges at the Point made redeveloping the area a particularly difficult design problem. Since the turn of the century, many plans, including those of illustrious designers Frederick Law Olmsted Jr.,

FIG. 1.1. Gateway Center. Testament to Renaissance I, Gateway Center anchors the end of Forbes Avenue, which along with paralleling Fifth Avenue awaits a controversial remake, ca. 1960. Courtesy of Carnegie Library of Pittsburgh.

E. H. Bennett, Robert Moses, and Frank Lloyd Wright, had been proposed to rejuvenate the Point in recognition of its geographical and historical significance. Efforts to designate it as a national park site had only recently collapsed. The design solution came with the bold decision to tear down the two bridges and build new ones upstream a short ways in order that more of the Point would be free of traffic and available for a park. The subsequent decision to go ahead with the construction of a thirty-six-acre state park in turn attracted the interest of private capital in an adjacent twenty-three-acre redevelopment parcel, which became known as Gateway Center (figure 1.1). The new Urban Redevelopment Authority acquired the land; the Equitable Life Assurance Society (of New York) became the developer. Between 1950, when construction began, and the mid-1960s, seven high-rise office buildings, a Hilton Hotel, a residential apartment tower, and an underground parking garage arose to comprise the redevelopment complex (Alberts 1980).

Point State Park and Gateway Center symbolized the rejuvenation of the city. Renaissance, as the postwar redevelopment became known, moved eastward up the Golden Triangle in the early 1950s with the announcement that the Mellon foundations would give the city a park and underground garage comprising nearly an entire block. Mellon Square opened up a densely developed uptown area and anchored two new corporate skyscrapers, one by ALCOA and the other housing both Mellon Bank and US Steel. At the same time, long-standing plans for redeveloping the lower Hill District, an old immigrant and now African American slum a few blocks east of Mellon Square, were dusted off and recast as a cultural center. Beginning in 1955, this project displaced more than 1,500 families and 400 businesses from a ninety-five-acre site, where, with the largesse of department store magnate Edgar Kaufmann, the Civic Arena with a retractable roof served as a combination sports arena and venue for the Civic Light Opera. Hopes that the arena would spark further development of other cultural activities did not materialize. Instead parking lots and the long-planned Crosstown Expressway isolated the Civic Arena from downtown. With the exception of two apartment buildings and a hotel, little additional development took place on the site for several decades (Lubove 1969, 106–41). The lower Hill project was a classic example of an urban renewal failure.

In the 1960s, however, as the twenty-year-old Renaissance moved away from downtown to large neighborhood renewal projects, no one could foresee that the lower Hill District site would not soon develop. The environmental successes, new infrastructure, and downtown projects had energized this older industrial city, giving Pittsburgh confidence that it would remain one of the nation's most powerful metropolitan centers. Although an extensive economic study published in 1963 warned that economic diversification had still not taken place and predicted a severely diminished steel industry within twenty years, civic leaders blithely moved forward with plans for a new all-sports stadium (across the Allegheny River from downtown), an innovative rapid transit system (focused on downtown and not built until the end of the 1970s), and many other projects about the city and county. With the aid of Point State Park, Gateway Center, Mellon Square, the Civic Arena, and new expressways, the Golden Triangle avoided the ravages of retail and office decentralization that debilitated so many other American downtowns. Several reasons account for this fact. The population of the Pittsburgh metropolitan area grew slowly in the 1950s and peaked in 1960. The region was not constructing or even planning a circumferential beltway. Corporate leaders still preferred downtown for their headquarters, and were under pressure from the Allegheny Conference to remain there. Thus, while suburbanization was putting stress on downtown retail stores, new suburban malls and office complexes were not yet growing so fast as to threaten the Golden Triangle's supremacy.

Renaissance II

Renaissance I represented a turning point in Pittsburgh's history. It reversed the downward trajectory in the Golden Triangle, began the critical cleanup of the city's environment, modernized several aspects of the infrastructure, and established a tradition of public-private partnerships. The legacy of Renaissance I is not only visible in downtown's landscape but is also palpable in the spirit of partnership, action, and success that civic leaders drew upon during the deindustrialization and social crises of the 1980s. Dubbed Renaissance II in 1977 by incoming mayor Richard Caliguiri, the second period of redevelopment lasted a little more than a decade, involved greater initiative by local government than in the previous period, was spread more widely about the Golden Triangle, and in the end probably had a greater effect on the downtown landscape. Some observers dispute that there was truly a second renaissance because there was not to the same degree a plan or an agency driving the process as there had been after World War II. Nevertheless, under the leadership of Mayor Caliguiri, both the Urban Redevelopment Authority and the newly created Mayor's Development Council (a body comprised of several city department heads and authority directors) attracted private investors, shepherded development projects through governmental steps, leveraged public funds, and generally nurtured continued downtown redevelopment. Thus, the public sector acted as catalyst for numerous skyscraper projects, upgraded downtown infrastructure to encourage private investment, welcomed redevelopment inspired by historic preservation, and cooperated fully with a nonprofit initiative to develop cultural attractions (Stewman and Tarr 1982).

Renaissance I ended with the election of Mayor Pete Flaherty in 1970. Capitalizing on the rising civil rights and anti–urban renewal sentiment of the 1960s, Flaherty attacked the Allegheny Conference for elitism, Renaissance's focus on downtown redevelopment, and the neglect of the neighborhoods. He terminated the public-private partnership, sued successfully to derail Allegheny County's innovative Skybus rapid transit system, instituted budgetary austerity, and shifted half of federal aid to the neighborhoods (Muller, Coleman, and Houston 1999). Despite the contentious relationships among civic leaders and the diminished focus on downtown, a few new projects came to fruition during the Flaherty years and a few others advanced in planning, which would later be associated with the Renaissance when they were finished in the 1980s (Lubove 1996, 58–61). US Steel erected its sixty-four-story headquarters building in 1971, and three thirty-plus-story towers went up in Oliver Plaza (containing two bank office headquarters). Disappointed that the Civic Arena project failed to generate a cultural complex, the Heinz foundation under the leadership of Heinz family scion, H. J. Heinz II, funded the renovation of an old movie theater into a concert hall for the Pittsburgh Symphony. Finally, before Flaherty left office in 1977 plans for both a new convention center and a limited conventional light-rail transit network were completed, and discussions begun on upgrading Grant Street into a grand corporate address (Stewman and Tarr 1982, 91–94).

Acrimony between city hall and the Allegheny Conference, the much-publicized failure of the Skybus transit proposal, darkening clouds over the steel industry, mounting population losses, inner-city social turmoil, and the fiscal distress of cities around the country produced a sense of stagnation and pending crisis for the city in spite of the apparent continuing development momentum in these interim years between the two Renaissance periods. Downtown seemed to be in need of additional help. Both districts paralleling the rivers had underutilized older buildings, growing numbers of surface parking lots, little new investment, and in one case a vigorous vice trade. The department stores had begun to struggle in their competition with suburban malls as white flight accelerated, especially after the 1968 Martin Luther King riot in the Hill District. The once vital Fifth Avenue retail corridor between the Horne's and Kaufmann's department stores began to look shabby and increasingly catered to lower-income African American shoppers, who had lost their neighborhood business district in the adjacent lower Hill District to urban renewal. The axis of upscale shopping had begun to gravitate to Smithfield Street, running perpendicular to Fifth Avenue.

Incoming Mayor Caliguiri tried to address this general malaise by invoking the Renaissance spirit. A second Renaissance, even one that would also include the neighborhoods, he argued, would rejuvenate downtown once again. He revived the public-private partnership, set up his Mayor's Development Council, and directed his departments to cooperate with developers. Construction began on the convention center in 1977 and on the light-rail transit line, including a short downtown subway, in 1981. The city rebuilt Grant Street with brick paving and expensive landscaping. Eight office towers went up, three of them in association with ground-level retail complexes and one with a new hotel. The most ambitious of them was the PPG Place complex adjacent to old Market Square, designed by Philip Johnson. The project consisted of a forty-story tower, six low-rise buildings, and a plaza, all covering six city blocks (figure 1.2). PPG Place would not have succeeded without the city's involvement in declaring property blighted and using its power of eminent domain. Similarly, the city cooperated with the developers of Grant Street Plaza with a fifty-four-story office tower by reconfiguring streets and assigning subsurface and air rights for the subway and parking. In the case of the Liberty Center project, a hotel and twenty-seven-story

FIG. 1.2. PPG Place.

office building next to the new convention center, the city initiated the development and found the developer. With the addition of privately developed Oxford Center with a forty-six-story tower, Fifth Avenue Place, and a few smaller office buildings, the supply of office and upscale retail space vastly expanded. These developments were scattered around downtown, not having the total impact on one district as Gateway Center had during Renaissance I (Lubove 1996, 57–85).

Despite the construction of several large building complexes since World War II, many older buildings with architectural merit and entire blocks of pre–World War I structures remained. Historic preservation, especially with federal tax incentives legislated in the 1970s and 1980s for the rehabilitation of commercial buildings, became an important force in downtown redevelopment during Renaissance II. Although public officials were irritated by preservation advocacy for buildings in the path of new construction, they were more than willing to encourage preservation when it promised to develop buildings or areas that were not the focus of new development. Preservation developers targeted the ten-block area paralleling the Monongahela Wharf, which contained some of oldest mercantile, warehouse, and office buildings in downtown. It had been a backwater ever since development moved away from the wharf to the center of the Golden Triangle in the late nineteenth century. The city responded by renaming the area Firstside, cooperating with its designation as a national historic district, discouraging the creation of surface parking lots, and encouraging the rehabilitation of many structures into professional offices and lofts. Today, Firstside is a stable complement to downtown. A few blocks north toward the heart of downtown, the city cooperated in maintaining the historical character of Pittsburgh's "little Wall Street." Fourth Avenue was once the center of dozens of banks, private investment houses, and savings institutions, which arose from lucrative investments in oil, gas, coal, and iron and steel. Although the local stock exchange closed early in the century and demolition had diminished the number of buildings, the street's designation as a national historic district has helped to preserve its turn-of-the-century office architecture and canyonlike streetscape reminiscent of lower Manhattan. Elsewhere in downtown, preservation incentives led to the rehabilitation of scattered individual buildings such as the Daniel Burnham–designed Pennsylvania Railroad station and the former Romanesque-style Old German Savings Bank on Sixth Avenue. The modest success of preservation in downtown has staved off the worst effects of classic urban renewal and modernism and helped to maintain the critical high-density development and diversity of buildings fabric that make downtown a successful landscape (Toker 1986, 33–41). Nevertheless, preservation advocates have to remain vigilant because city officials and developers frequently do not value or respect the contribution of older buildings to the Golden Triangle's success.

Preservation also played a key role in the strategy for redeveloping the fourteen square blocks paralleling the Allegheny River between Stanwix and Eleventh streets, known as the Penn-Liberty corridor. However, the primary means for redevelopment involved the cultivation of cultural amenities such as the symphony, opera, ballet, and theater, which, it was argued, would enhance both the city's competitive edge for economic investment over other metropolitan areas and downtown's distinctiveness within the metropolitan area. The success of Heinz Hall (1971) and the adjoining Heinz Plaza parklet (1979) pointed out the potential of cultural attractions, but the concert hall's location in the Penn-Liberty corridor left it isolated from other downtown facilities and embedded in a deteriorating area of warehouses, wholesalers, and vice activities. Moreover, when downtown's remaining movie theater closed during the 1970s, nightlife besides the vice trade nearly disappeared. Acting on consultants' advice, the leadership of H. J. Heinz II, and the financial support of the Howard Heinz Endowment foundation, the Allegheny Conference incorporated the Pittsburgh Cultural Trust in 1984 to oversee the transformation of the Penn-Liberty corridor into a cultural district. The Cultural Trust acted as developer, facilities manager, and service provider to arts organizations. With the city's financial and planning cooperation the Cultural Trust became the central actor in the redevelopment of a major portion of downtown. Its goals were to remove the vice trade, support both Heinz Hall and the new convention center (also located in the area), enhance the city's cultural institutions, and restore nightlife in downtown (Lubove 1996, 194–201).

Between 1984 and 1987, the Trust engineered the conversion of the old Stanley Theater into the Benedum Center for Performing Arts and the construction of the CNG (Consolidated Natural Gas) Tower, from which the Trust received substantial income. The city and the Trust then obtained the designation of a sizable portion of the area as a national historic district and with that in place undertook a street and building facade improvement program. While the office construction of Renaissance II ended with the recession that swept across the nation at the end of the decade, the Trust continued its redevelopment of the Penn-Liberty corridor or Cultural District, as it has become known. During the 1990s it converted another movie house into a theater for smaller arts companies (the Byham), turned an X-rated movie theater into a venue for foreign and specialty films (the Harris), opened an art gallery, completed the construction of a new facility (the O'Reilly) for the popular Pittsburgh Public Theater, which allowed it to move into the district, and built the first phase of a riverfront park. Other indications of the success of the redevelopment process include rehabilitation of some historic buildings for loft apartments; the transformation of the Fulton office building into an upscale hotel; new restaurants; the architecturally noteworthy expansion of the convention center; a planned new hotel; and the opening of a high school for the performing arts. Still, considerable work remains to be done in the district.

While Mayor Caliguiri hoped in 1977 that a second renaissance would breathe life into a city experiencing long-term decline, he articulated a more ambitious goal at Renaissance II's mid-point in the 1980s. Surveying the carnage of deindustrialization, the mayor declared that downtown's new office towers, streetscapes, cultural amenities, rapid transit, and historic rehabilitation were aiding the city and region's transformation to a vigorous urban economy built around education, research, health care, advanced technology industries, and professional and business services (Lubove 1996, 61). The city assisted private and nonprofit developers with tax abatements, land assembly, low-interest loans, street improvements, and cooperation in many other ways. By 1990 large sections of downtown had undergone substantial redevelopment and office occupancy rates remained above 80 percent, but problems remained in the retail and entertainment functions. Nightlife was minimal and concentrated in the emerging Cultural District, and there were too few residential opportunities.

Post-Renaissance Developments

Mayor Caliguiri's untimely death in 1988 coincided roughly with the end of Renaissance II. The accumulating pressures of increased population loss, plant closings, rising unemployment, declining tax revenues, and the na-

FIG. 1.3. Fifth Avenue corridor.

tional recession caused the next administration to become far less entrepreneurial. Development activity in downtown subsided, and a few projects planned in the 1980s collapsed for lack of funding. Nevertheless, pressure built for completing the Cultural District, improving the dilapidated Fifth Avenue retail corridor, expanding convention business, and stimulating more nightlife and a downtown residential community. By the mid-1990s the burgeoning national economy renewed the demand for downtown office space. With his election as mayor in 1994, Tom Murphy actively addressed these issues with the full satchel of governmental assistance strategies and even, as in Renaissance II, some initiation of projects. The concentration of new or planned projects in an expanded downtown area has observers beginning to talk about a third renaissance.

The city's major downtown initiative at the end of the century has been the effort to revive retailing in the Fifth Avenue corridor (figure 1.3). It helped Lazarus close its old department store adjacent to Gateway Center (formerly Horne's) and construct a new one on Fifth Avenue. One block further up Fifth, the city encouraged Lord & Taylor to come to downtown and adaptively reuse the historic Mellon Bank building (1924). In a controversial move, the city and Urban Redevelopment Authority negotiated a deal with a Chicago developer to assemble several blocks at the lower end of Fifth and permit the removal of many businesses and demolition of numerous older buildings in order to develop a mall-like complex of national retail shops and entertainment attractions. Preservationists opposed the potential destruction of so much of downtown's older building fabric; others doubted the wisdom of turning over so much space to stores that duplicate those found in suburban malls. Both opponents believed that downtown would lose some of its distinctiveness if this plan were implemented. The deal collapsed. The city in cooperation with local businesses and preservationists created a set of principles for redevelopment, and has contracted with a new developer for reviving the area.

The city also helped both Mellon Bank and PNC Bank find downtown locations for new large-operations office buildings. The city worked closely with the state to enact a plan that more than doubled the size of the convention center and reoriented it towards the Allegheny River. Since the convention center is located in the Cultural District, civic leaders believed that it would enhance the viability of the area's cultural attractions and nightlife. The securing of state financial support became entangled with the city and county's efforts to fund two new sports stadiums. Together the package of funding for the stadiums and convention center affirmed a trend towards the expansion of downtown's boundaries beyond its historic limits. Perhaps, the initial expansion of downtown occurred in the 1970s when the Pittsburgh History and Landmarks Foundation purchased the Pittsburgh and Lake Erie Railroad station and freight buildings on the south shore of the Monongahela River directly across from downtown (and Firstside). The development of the properties into a retail, entertainment, office, and hotel complex created a successful destination point and a complement to downtown (Lubove 1996, 218–23). In the 1980s, lawyers and other professionals rehabilitated older buildings to the east along Forbes and Fifth avenues, pushing downtown a few blocks beyond the Crosstown Expressway that had acted as a barrier since its completion in 1964. The construction of Two Chatham Center added to this eastward movement.

The biggest expansion of downtown, however, is north across the Allegheny River (see also chapter 8). The city and county are intent on creating a corridor of activities on both sides of the river. This strategy reflects the realization by civic leaders that the rivers are once again essential to the city's future, but this time as both a natural and recreational amenity rather than simply part of the region's industrial infrastructure (Muller 2003). The new stadiums and reoriented convention center are the centerpieces of the plan. They are joined on the north shore by Alcoa's new corporate headquarters, a few older warehouses rehabilitated into offices, planned development around the stadiums, the Andy Warhol Museum, and the Carnegie Science Center and Heinz corporate complex at each end. On the Allegheny River's south shore, in addition to the convention center, the Cultural District complements the new north shore developments and is linked to the stadiums on game days by the limiting of the Roberto Clemente Bridge (formerly the Sixth Street Bridge) to pedestrians. The conversion of older riverfront properties into new developments has enhanced the vitality of the corridor, and the inevitable development of several prime riverfront acres of what is now surface parking upriver between Eleventh Street and the vibrant Strip District will extend the corridor and with it downtown. On both shores, riverfront trails, completed or in planning stages, tie the activities together.

The landscape of Pittsburgh's Golden Triangle still reflects its origins as an eastern North American downtown. It has a marvelous mix of architectural styles, ornamental sculptures, and building facades of different textures and colors. Constrained by the three rivers, it is densely developed with many skyscrapers and relatively few surface parking lots creating gaps in the block fronts. Streets and sidewalks are narrow. And the awkward, angular conjunction at Liberty Avenue of the two original rectangular street plans, one fronting the Monongahela River and the other the Allegheny River, has created visual delights for pedestrians and architects, but headaches for traffic engineers. Each weekday the sidewalks are crowded with people bustling about, the streets filled with cars and buses. The intensity of activity says this is downtown.

Degraded by smoke, flooding, and railroads, ill-suited for the automobile, and minimally affected by planned improvements, downtown entered the post–World War II era in need of massive new investment and imaginative planning. Suburbanization, a declining metropolitan population, contentious race relations, deindustrialization, and the loss of several major corporate headquarters over the second half of the century added further pressure on downtown. (See also chapter 9.) Adopting current fashions in planning, architecture, and redevelopment, a proactive civic leadership managed to maintain the Golden Triangle's vibrancy, enhance its usability, and position it well for continued success early in coming decades. Mistakes in design, demolition of older buildings, and traffic planning have been made, of course, along the way. But without the involvement of local government, foundations, and nonprofit organizations in initiating redevelopment, nurturing private investment, and obtaining state and federal financial support, the Golden Triangle would probably not be so golden at the dawn of the twenty-first century.

References

Alberts, Robert C. 1980. *The Shaping of the Point: Pittsburgh's Renaissance Park.* Pittsburgh: University of Pittsburgh Press.

Lubove, Roy. 1969. *Twentieth-Century Pittsburgh: Government, Business, and Environmental Change.* New York: John Wiley and Sons.

———. 1996. *Twentieth-Century Pittsburgh.* Vol. 2, *The Post-Steel Era.* Pittsburgh: University of Pittsburgh Press.

Muller, Edward K. 2003. River City. In *Devastation and Renewal: An Environmental History of Pittsburgh and Its Region*, ed. Joel A. Tarr, 41–63. Pittsburgh: University of Pittsburgh Press.

Muller, Edward K., Morton Coleman, and David Houston. 1999. Skybus: Pittsburgh's Failed Industry Targeting Strategy of the 1960s. Center for Industry Studies, University of Pittsburgh, 2002, www.industrystudies.pitt.edu.

Stewman, Shelby, and Joel A. Tarr. 1982. Four Decades of Public-Private Partnerships in Pittsburgh. In *Public-Private Partnerships in American Cities*, ed. R. Scott Fosler and Renee A. Berger. Lexington, MA: D. C. Heath and Company.

Teaford, Jon C. *The Rough Road to Renaissance: Urban Revitalization in America, 1940–1985.* Baltimore: Johns Hopkins University Press, 1990.

Toker, Franklin. 1986. *Pittsburgh: An Urban Portrait.* University Park, PA: Pennsylvania State University Press.

TWO

Pittsburgh as a Concentric Triangle

Kevin J. Patrick

In 1925, Ernest W. Burgess formalized a descriptive model of the American city that was first discussed by Robert Hurd as early as 1903 (Ley 1983, 23). The model described urban social landscapes as a series of concentric rings arrayed around a central business district (Burgess 1967, 50–51). It was the seminal piece of research in what came to be known as the Chicago school of urban ecology (Knox 1994, 221). Burgess's zonal rings were more the product of a radial, rail-based transportation system that made up the infrastructural framework of all the great North American industrial cities of the early twentieth century. This chapter poses a slightly different question: What if Burgess had done his landmark research at the University of Pittsburgh instead of the University of Chicago? The influential nudge of site-specific geomorphology may have given us a concentric *triangle* instead of something that looked like an abstract dartboard, or in the case of Chicago, half a dartboard (figure 2.1).

While the concentric triangle is a bit of a stretch, it is an adequate template for trying to comprehend the urban morphology of Pittsburgh. Burgess's model describes the North American city at a specific period in time, the 1920s, the high-water mark of the mature industrial metropolis shaped by capitalist land use competition and a nodal transportation system of intercity railroads and intracity streetcar and commuter lines. Subsequent urban growth and development has not effaced the urban landscapes assembled under these conditions. In fact, the pattern anticipated by descriptive land use models of the Chicago school is still apparent on a modern map of median house values (figures 2.2 and 2.3).

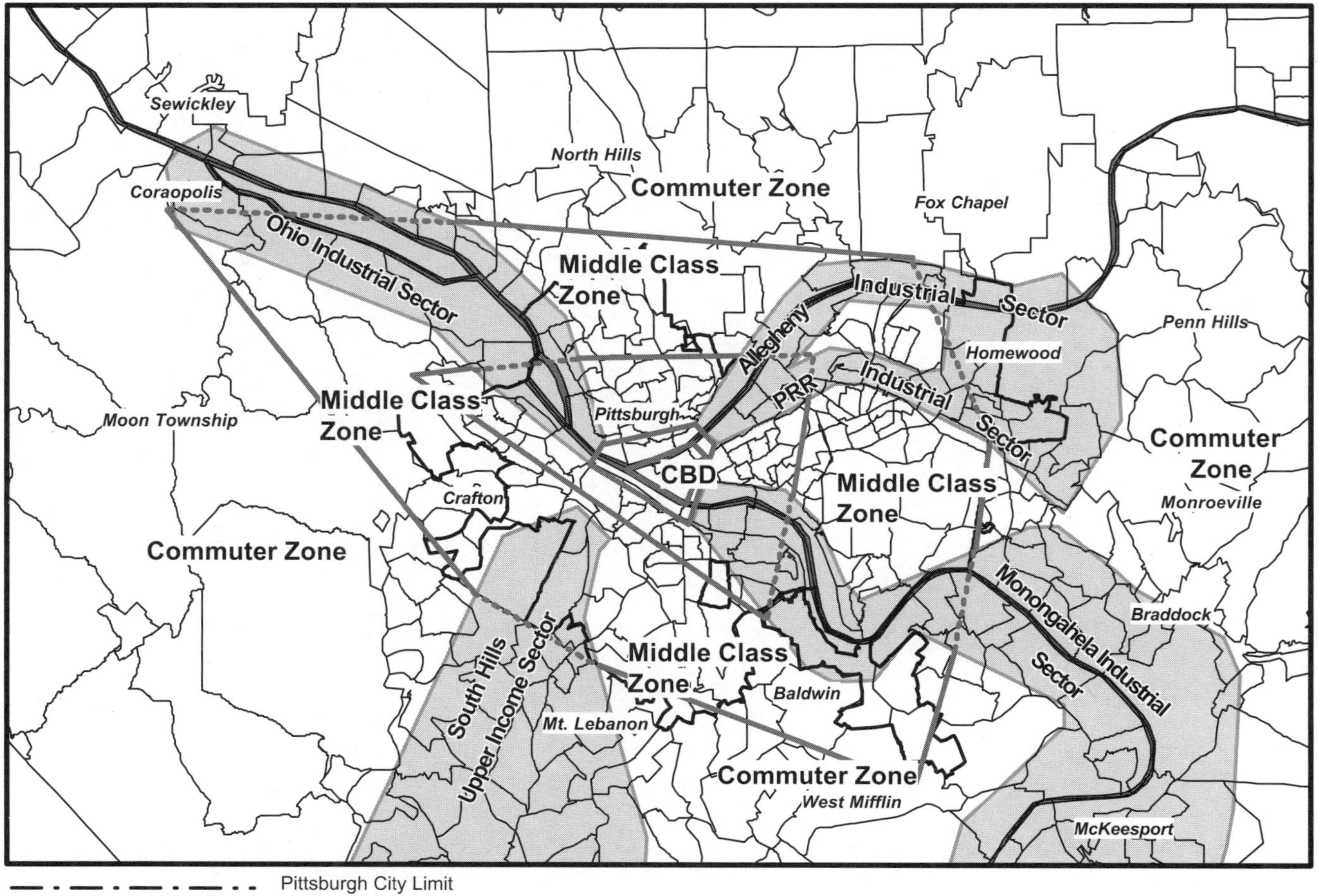

FIG. 2.1. This map of Pittsburgh as a concentric triangle shows the industrial/working-class sectors that follow the rivers and major rail corridors, as well as the upper-income sector that originally developed along the streetcar lines that extended into the South Hills.

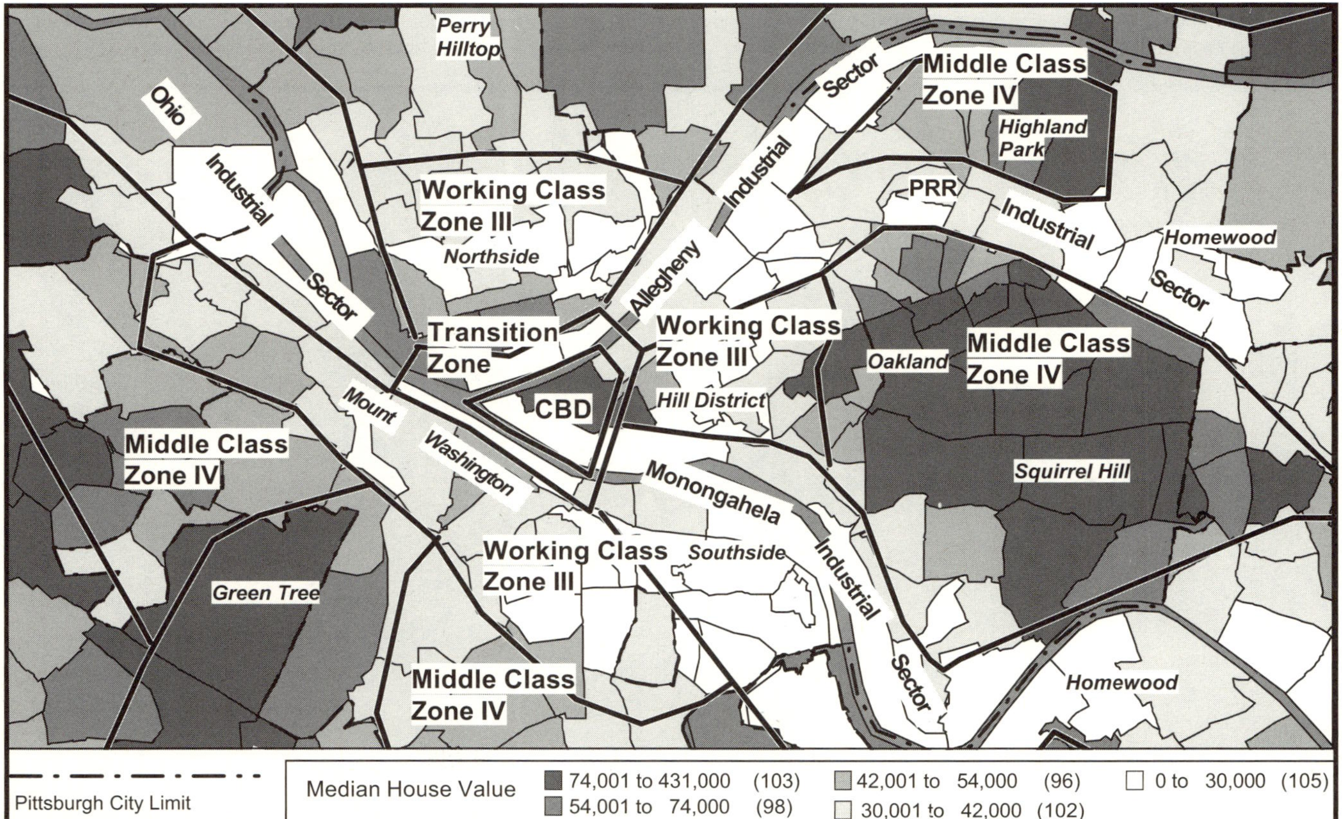

FIG. 2.2. The concentric zones and sectors within the City of Pittsburgh are discernable on this 1990 map of median house values by census tract. The lowest median house values are in the industrial sectors and the working-class zone. The highest median house values are in the middle-class zone, and in the South Hills upper-income sector extending south from Green Tree.

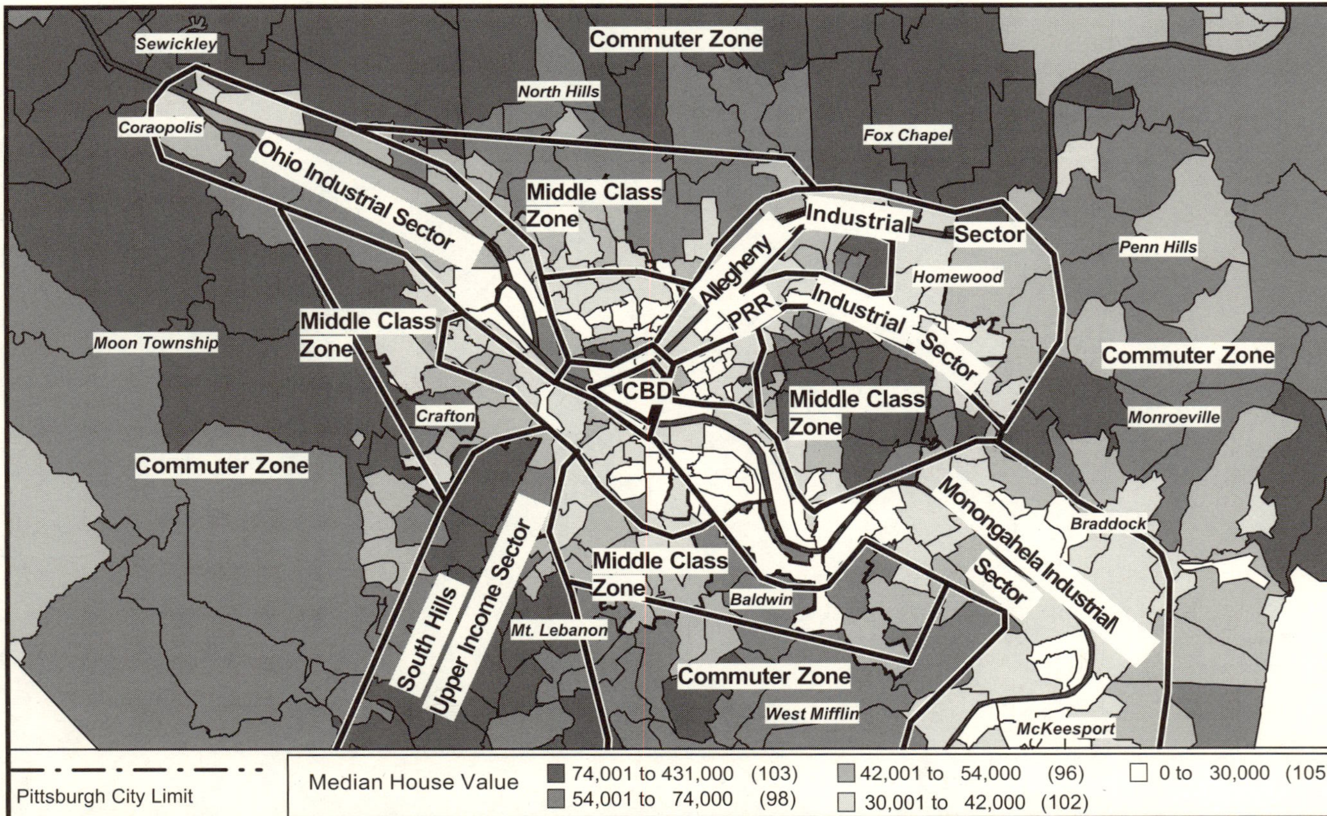

FIG. 2.3. This map of median house values by census tract shows Pittsburgh's zones and sectors at the regional scale, including the suburban commuter zone that was just emerging during the 1920s, but has since come to be the largest and wealthiest zone in the metro area.

Pittsburgh's Golden Triangle and Transition Zone

The Golden Triangle is Pittsburgh's zone I. Whereas Chicago's concentric rings are truncated to the east by Lake Michigan, Pittsburgh's Golden Triangle is pinched to the west by the joining of the Allegheny and Monongahela rivers to form the Ohio River. The downtown sits on a floodplain bounded on three sides by steep-sided hills carved by erosion of the Allegheny plateau. Of the three rivers, the Monongahela was the most significant to the development of Pittsburgh's Golden Triangle, which was initiated by the commercial activity centered along the Mon Wharf. Back from the wharf, a row of neoclassical bank buildings along Fourth Avenue still marks the location of Pittsburgh's original financial center. By the early twentieth century, the financial district and a burgeoning retail district made up the core of a triangular zone I, bordered to the south by the Monongahela River, to the northwest by Penn Avenue, and to the east by Grant Street (figure 2.4).

Borrowing the idea of succession from plant ecology, Burgess wrapped his central business district in a "zone in transition" (Burgess 1967, 50). It was into this zone that the more capital-intensive activities of the central business district would expand. In the meantime, the area would support an inner "factory zone" of light manufacturing and wholesaling critical to the downtown but too extensive to compete for land in zone I. A freight-hauling network of railroads evolved that literally ringed the downtown to serve the factories and warehouses bordering the Golden Triangle.

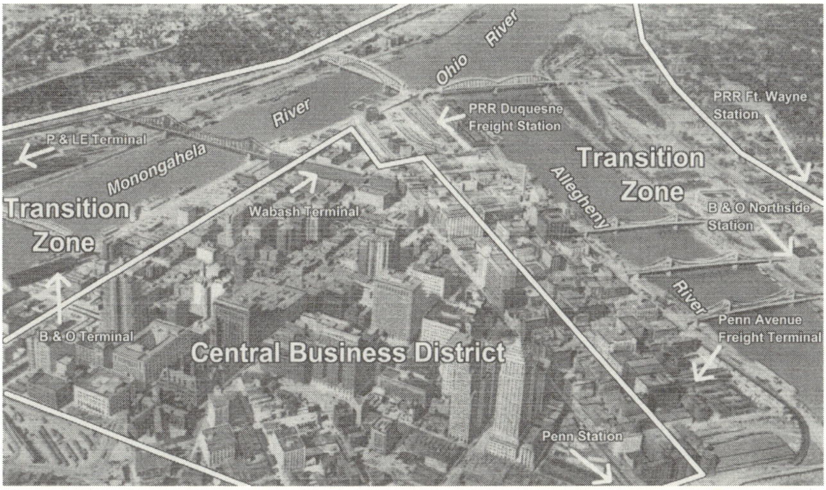

FIG. 2.4. This vintage overview of downtown Pittsburgh shows the concentric triangle boundaries around the central business district and transition zone as they existed in 1935.

The Monongahela leg of industrial age Pittsburgh's transition zone included the activity of the wharf and an industrial corridor of glassworks and iron forges served by two railroads that ran along the far shore. The older of the two lines was the Panhandle Division of the Pennsylvania Railroad (PRR), which connected Pittsburgh with Ohio via the panhandle of West Virginia in 1865. The other was the Pittsburgh and Lake Erie Railroad built in 1879.

Flush against the toe of Grant's Hill is the eastern leg of the triangle. The physical limitations of this leg preclude its use as an industrial corridor, but the economic power of zone I, as dictated by Burgess, nonetheless slated it for transportation. Constructed at what in 1865 was the edge of the city, the Pennsylvania Railroad's Panhandle line tunneled through Grant's Hill and over the Monongahela River on a bridge that now carries Pittsburgh Area Transit's trolley line into downtown. The railroad was preceded by an extension of the Pennsylvania Main Line Canal, which had also tunneled through Grant's Hill from its terminus at the Pittsburgh end of an aqueduct across the Allegheny River to interface with the river traffic plying the trade on the Mon Wharf.

Northwest of Penn Avenue, the Allegheny leg of the Golden Triangle was once a quintessential "factory zone" that functioned as part of Pittsburgh's wholesale district (figure 2.5). The Point was dominated by the Pennsylvania Railroad's main freight depot, Duquesne Station, which was connected to Union Station, the railroad's main passenger terminal, by a set of tracks laid down the center of Liberty Avenue. In a Burgessian case of urban land use succession, the tracks were relocated to an elevated structure along the Allegheny River in 1906 when the northward expansion of the central business district began to change the nature of Penn and Liberty avenues. Literally clinging to the Allegheny edge of the Golden Triangle, this last remnant of transition zone was pushed out of downtown during the 1950s Renaissance I urban renewal project and related creation of Point State Park. A zone of light manufacturing and wholesaling was nonetheless maintained farther up the Allegheny in the Strip District and along the north shore floodplain between the river and the tracks of the Pittsburgh, Ft. Wayne and Chicago Railroad (Lorant 1980).

Like the great intercity rail terminals that surrounded Chicago's Loop, industrial age Pittsburgh spawned similar grand edifices to act as competing pedestrian portals at the edge of its central business district prior to World War II. The Baltimore and Ohio Railroad depot anchored the southeastern apex of the Golden Triangle. It operated at the north end of the Smithfield Street Bridge. The Pittsburgh and Lake Erie Terminal was across the Monongahela River at the south end of the bridge. The Wabash Terminal of the

FIG. 2.5. Absorbed into an expanding central business district in the 1950s, Pittsburgh's Point and Allegheny waterfront were still a part of the transition zone in 1929, then a mixed-use strip of warehouses, light manufacturing, and transportation facilities.

Pittsburgh and West Virginia Railroad stretched four blocks between First and Liberty avenues along what is now Stanwix Street. This railroad entered downtown via the Wabash tunnel (through Mount Washington) and bridge (over the Monongahela River). The Pennsylvania Railroad's Duquesne Freight Station was at the Point apex, and its Union Station, later known as Penn Station, secured the northern apex of the triangle near the intersection of Liberty Avenue and Grant Street.

As the dominance of the railroads declined, the expansion of the central business district determined the fate of these terminals. The Wabash Terminal burned in 1946, clearing the property for the Renaissance project's Gateway Center office complex (Lorant 1980, 385). Road builders bulldozed the Smithfield Street B&O depot for the Penn-Lincoln Parkway constructed along the Mon Wharf in the 1950s. This was the first of a somewhat triangular network of limited-access highways predictably laid within the old rail corridor of the transition zone. Private investors renovated the spectacular 1901 Pittsburgh and Lake Erie Terminal as a hotel, restaurant, and shopping mall in 1977 (Van Trump 1978, 23–25). This waterfront redevelopment project was essentially a beachhead expansion of the central business district into the then derelict factory zone on the far side of the Monongahela River (figure 2.6).

The Penn Station triangle apex is representative of both Burgess's transportation-dependent transition zone as well as the postindustrial fate of such

FIG. 2.6. Located at the south end of the Smithfield Street Bridge, the Pittsburgh and Lake Erie Railroad Terminal was redeveloped into Station Square in 1977.

zones. Beginning in the 1830s, the site functioned as the terminus of the Pennsylvania Main Line Canal, Pittsburgh's first heavy-freight link to the trans-Appalachian east. The Pennsylvania Railroad came to dominate this location on the edge of town after 1852. The PRR built Union Station here to join its eastern Main Line and Conemaugh Division with its western Panhandle Division, and its extension to Chicago, the Pittsburgh, Ft. Wayne and Chicago Railway (Kobus and Consoli 1997, 5).

The renowned architect and planner Daniel Burnham designed Penn Station, with its impressive rotunda, in 1901 to replace Union Station. Although Amtrak trains still stop in its shadow, developers renovated Penn Station as a commercial property in the 1980s with no functional links to the railroad. It stands as a showpiece of historic preservation on the leading edge of Pittsburgh's downtown. Essential to the functional nature of the Industrial Age Transition Zone was the Penn Avenue freight terminal, located a block from Penn Station between Tenth and Eleventh streets. Just as critical to Golden Triangle's twenty-first-century economy is the David Lawrence Convention Center (host of the Year 2000 Association of American Geographers meeting), which replaced the moribund freight terminal in 1981. The convention center sits in what was Pittsburgh's "Zone of Discard" (Ford 1994, 65–73), a corridor of single room occupancy hotels, low-rent office buildings, cafes, adult theaters, warehouses, and railroad tracks along Penn and Liberty avenues between the Golden Triangle and the Strip District. This onetime skid row is in the midst of revitalization with the expansion of the central business district along Liberty Avenue and the gentrification of the Strip District.

Within or adjacent to the central business district, Burgess described a "main stem" of "hobohemia," a "teeming Rialto of homeless migratory men" (Burgess 1967, 54). This could have been a synopsis of the Great Depression Hooverville that formed in the Strip District between the PRR's Pittsburgh terminal yard and the banks of the Allegheny River. Named for the narrow corridor of Allegheny floodplain squeezed between the river and the steep bluffs of Grant's Hill, the Strip District evolved as an industrial corridor along the PRR's Main Line to the east. In the early twentieth century, the Strip emerged as the city's premier wholesale district and food distribution center after these activities were pushed out of the Golden Triangle by the expanding central business district. In a more recent era of truck transportation and fragmented metropolitan space, the Strip District's wholesaling and light manufacturing role has diminished relative to its more recent identity as a tourist-oriented nightclub and retail district addendum to downtown.

Pittsburgh's Sinuous Sectors and Working-Class Zone III

Extending up the shores of the Allegheny from the Golden Triangle, the Strip District is part of an industrial, working-class sector of the type described by Homer Hoyt in his 1939 adjustment of Burgess's concentric ring model. Heavily oriented toward the sinuous course of the region's rivers and railroads, Pittsburgh's most significant working-class sectors exist as industrial corridors meandering through the zonal fabric of the city. Like the tentacles of an octopus, the primary industrial corridors extended outward from the transition zone along the floodplains of the Ohio, Allegheny, and Monongahela rivers. A fourth sector follows the PRR Main Line eastward through the working-class neighborhoods of Homewood and Wilkinsburg. Beyond the urban fringe, McKees Rocks, Ambridge, and Aliquippa along the Ohio and Homestead, Braddock, Duquesne, McKeesport, and Clairton on the Monongahela developed within these valley bottom sectors as industrial satellite cities centered on huge integrated steel mills.

In addition to the factory zone, Ernest Burgess's zone in transition also included a "zone of deterioration encircling the central business section" where so-called slums and bad lands exist with their "submerged regions of poverty, degradation, and disease, and their underworlds of crime and vice" (Burgess 1967, 55). Like the shantytowns that covered the Hill District, Pittsburgh produced poverty-stricken ghettos adjacent to its rail-laced factory

FIG. 2.7. The success of the nearby mixed-residential development, Crawford Square, has yet to filter down to the Hill District's Centre Avenue, one of the city's most notorious neglected social spaces.

zone every bit as bleak as Burgess's description, but with no clear distinction between them and his more stable "zone of workingmen's homes" beyond. Workers who had "escaped from the area of deterioration but who desire to live within easy access of their work" inhabited this third zone. Relative to Pittsburgh's concentric triangle, zone III would encompass the Hill District to the east (figure 2.7), the North Side neighborhoods beyond the Allegheny River, and the South Side over the Monongahela River.

Zone III is classic Pittsburgh, rank upon rank of modest, gabled houses marching up steep-sided bluffs and set cheek by jowl along narrow, winding brick streets. As in other industrial cities, these high-density neighborhoods were extended outward along electric streetcar lines, but specific to Pittsburgh's dissected geomorphology, the hillside neighborhoods were also connected to the jobs in zones I and II by inclined railways. The Duquesne and Monongahela inclines on Mount Washington are the only two that remain. Representative of Harris and Ullman's multiple nuclei model (1945), Pittsburgh's working-class zone evolved as a patchwork of ethnic neighborhoods, each with its own retail district functioning as a small downtown subservient to the Golden Triangle.

The gradation of slums and stable working-class enclaves that straddled zones II and III were targeted for urban renewal in the 1950s and '60s. Most tragic was the "reconstruction" of the Lower Hill starting in 1955. This urban renewal project gutted the once vibrant black business district along Wylie Avenue and replaced it with a sea of parking lots surrounding the igloo-shaped Civic Arena and the Crosstown Expressway, which walled off the Hill District from downtown like a moat. Thirteen hundred buildings were demolished and eight thousand residents, largely African American, were displaced before public outcry stopped the project (Toker 1986, 234). The decentralization of African Americans from zone II has created a "Black sector," in Hoyt's terms, extending from its most concentrated apex in the Hill District eastward to its more diffuse outer margins in Penn Hills. Another black sector extends up the industrial Mon Valley to McKeesport and Clairton.

Pittsburgh's other massive, clean-sweep planning project occurred on the North Side where 518 buildings in the center of the Allegheny City retail district were scuttled for the modernist malls, office buildings, and apartment buildings of Allegheny Center. The trauma of urban renewal in the 1950s and 1960s spared the South Side. It lies a bit remote from the expansionist influences of the Golden Triangle. However, it suffered from the deindustrialization of the 1970s and 1980s. The South Side's postmodern rebirth in the 1990s, similar to that of the Strip District on the other side of town, emphasizes gentrification and modest conspicuous consumption that includes bars, eateries, and music clubs. Playhouses, coffee shops, nightclubs, and gift shops along its main drag, Carson Street, replaced the movie theaters, lunchrooms, taverns, and drug stores that lined the street in the past.

Pittsburgh's Zone of Better Residences and Commuter's Zone

Residential zone IV of Pittsburgh's concentric triangle spreads out over the hills where the distant office spires of the Golden Triangle can only be seen in shadowy glimpses. Like Burgess's concentric ring model, the integrity of the concentric triangle disintegrates with distance from zone I. Representative examples of Burgess's "high-class apartment buildings," "restricted residential districts," "bright light" areas, and "single family dwellings" exist at the appropriate distance, but not as a clear-cut band that circumscribes the entire city. Pittsburgh's zone IV is nonetheless best represented in three locations situated just beyond the working-class zone III. As in other cities, this "Zone of Better Residences" was the product of commuter railroads and electric streetcar lines which opened up amenity-oriented residential space in the borderland between city and country for those who could afford a single-family home and the daily commute downtown.

Pittsburgh's first and foremost zone of better residences was to the east along the high ground of the Pennsylvania Railroad and the streetcar line that followed Fifth Avenue. Adjacent to Homewood, the first suburban station

Fig. 2.8. Greenfield's high-density built environment is typical of the middle-class streetcar suburbs built during the early twentieth century.

out from the Golden Triangle, Point Breeze became the exclusive address of Pittsburgh's elite during the latter part of the nineteenth century. Dozens of millionaires enriched by Pittsburgh industries, including Carnegie, Frick, Mellon, Heinz, Westinghouse, and Armstrong, built mansions in the Penn Avenue neighborhood. Most of these millionaires had moved away by the dawning of the twentieth century, leaving their mansions to be demolished and their estates to be cut up into middle-class streetcar suburbs (figure 2.8). Among the bungalows and Hully houses (a local variant on the bungalow) of this 1920s-era commuter zone, only Clayton, the home of Henry Clay Frick, remains as a representative example of the Gilded Age.

Even without the name-brand millionaires, the East End was a well-established zone of better residences with enough influential movers and shakers in the 1890s to develop two Olmstead-inspired parks, Schenley and Frick. In addition, a neoclassical second city center developed at Oakland and served as the cultured counterpart to the Golden Triangle. Constructed around the University of Pittsburgh and Carnegie Institute of Technology and Mellon Institute (merged as Carnegie Mellon University in 1967), this second nucleus of commercial activity reflects the best of the City Beautiful movement. Oakland still anchors an island of high income surrounded by the working-class corridors of the Pennsylvania Railroad and Mon Valley.

To the south, trolleys still glide through the Mount Washington Tran-

FIG. 2.9. Middle-class tract housing, like this West Mifflin plan, sprawled across the plateau surfaces of Pittsburgh's commuter zone in the 1950s and 1960s.

sit Tunnel that linked the Golden Triangle to what in the early twentieth century were exclusive neighborhoods in Banksville, Beechview, Brookline, Overbrook, and Carrick. To this day, these neighborhoods display an average household income that exceeds the average for the city (Department of City Planning 1992). By the 1920s, a distinct upper-income sector developed along the interurban lines of an emergent commuter zone that stretched out to South Park and included Baldwin, Mt. Lebanon, and Bethel Park.

A similar zone of better residences developed on the hilly fringes of the North Side in the Perry Hilltop neighborhood adjacent to Riverview Park. Evergreen Hamlet in the commuter zone beyond predates Edward Burgess by seventy-five years, reaching back to the earliest days of the romantic Victorian suburb (Toker 1986, 300–301). Closer to the Ohio River, the Pennsylvania Railroad induced a string of railroad suburbs that evolved into the most exclusive segment of Pittsburgh's upper-income commuter zone. This zone of wealth expanded northward when auto-oriented suburbs around Sewickley Heights and Sewickley Hills joined the older railroad towns of Avalon, Ben Avon, Emsworth, Sewickley, and Edgeworth.

Auto-oriented suburbs came to dominate the commuter zone after World War II when middle-class housing plans typically consisting of modest brick Cape Cods sprawled over Allegheny County's undulating plateau surfaces after World War II (figure 2.9). Mill town retail districts faded with the construction of shopping centers along arterial highways, like the Miracle Mile Shopping Center in Monroeville. Depending on their locations, these borderless communities were collectively known as the East Hills, South Hills, or North Hills suburbs, a tripartite, suburban extension of the Golden Triangle.

Metropolitan Pittsburgh at the Threshold of a New Millennium

Pittsburgh's peak period of growth occurred during the rail-dominated industrial age. As a result, Pittsburgh's current urban morphology is a shadow of cities past. The power of the concentric triangle, however, dissipates for landscapes shaped after 1970. Over the last thirty years, the diminishing role of the central city relative to the ever-expanding boundaries of the metropolitan environment has caused newer descriptive models to be more appropriate. James Vance's urban realms model (1964) is apparent in the suburban downtowns that have emerged around interchanges of the Pennsylvania Turnpike (Pittsburgh's de facto cross-suburban expressway) at Monroeville, Cranberry, and in the vicinity of the Pittsburgh International Airport to the west. At the macro scale, the sinew and fabric of these "restless urban landscapes" (Knox 1991, 1) are representative of Pierce Lewis's galactic city, each business park, housing development, and shopping mall tied together by a ganglion of roads and held in tension by their mutual gravitational attraction (Lewis 1983, 35).

Like other American cities, metropolitan Pittsburgh continues to be shaped by ever-changing socioeconomic paradigms that challenge the geographer's powers of description. Elements of the postmodern metropolis, as described by an emerging Los Angeles School (Dear and Flusty 1998, 52), are apparent in Pittsburgh. The metropolis can be read as a complex game board consisting of winners and losers, where rapid revitalization in the Strip District or South Side occurs alongside the persistent poverty of the Upper Hill District and Braddock. Entire neighborhoods have been given over to "spectacle," like the North Shore, which was buried (or maybe resurrected) by the construction of two new professional sports stadiums. Others, like Station Square with its collection of restaurants, shops, industrial age artifacts, boat and incline rides, are being redesigned as theme parks. Examples of Dear and Flusty's "ethnoburbs," "edge cities," "consumption opportunities," and "corporate citadels" are just as evident in Pittsburgh as they are in Los Angeles. A trip inward, however, toward the Golden Triangle, is a trip back in time through landscapes shaped by the geography of changing technology.

References

Burgess, Ernest W. 1967. The Growth of the City: An Introduction to a Research Project. In *The City*, by Robert E. Park, Ernest W. Burgess, and Roderick D. McKenzie. 4th ed. Chicago: University of Chicago Press.

Dear, Michael, and Steven Flusty. 1998. Postmodern Urbanism. *Annals of the Association of American Geographers* 88 (1).

Department of City Planning. 1992. *Department of City Planning 1990 Census of Population and Housing Reports*. Pittsburgh: City of Pittsburgh.

Ford, Larry. 1994. *Cities and Buildings: Skyscrapers, Skid Rows, and Suburbs*. Baltimore, MD: Johns Hopkins University Press.

Harris, C. D., and E. Ullman. 1945. The Nature of Cities. *Annals, American Academy of Political and Social Science* 242:7–17.

Hoyt, Homer, 1939. *The Structure and Growth of Residential Neighborhoods in American Cities*. Washington, DC: Federal Housing Administration.

Hurd, Richard M. 1903. *Principles of City Land Values*. New York: The Record and Guide.

Knox, Paul L. 1991. The Restless Urban Landscape: Economic and Socio-Cultural Change and the Transformation of Washington, DC. *Annals, Association of American Geographers* 81 (2): 181–209.

———. 1994. *Urbanization: An Introduction to Urban Geography*, Englewood Cliffs, NJ: Prentice Hall.

Kobus, Ken, and Jack Consoli. 1997. *The Pennsy in the Steel City: 150 Years of the Pennsylvania Railroad in Pittsburgh*. Publication of the Pennsylvania Railroad Technical and Historical Society. Kutztown, PA: Kutztown Publishing.

Lewis, Pierce F. 1983. The Galactic Metropolis. In *Beyond the Urban Fringe*, ed. R. H. Platt and G. Macinko. Minneapolis: University of Minnesota Press.

Ley, David. 1983. *A Social Geography of the City*. New York: HarperCollins.

Lorant, Stefan. 1980. *Pittsburgh: The Story of an American City*. 3rd ed. Garden City, NY: Doubleday.

Toker, Franklin. 1986. *Pittsburgh: An Urban Portrait*. Pittsburgh: University of Pittsburgh Press.

Van Trump, James D. 1978. *Station Square: A Golden Age Revisited*. Pittsburgh: Pittsburgh History and Landmarks Foundation.

Vance, James E., Jr. 1964. *Geography and Urban Evolution in the San Francisco Bay Area*. Berkeley: Institute of Governmental Studies.

THREE

The Steel Valley

Edward K. Muller

Industrial restructuring has swept through the Monongahela River Valley of Pennsylvania twice in the past one hundred years, rearranging the landscape each time. In the closing decades of the nineteenth century, Pittsburgh iron and steel owners adopted mass production techniques and organization, requiring massive capitalization, all of which led to the industrialization of the valley. By the beginning of World War I, enormous iron and steel mills, various other industrial plants, railroads, and adjacent mill towns occupied the floodplains nestled within the Monongahela's meandering curves for the final thirty miles of its journey to meet the Allegheny River, where it forms the Ohio River at Pittsburgh (figure 3.1). Interspersed between the mill sites and for another thirty miles upriver, coal mines, coke works, and coal-loading facilities studded the river valley and the surrounding countryside.

One hundred years later the traditional smokestack industries of the Pittsburgh metropolitan region succumbed to the new requirements of the global economy, and one by one, owners shuttered the mills and mines. By the 1990s, brownfields and tired mill towns were strewn the length of the lower Monongahela Valley (figure 3.2). However, a new landscape is slowly and unevenly emerging on the ruins of the older industrial one. The success of advanced technology and service industries in the Pittsburgh metropolitan region is slowly reaching down into the Mon Valley and spreading upriver, while the rejuvenation of the valley's ecology is opening up recreational opportunities.

FIG. 3.1. The Duquesne Works in 1945 and the adjacent city of Duquesne. They were originally part of Carnegie Steel and later US Steel. Courtesy of Steel Industry Heritage Corporation.

The First Industrial Restructuring

Arising in the West Virginia mountains not far from the headwaters of the Potomac River and flowing northward for 128 miles to its junction with the Allegheny River, the Monongahela became one of the main pathways by which Euro-Americans reached the Ohio River, the primary river route of the trans-Appalachian West. Fur traders, Indian agents, and land speculators converged on southwestern Pennsylvania in the mid-eighteenth century. After the British dislodged the French from the region in the French and Indian War in the mid-eighteenth century, settlers poured into the region. Peace did not come until after the American Revolution, but farming already dominated the life of this corner of Pennsylvania and continued to do so throughout the first half of the nineteenth century. The river provided one means of commercial movement for this modestly prosperous agricultural economy. River landings and towns such as Elizabeth and Brownsville, where the National Road crossed the Monongahela River, served as marketing and boat-building centers (Baldwin 1937).

Small, largely rural industrial establishments were scattered about the countryside. In addition to grist and flour mills and the usual array of artisan shops (for example, blacksmiths, wheelwrights, and saddle and harness mak-

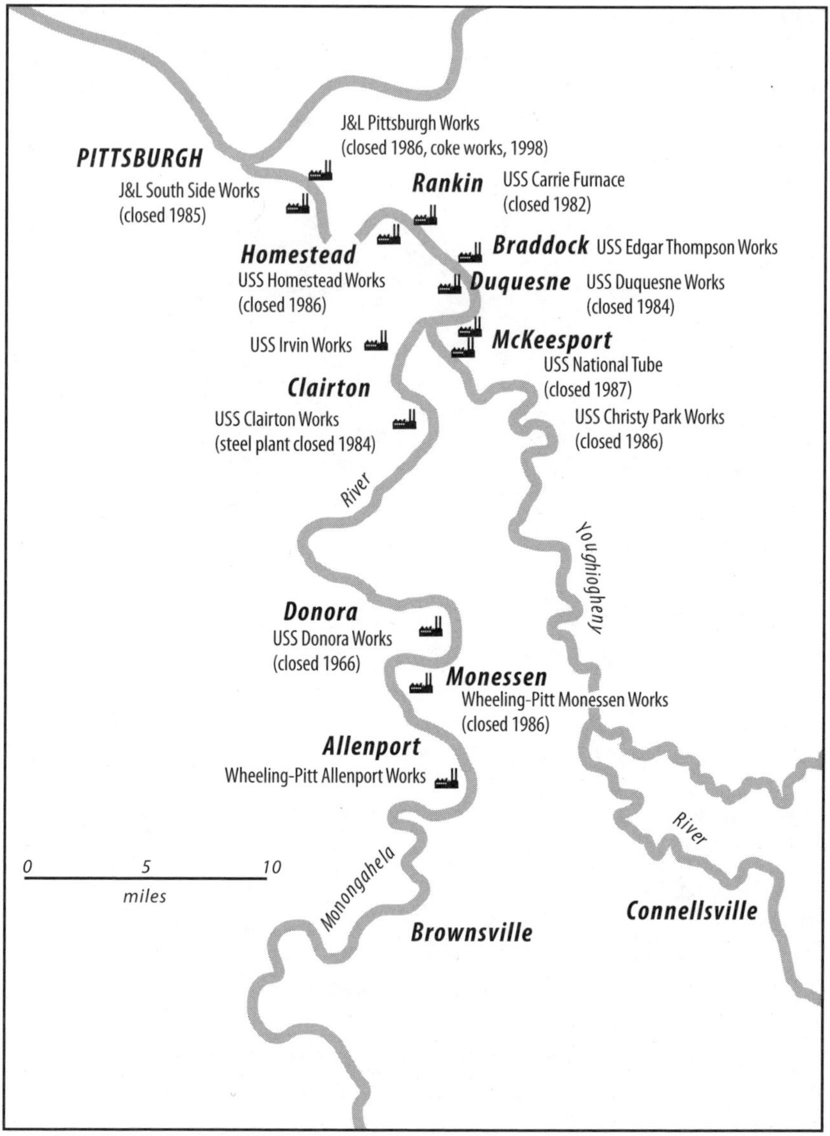

FIG. 3.2. The Steel Valley and its mill closings.

ers) serving the rural economy, iron furnaces in the foothills of the Allegheny Mountains produced pig iron for local and Pittsburgh iron mills, one-man mines shipped small amounts of coal to Pittsburgh and the Ohio Valley, and rye whiskey distillers carried on a regional export specialty. Pittsburgh, at the mouth of the river, was a growing market, transit point, and banking center, but it was relatively remote from the everyday lives of Mon Valley residents.

The second industrial revolution, coming after the Civil War, drew the Monongahela Valley and the city together. Perhaps, the investment in 1851 by the partnership of Philadelphians William Wood and Richard Gilpin in a new iron rolling mill at McKeesport, twelve miles upriver from Pittsburgh where the Youghiogheny River meets the Monongahela, foreshadowed the changes that would sweep through the lower valley (Ingham 1991, 225). Or, perhaps, one might point to the construction of the huge and vertically integrated American Iron Works, later the Jones & Laughlin (J&L) Company, in the 1850s and 1860s on both sides of the river only a couple of miles from Pittsburgh's Monongahela Wharf as the beginning of the lower valley's restructuring (Porter and Livesay 1971, 65–68). In the 1850s, the city of Pittsburgh contained a large number of iron rolling mills and foundries, but there were no blast furnaces or railroad rail mills, the latter reflecting the new market sector that drove the industry for the next quarter century. Either Pittsburgh ironmasters had to move into these new product lines and vastly expand their mills or remain in their familiar, though profitable, market niche and watch the new segment of the industry pass them by (Temin 1964).

Drawing on local capital resources and skilled craftsmen, ironmasters such as Benjamin F. Jones and the irrepressible Andrew Carnegie did enter the markets for railroad rails and equipment. Theirs and other firms also expanded to meet Civil War demands for iron products. The tremendous growth of local iron mills overwhelmed the ability of rural iron furnaces to meet the demand for pig iron. Beginning in 1859, a few ironmasters erected blast furnaces in Pittsburgh, which in turn stimulated the development of the coke industry in the Connellsville area (eventually to be known as the famous Connellsville coke district) forty miles southeast of the city (figure 3.3). Coke moved by rail and the Monongahela River to Pittsburgh mills (Warren 1996). By 1870 the burgeoning iron industry along with glass factories and other industrial firms crowded the floodplains of the city's three rivers.

The fundamental change in the urban geography of the iron and steel industry came with the introduction of the Bessemer steelmaking process. Recognizing the enormous profit potential in substituting steel for iron in railroad rails and other products, Carnegie and a few other iron manufacturers around the country aggressively experimented with the Bessemer technology. In 1872 Carnegie and several investing partners decided to build a Bessemer steelworks and rail mill at Braddock's Field, where the Pennsylvania Railroad met the Monongahela River twelve miles south of Pittsburgh. The Edgar Thomson Works at Braddock opened in 1875 and was soon acclaimed as the leader in the field (Wall 1970). The huge success of this works drew

FIG. 3.3. Hand-drawing coke from the Lemont Ovens in Fayette County. Courtesy of Steel Industry Heritage Corporation.

competitors, who understood that mass-produced steel was rapidly replacing iron. A group of investors, including disgruntled former Carnegie partners, constructed a Bessemer works at a site across and slightly downriver from Braddock. Opened in 1881, the mill at Homestead soon ran into a variety of problems, giving Carnegie the opportunity to purchase this competitor. Carnegie restructured the mill into one that produced structural steel shapes. A few years later he purchased the Carrie blast furnaces across the river at Rankin and connected them by bridge to the Homestead Works. In the late 1880s investors tried again to compete with Carnegie by erecting another innovative and integrated Bessemer rail mill at Duquesne, a few miles upriver from Braddock and on the same side as Homestead. Carnegie bought this group out as well and over the years added more blast furnaces at the site. By the end of the century Carnegie had three fully integrated steelworks spanning a short stretch of the Monongahela River (Ingham 1991).

Others recognized the advantage of locating mills at Monongahela River sites close to the essential Connellsville coke district. The Pittsburgh Steel Company, for example, opened a large integrated iron and steel works at Monessen, thirty miles from Pittsburgh, as part of a speculative industrial development that also included a steel wire firm, steel hoop mill, a tin-plate plant, and a foundry and machine company (Magda 1985). Over the years, steelworks operated at McKeesport, Clairton, Donora, and Allenport.

FIG. 3.4.
Coal mine tipplers like this one dotted the landscape. Courtesy of Steel Industry Heritage Corporation.

Numerous specialized and smaller plants such as those at Monessen, boat-building yards at Elizabeth and Dravosburg, a wire factory in Braddock, and glassworks at Glassport, Charleroi, Monongahela, and New Eagle filled in the valley's industrial complex. US Steel, formed in 1901, which included Carnegie Steel under its corporate umbrella, built an enormous by-product coke works at Clairton in 1918 and ran pipelines for miles down the river-front to use the surplus gases for fuel in its former Carnegie mills (Warren 2001). Tows pushing barges loaded with coal and coke jammed the river, and railroads lined the valley (figure 3.4). While the river and rail network knit the coke and steel industrial complexes together, the expansion of the coke district after 1890 westward to and across the Monongahela brought them into direct physical contact (Muller 2001). Above Brownsville in the middle Monongahela Valley, coal loading and mining facilities dotted the verdant hillsides and floodplains. Below this older river city the concentration of heavy industry, especially approaching Pittsburgh, polluted the river, darkened the skies, scarred the hillsides, filled every available flat site, and rendered labor relations tense and sometimes violent. With each turn of the river, one encountered yet another industrial complex and adjacent mill town.

The Second Industrial Restructuring

Crossing the bridge over the Monongahela River to Donora in the 1970s, one might have been struck with a vision of the valley's future. Set far back from the river and defying its smoky reputation gained from the infamous 1948 killer smog, the town seemed to sparkle under the sunlit blue skies, while the floodplain in the foreground appeared like a meadow with a few corrugated steel warehouses isolated in its midst. Closer inspection revealed, however, not a meadow but a brownfield site and a town with boarded-up storefronts struggling to survive. Demolition of the Donora mill in the 1960s sent a shudder through the valley, but few dared truly believe that such a fate could await the region's other historic and powerful facilities.

Unbelievably, much of the Steel Valley soon convulsed with the onslaught of deindustrialization (figure 3.5). Cheaper imported steel, outmoded technologies, competition from more efficient domestic mini-mills, high labor costs, expensive pollution controls, and arrogant and stubborn management doomed the giant works of the valley. In the 1980s layoffs, rumors of closings, tense labor relations, and often sudden shutdowns stunned lower valley mill towns. An eerie calm settled over the lower valley, where once the cacophony of heavy machinery, warning whistles, and rumbling trains created a constant but comforting din. Brightening skies and cleaner river water did little to assuage lower valley residents. The unthinkable had happened; the valley was in a state of shock (Hoerr 1988).

Huge industrial hulks stood quietly above the river and loomed menacingly over the towns. Public officials frantically and futilely discussed what to do. As severance checks and unemployment compensation ran out, adjacent diners, cafes, taverns, gas stations, barbershops, and a host of other services watched their customers slip away. Soup kitchens and food pantries opened their doors to hungry families. Younger men and women began leaving the region for jobs across the Sunbelt. Older residents kept waiting for this most recent downturn to end, as others had, and the mills to spring back to life. A new pall hung over the lower valley, this one psychological rather than visual.

All was not lost. US Steel modernized its oldest mill, the Edgar Thomson Works in Braddock, which continues to ship steel a few miles upriver to the Irvin strip mill that was originally opened in 1938. Three large coke plants stayed open in Monessen, Clairton, and the Hazelwood neighborhood of Pittsburgh, despite constant struggles over air quality standards. LTV's

FIG. 3.5. Vacant US Steel mill, ca. 1980s. Courtesy of Steel Industry Heritage Corporation.

Hazelwood plant closed; the Monessen operation is up for sale. Although no beehive coke works remain open and many mines have closed, a few tows push coal-laden barges downriver and coal trains pass through the valley. But, this remnant of the once vigorous Steel Valley cannot mask the economic and social devastation of the second wave of industrial restructuring and the abandoned landscape that followed in its wake.

Civic leaders reflexively tried to replace the iron and steel industry with new industrial jobs. However, the closed mills themselves, toxic wastes, the lower valley's image of aggressive unionism, an unattractive environment, inadequate infrastructure, and the sheer scale of the devastation impeded the marketing of these sites to new industries. Although a few private industrial salvagers jumped at the opportunities, local government agencies with state aid have had to acquire most sites, undertake demolition, and initiate redevelopment. The snail's pace of this process has allowed consideration of more imaginative reuses of the riverfronts than was possible in the years immediately after the collapse (Muller 1989). But it also deepened the discouragement of valley residents and left the communities to deteriorate further. Housing values declined, structures decayed, and some were abandoned. Many churches and affiliated parochial schools closed. Low-income renters moved in; drug trafficking and crime increased. In some places African American populations increased and racial divides deepened. School and municipal budgets declined, and in a few instances the state declared emergencies and took control. Boarded-up storefronts appeared along main streets (Modell 1999).

For many public officials the prerequisite for redevelopment has been the improvement of the lower valley's access to the interstate highway network. Monongahela Valley industries traditionally relied on the river and railroads. After World War II regional expressway planners avoided the densely settled Monongahela bottomlands. In the 1980s civic leaders implored highway officials to drive an expressway through or near the lower valley, so that communities would have competitive access to Pittsburgh and the regional interstate highways. Political battles ensued over the proposed expressway's alignment in the lower valley, but according to plans being finalized, the route will consume some former industrial riverfront lands. In a manner more reminiscent of the 1950s than the 1990s, most residents valued anticipated economic benefits over the loss of riverfront access and environmental quality.

Location with respect to Pittsburgh has influenced the rate and kind of redevelopment of lower Mon Valley brownfields. The city of Pittsburgh took control of the former J&L mill sites on both sides of the river. The former blast furnace site on the river's north shore lies a few miles from both downtown and the two research universities in the city's Oakland section. After overcoming toxic waste issues and with considerable help from the state, the city partnered with Carnegie Mellon University and the University of Pittsburgh to develop an advanced technology industrial and research park. Besides the university research facilities, several companies and regional advanced-technology nonprofit organizations have located in new buildings on the site. The city proudly displays this research park as a model of successful brownfield conversion and public cooperation with the region's advanced technology industries focused on robotics, software engineering, bioengineering, and precision manufacturing. The former coke works adjacent to the research park closed and came under control of the city. Its future is not yet clear.

Development of the site across the river on the South Side has moved more slowly because of weaker consensus on objectives and the private developer's funding difficulties. The city's initial flirtation with gambling interests aroused vigorous neighborhood opposition. Indeed, the city can accomplish little without the cooperation of the politically potent South Side community organizations. The site now houses a sports complex providing sports medicine and practice facilities for the University of Pittsburgh and the Pittsburgh Steelers professional football teams. Other office, retail, and entertainment activities have opened or are planned, but the final mix and form of development will ultimately reflect both neighborhood input and its integration into the older neighborhood by the street network.

Unlike the J&L mill sites in Pittsburgh, the mammoth Homestead Works was sold to an out-of-town private salvager, who showed little concern for community needs. For a decade, the company scrapped the buildings, sold and reconditioned machinery, built some infrastructure, squabbled with community groups and local governments, and managed a few land sales before finally selling the bulk of the site to a developer who constructed a large retail and entertainment complex. The mall wisely took advantage of the site's location within a few miles of Pittsburgh's affluent East End neighborhoods. The Waterfront—a combination of huge big box stores surrounded by acres of parking, a small outdoor cluster of retail shops and restaurants, a few office buildings, a townhouse complex, and a string of chain restaurants—feels like a suburban development, featuring access only by automobile, a low-density built environment, and familiar brand names. Despite its name, the Waterfront all but ignores the river running along the entire northern edge of the complex. Enormously successful in its initial years, the mall's design and access points limit integration with the adjacent Homestead communities, and so far the development has had little direct positive impact on their deteriorating business streets.

Further up the river, and therefore a few miles further away from Pittsburgh, the control of US Steel's former Duquesne and McKeesport works by the Regional Industrial Development Corporation (a county-wide public authority) has resulted in a focus on manufacturing firms and business incubation. Scrapping old mills, the authority has decongested the sites, built new infrastructure, rehabbed masonry buildings whenever possible, and begun marketing the sites. Beyond McKeesport, brownfield redevelopment has moved even more slowly. Thus, ten to fifteen years after plant closings, most sites are only now either beginning to show redevelopment or remain vacant.

The reviving riverine ecology of the Monongahela Valley has also created new opportunities. During the gloomy initial years of deindustrialization, few residents could envision the economic value of the valley's ecological assets. Industry had blocked access to the river and degraded the environment for decades, in some places for nearly a century (Muller 1989). New jobs took priority over conservation and recreation. Nevertheless, river recreation has burgeoned almost in the shadow of regional economic development efforts. Boaters overwhelmed Pittsburgh's small river landing built on the J&L site in the late 1980s, and police had to control traffic at the ramp on the weekends. Marinas and other river-oriented services sprouted up throughout the valley to handle the rapid growth of leisure boating. Game fish returned to the river, and blue herons competed with fishermen for its bounty. Small groups of activists assisted by state grants doggedly pursued rails-to-trails

FIG. 3.6. US Steel Homestead Works' brownfield site, 1999. The roof of the Homestead Carnegie Library is in the center background. Courtesy of Steel Industry Heritage Corporation.

conversions through the lower valley and around the region. As the trails have appeared, so have cyclists, hikers, in-line skaters, and their service businesses. Most remarkable is the successful water park at the western end of the Homestead area riverfront. Although traditional development projects remain the priority, recreational and quality of life advocates are no longer simply dismissed, and the river should become an increasingly important part of redevelopment strategies (Muller 2003).

Signs of new life along the Monongahela riverfront also signal stirrings in the adjacent communities. With grants from local foundations, the state, and the federal government, community organizations have labored to rekindle the spark of depressed communities (figure 3.6). Dependent for years on corporate largesse, older local officials were bewildered by the crisis facing them and reflexively remained suspicious of outsiders' proposals. Cultural and historical conservationists tried to rally community spirit around proud heritages. Community organizers focused energies on housing rehabilitation and small economic development projects and quietly trained a new generation of leaders. Main street programs spruced up waning business districts (Lubove 1996). However, until redevelopment strategies truly revitalize the lower valley's economy, these small communities will continue to struggle.

The new character of the lower Monongahela Valley landscape in the twenty-first century is not yet clear. Emerging activities and populations have not had time to interact with, encompass, or sweep away the populations, buildings, traditions, and politics of the past. The lower valley's revitalization depends in part on the success of the metropolitan Pittsburgh region, just as its earlier industrialization had. Regional growth since 1985 has concentrated in outer suburbs, the new airport, the greater downtown area, and the university section, none of which is close to most of the lower valley. The city and Allegheny County have pursued economic, cultural, and entertainment projects that have not been particularly directed towards the Monongahela Valley. Most valley communities will have to find their niches with respect to a region growing around advanced technology, business services, higher education, tourism, small specialized manufacturers, and river recreation. The convergence of the new interstate highway and the improved river environment may well give many communities a new attractiveness for small industries and prospective residents. The lower valley near Pittsburgh has the greatest access to the emerging regional economy. As the former J&L and Homestead works show, the brownfield sites offer land for redevelopment that is embedded in the core of the urban region and therefore potentially advantageous. The trick will be to leverage the site's access to the river, while not turning a cold shoulder to the older adjacent communities. Successful redevelopment will require good design, imaginative site planning, and a commitment to urban living by public and private interests. The middle Monongahela Valley, where industrialization left a lighter footprint, has the greatest opportunity to take advantage of ecological assets. These communities will regain access to the river, enjoy a more hospitable environment, depend less on industry, and have a lower-density settlement pattern. Where one of the world's centers of iron and steel production shaped both life and the landscape, a new postindustrial settlement pattern is emerging, as competing visions, economic interests, and political ambitions contest the future.

References

Baldwin, Leland D. 1937. *Pittsburgh: The Story of a City, 1750–1865.* Pittsburgh: University of Pittsburgh Press.

Hoerr, John P. 1988. *And the Wolf Finally Came: The Decline of the American Steel Industry.* Pittsburgh: University of Pittsburgh Press.

Ingham, John N. 1991. *Making Iron and Steel: Independent Mills in Pittsburgh, 1820–1929.* Columbus: Ohio State University Press.

Lubove, Roy. 1996. *Twentieth Century Pittsburgh.* Vol. 2, *The Post-Steel Era.* Pittsburgh: University of Pittsburgh Press.

Magda, Matthew S. 1985. *Monessen: Industrial Boomtown and Steel Community: 1898–1980.* Harrisburg: Pennsylvania Historical and Museum Commission.

Modell, Judith. 1999. *A Town Without Steel: Envisioning Homestead.* Pittsburgh: University of Pittsburgh Press.

Muller, Edward K. 1989. The Legacy of Industrial Rivers. *Pittsburgh History* 72:64–75.

———. 2001. Industrial Suburbs and the Growth of Metropolitan Pittsburgh, 1870–1920. *Journal of Historical Geography* 27:58–73.

———. 2003. River City. In *Devastation and Renewal: An Environmental History of Pittsburgh and Its Region,* ed. Joel A. Tarr, 41–63. Pittsburgh: University of Pittsburgh Press.

Porter, Glenn, and Harold C. Livesay. 1971. *Merchants and Manufacturers: Studies in the Changing Structure of Nineteenth-Century Marketing.* Baltimore: Johns Hopkins Press.

Temin, Peter. 1964. *Iron and Steel in Nineteenth-Century America: An Economic Inquiry.* Cambridge: M.I.T. Press.

Wall, Joseph Frazier. 1970. *Andrew Carnegie.* Oxford: Oxford University Press.

Warren, Kenneth. 1996. *Triumphant Capitalism: Henry Clay Frick and the Industrial Transformation of America.* Pittsburgh: University of Pittsburgh Press.

———. 2001. *Big Steel: The First Century of the United States Steel Corporation, 1901–2001.* Pittsburgh: University of Pittsburgh Press.

II CITY OF SPECIAL PLACES

PITTSBURGHERS CHERISH their city as a special place of unique neighborhoods, diverse ethnic heritage, powerful industries, and stunning achievements in engineering and design. Part II celebrates Pittsburgh's one-of-a-kind character with five chapters highlighting local legends, soaring bridges, rich communities, and place identity.

Kevin Patrick opens the section by unraveling the mythology surrounding the city's renowned steelworkers. Joe Magarac embodies the old adage that the greatest compliment the world gave America was its immigrants. This good-hearted, hard-working figure of Eastern European heritage is depicted during Pittsburgh's heyday as a leading steel producer and reflected upon in the aftermath of the city's industrial decline. Like other newcomers to America's industrial revolution—African Americans from the Deep South, Italian immigrants, and Scotch-Irish workers from various city neighborhoods—Joe Magarac sustained heavy industry. His sweat and sacrifice helped to line the pockets of corporate America and afford a livelihood for tens of thousands of workers over more than a century of industrial prowess. Joe Magarac is Pittsburgh's own Paul Bunyan–like Hunkie hero whose labor in the steel mills of the Mon Valley made Pittsburgh famous.

Chapter 5 explores the evolution of the city's produce yards. The Strip District, with its voluminous redbrick warehouses, railroad terminals, and freight yards, emerged as Pittsburgh's wholesaling center around the turn of the last century. The Strip's evolution from an industrial and manufacturing center and produce warehouse district to a stylish place of greengrocers, restaurants, and nightclubs has not eroded its primary warehousing function. It is a tristate tourist attraction and a must-see neighborhood when out-of-towners come to the city. The scarce number of residents there aids its 24/7 industrial party atmosphere. Even though vestiges of its ethnic produce suppliers remain today, it has managed to adapt to the corporatization of produce wholesaling while offering up a landscape that suburban shopping outlets simply cannot emulate.

Few architectural and engineering aspects of Pittsburgh and the Appalachians are as important to the region as are the bridges that link its towns and neighborhoods. Kevin Patrick dissects Pittsburgh's iconographic bridges to weave together a story about how transportation, topography, and urban history complement each other. Few urban vistas in America are as striking as the view seen by motorists emerging from the Fort Pitt Tunnel; a panorama that takes in the Point fountain, Pittsburgh's three rivers, and the North Side sports complexes, all against a backdrop of the skyscrapers of the Golden Triangle. From George Washington's near drowning in the frozen Allegheny and fires that consumed wooden bridges, to multilevel steel bridges carrying more than 130, 000 vehicles, Patrick shows that "Pittsburgh is all about bridges."

Christopher Cusak and George Pomeroy highlight a remarkable neighborhood not far from downtown. Chatham Village embodied the urban design principles of the Garden Cities movement that swept through Europe, North America, and Latin America a century ago. What better city with which to employ these principles than smoky Pittsburgh? The authors trace the history of Chatham Village conceptualized by Charles F. Lewis, former executive director of the philanthropic Buhl Foundation. He was influential in showing that good housing did not require government involvement. Chatham Village reflects many of the design principles of what today is called New Urbanism, like a pedestrian-friendly neighborhood that co-locates work, retailing, and housing in a setting that downplays reliance on the automobile. Although Chatham Village has no industry, schools, churches, or library, it is an alternative to suburban cookie-cutter urban development as well as to the more conventional in-city residential neighborhoods found in most American cities. The authors argue that Chatham Village has the potential to provide multifamily housing while preserving open space and fostering a strong sense of community.

Part II concludes with a David-and-Goliath tale of how a Pittsburgh neighborhood challenged powerful corporate and city interests. Pittsburgh native, historian, and local activist John Canning relates how Pittsburgh's North Side tried to control the terms and conditions surrounding two new sports complexes: Heinz Field for football and PNC Park for baseball. One community organization invested in the services of an internationally renowned consulting firm to help compile a list of conditions that local residents wanted to see fulfilled. The demands they made reflected community concerns without imposing a nonnegotiable and no-growth position. Written from a grassroots perspective, the chapter typifies the seemingly never-ending demand for cities in the United States and Europe to build state-of-the-art facilities that satisfy sports fans and promise big economic payoffs.

FOUR

Joe Magarac and the Spirit of Pittsburgh

Kevin J. Patrick

"My name is Joe Magarac, what you tink of dat, eh?"
Everybody laughed, for magarac in Hunkie means jackass donkey. They know this is a fine fellow alright when he says his name is Joe Jackass.
"Sure! Magarac, Joe. Dats me. All I do is eat and work same like jackass donkey."
—*Owen Francis, "The Saga of Joe Magarac, Steelman"*

Meet Joe Magarac

Carved from the same legendary mold as Paul Bunyan, John Henry, and Old Stormalong, Joe Magarac is the titan miracle man of the Pittsburgh steel mills (Botkin 1944). Made entirely of steel, Joe was born inside an iron mountain. One day he rode the ore train to Pittsburgh and emerged from the materials pile next to the blast furnace to be the greatest steelworker that ever existed. Like his folklore brethren, Joe Magarac was of uncommon dimensions and superhuman strength, forged from the stories told by workmen at the height of America's unbridled industrial expansion.

Joe Magarac, however, stands in contrast to the traditional folk heroes, those tragic paragons of human spirit, individualism, and might who pitted their brawn against the inevitable flood of mechanization only to be overwhelmed in the end. John Henry's great heart burst against the power of a steam drill. Mose, the most valiant fireman, disappeared from the streets of New York after the introduction of the steam fire engine, and fifty sailors carried Alfred Bulltop Stormalong to his grave sometime after the steamship replaced the Yankee clippers.

Joe Magarac came later, and reflects the experience of the Slavic im-

FIG. 4.1. This 1933 postcard of US Steel's Homestead Works shows an idyllically tinted view of Joe Magarac's world.

migrants who created him relative to their adopted home, the steel mill towns of the Pittsburgh district. Unskilled laborers from Eastern Europe poured into the mine- and mill-laden hills of western Pennsylvania during the late nineteenth and early twentieth centuries. Their collective consciousness contained no recollection of the master craftsman's halcyon days at the dawn of the Industrial Revolution. The industrial age had beaten the Slavs to America, setting up a siren song in the form of a shrill shift whistle that beckoned them forth into the maw of the machine. In 1870, there were already eleven blast furnaces in Pittsburgh and thirty-three rolling mills in Allegheny County. Jones and Laughlin's American Iron Works covered twenty acres of ground along the banks of the Monongahela River. By 1900, the Pittsburgh district supplied half of the nation's open-hearth steel, and more than half of its coke. The Carnegie mills produced nearly as much steel as England (Lorant 1980, 178). A boat moving up the Monongahela River from Pittsburgh would not be out of sight of a steel mill for twenty miles. Six great, integrated steel mills would come to occupy the valley floor. At Pittsburgh, Homestead, Braddock, Duquesne, McKeesport, and Clairton, each mill was a monster in its own right, a sprawling complex of steam-seething furnaces, oversized sheds, and stacks belching fire and smoke (figure 4.1). This was the surrealistic industrial world that awaited the Slavic peasant. Pittsburgh's spirit was tempered here.

With the exception of the African American John Henry, the man-against-the-machine folk heroes have a decidedly Anglo-American origin, emerging from a population that witnessed the urban-industrial overshadowing of Jeffersonian agrarianism. By the turn of the century, however, Anglo-Saxon immigration had subsided. Between 1881 and 1900, Irish immigration to Pittsburgh was cut in half, Scandinavian by nearly two-thirds. British immigrants went from 81,736 to 12,509, and the tide of Pittsburgh-bound Germans collapsed from over 200,000 to less than 20,000 (Lorant 1980, 187–88). Taking their place as the labor input for the newer, more massive mills were unskilled laborers from eastern and southern Europe. Over the same time period, the number of nationals arriving in Pittsburgh from Poland and Austria-Hungary grew from under 10,000 to over 100,000.

The Slavs were an ethnically diverse lot, including Slovaks, Hungarians, Magyars, Romanians, Bulgarians, Serbs, Croats, Polish, Ukrainians, and Russians, as well as people from the Baltic states. To their English-speaking neighbors, co-workers and bosses, however, they were all "Hunkies," "bohunks," or "mill hunks," human factory fodder who lived in the meanest, most unsanitary, and overcrowded parts of town. Their language, cultural differences, and poverty-stricken existence were generally accepted as evidence of the race's brutish ignorance (Byington 1974, 15).

In 1907, Slavs made up 53 percent of the workforce at US Steel's Homestead mill. They were required to do the heaviest, most dangerous labor for the least pay, with little chance for advancement but a good chance of being laid off first with each downturn in the economy. Slavs were given jobs that required above all strength and stamina. Many worked in the cinder pits, loaded trains, and handled heavy steel billets and bars for ten or twelve hours a day, six days a week. Concern for their safety was minimal. A mill worker weary of dodging the engines that fed raw materials to the furnaces and carried off the steel described their reckless wanderings: "No choo choo! No ling ling! No God damn you get out of the way! Just run over!" (Bowen 1968, 82).

From this environment rose the legend of a giant imbued with all of the qualities required of the Slavic mill worker: brute strength, tireless stamina, and boastful pride. Joe Magarac would work all night and all day without rest, throwing coke, ore, limestone, and scrap into the furnace. Then he would sit in the furnace door and let the flames lick around his chin. He would stir the molten batch with his bare hands until it was ready to tap, and then crawl into the furnace and scoop up big handfuls of steel and dump them into the ingot moulds. After that, he would run down to the rolling mills and make rails eight at a time by grabbing fistfuls of steel and squeezing them out between his clenched fingers (Francis 1931).

Like his Slavic creators, Joe Magarac realized his position relative to the work of the mill and the English-speaking world around him, and he combated this awareness of a bleak life of toil and drudgery with fatalistic, good-natured humor. He was the heroic personification of the meager life meted out to the Slavs, who saw their working existence as not much different than that of pit ponies and jackass donkeys. And through it all they could somehow laugh at the tragic irony of it. Suffering the abusive epithets thrown at them daily by English-speaking foremen, it was commonplace for Slavic mill workers to call each other "*magarac*" and have it be accepted as a term of camaraderie rather than an insult (Francis 1931).

Like most of the single Slavic men of the mill towns, Joe Magarac was a boarder in a house run by a woman who undoubtedly had her own kin to look after as well. As the quintessential "*magarac*," Joe explained his needs to Mrs. Horkey; "Dis place look all right for me. I gone work in mill and I want good place for eat. I no want room, just five big meals a day, dats all, for I work night turn and day turn all at same time" (Francis 1931).

In her 1910 Russell Sage Foundation report on Homestead (1974, 149), Margaret Byington described the family life of the Slavs:

> Families who live in narrow quarters have no room for festive gatherings. In the evening a group often gathers around the stove gossiping of home days, playing cards, drinking, and playing simple instruments. On the Saturday after payday the household usually clubs together to buy a case of beer which it drinks at home. These ordinarily jovial gatherings are sometimes interrupted by fights and the police have to be called in. One officer who had been on the force for nine years said that these men were generally good-natured and easy-going, and in all his experience he had never arrested a sober Hunkie; it was when they were drunk that the trouble began. The punishment usually inflicted for disorderly conduct in Homestead, a small fine, has little deterrent among the Slavs. It is indeed currently said that some are proud of having a large fine imposed, as they feel it indicates increased importance. . . .
>
> Almost the only time the house is really the scene of festivity is when those primal events, birth, marriage, and death, bring together both old-time friends and new neighbors. On most of these occasions, whether weddings, christenings or funerals, joy and grief and religious ceremony are alike forgotten in a riotous good time.

Some sixty-eight years later, director Michael Cimino would tell the tale of Pittsburgh's Slavic working class during the Vietnam War era. His movie, *The Deer Hunter*, understandably commits the first thirty minutes to a wedding.

Joe Magarac made his first appearance at a party thrown by Hunkietown resident, Steve Mestrovich, who arranged a contest of strength to determine who was the best man to marry his daughter Mary, "best" being synonymous with "strongest." It is inconceivable that Mary would marry anyone but a

Hunkie steelworker, and in that respect brute strength is directly equated to familial security. Essential to the party were two barrels of beer, plenty of "prune-jack" and cakes. Because Mary was "prettier as Hunkie girls from any place," men came from all the mill towns—Homestead, Duquesne, Monesson, even Johnstown—to compete for her affection by attempting to lift three dolly bars (borrowed from the eighteen-inch mill) of differing weight. Needless to say, no one could beat the man made of steel. But Joe wasn't interested in taking Mary for his wife, his sole concern being to eat and work, like "jackass donkey."

In the Shadow of Magarac

The origins of the Joe Magarac stories are unclear. They were first penned by Owen Francis in the 1930s, but it is unknown how much Francis created and how much came from the early twentieth-century folklore of southwestern Pennsylvania. By 1948, when William Gropper painted "Joe Magarac" (currently in the University of Pittsburgh's Gimbel Collection), Pittsburgh's Man of Steel had been thoroughly integrated with the city's historical identity.

Joe's sketchy genesis, however, fits the Pittsburgh of my earliest recollection, the Pittsburgh of the late 1960s and early 1970s. The steel mills of the Monongahela Valley were running full tilt back then, smearing the nighttime sky orange, and filling the air with the smell of sulfur. A simple ride to the grocery store down rumbling brick streets would pass sweeping vistas of factory-filled valleys, huge machinery that let loose screaming blasts of steam at random, mammoth slag dumps that smoked by day and glowed red at night, coal-laden barge tows, and miles of trains that crossed each other over soaring bridges.

And in all of this, Joe Magarac was a footnote that would occasionally appear in a Sunday supplement to the newspaper, or as a casual historic reference on a sign at Kennywood Amusement Park. He was one of the titans, like John L. Lewis, vaguely remembered as somehow being responsible for all that was currently taken for granted. His incredible feats were part of the distant past when it was still possible for a godlike hero to erect a bridge in a single day or forge steel with his bare hands. In the comparatively mundane Mon Valley of the 1960s, however, everybody just worked for a living, drawing a paycheck from seemingly eternal mills covered with the red dust of antiquity.

As a kid, it was hard to figure out whether the grown-ups thought the steel mills were a good thing or a bad thing. More times than not it was "that goddamn mill" whether in reference to the noise, the dirt, the smell, the strike, or the layoffs. But at the same time, locals reveled in taking out-of-towners past the mill to marvel at its immensity and be regaled with facts and figures about steel tonnage, boiler plate, and furnaces that always held the record for being the biggest in the world. Even the slag dumps were proudly pointed out as among the world's biggest.

From the appearance of some of the workers, however, there was apparently a price to pay for a job in the world's biggest steel mill. Through the mill gate you could sometimes see scary-looking guys with just their eyes peering out of faces colored black with soot, like photographs of factory workers from the nineteenth century. The open door of a corner tavern would occasionally reveal an ancient mill worker hunched over a glass of beer at the bar. Quite a few of them looked pretty beaten up. It seemed like a hard life, but this too was fraught with contradiction. Loosened up by a six-pack, guys from the mill could at times tell Magarac-like tales of hard work, Herculean accomplishments, and grisly stories of death by molten steel. At other times, they would brag—with equal passion and pride about the number of hours of shift work actually spent sleeping, or of competitions among workers in petty larceny, or of the salary time used playing golf (Serrin 1993, 299–301).

Sure enough, generations of Pittsburgh sons followed their fathers into the mill. In the 1960s and '70s, however, few children aspired to a life in the steel mills when they grew up, and thanks to thirty years of strong union bargaining, their fathers could ensure that they didn't have to. The mills were a fallback position. If you flunked out of college, you could always go to work in the mill. If you needed some extra money over the summer, you could always go to work in the mill. If you got back from Vietnam alive, you could always go to work in the mill. And many people did. The steel plants were notorious for overstaffing (Hoerr 1988, 296). It was as if every Pittsburgher's birthright was to be able to work in the mill any time they needed a few bucks. The mills were like cities unto themselves, maybe even countries, and somewhere in the facility there was always a broom to push, a shovel to throw, or a stack of pipes to goof off behind. And the competition? What competition? After World War II, the steel mills of Europe and Japan were in shambles, and the United States had economic hegemony over the entire industrial world (Dicken 1998, 22). It seemed so right that America should be on top of the world that the mills coasted right through the 1960s on borrowed time, unaware that the clock was ticking. The endless strikes and strike threats of the postwar years, however, took its toll on consumer confidence. After the 1959 mother of all strikes, which idled half a million steelworkers and a quarter million more in related industries (Hoerr 1988, 101), steel consumers started searching overseas for alternative supplies. What they found in the rebuilt world of global steel was good, and cheap. By the 1970s, with its runaway inflation, stagnant economies, and various energy crises (Harvey 1989, 141–45), the cracks in America's steel fortress were beginning to show.

If the labor force was complacent about the mills, so were the companies. US Steel's own labor-intensive, top-down bureaucracy had ten levels of operating management from the executive staff downtown to the foreman on the production lines (Hoerr 1988, 304–12). It emphasized control over commitment and quantity over quality up into the 1980s, when too little change came too late. In a way, the steel industry's obsessive need for control helped forge the legend of Joe Magarac. Armies of unskilled laborers, many speaking different languages, were managed by being told in no uncertain terms what to do to increase production. Critical analysis of and responsibility for the production process were part of few job titles. Quality slid and the plants passed out the poor product (Hoerr 1988, 321–24) until the sons of Magarac found themselves unemployed and frustrated, expending their energies beating up Japanese cars with sledge hammers in parking lot fundraisers: three whacks for a dollar.

Fall of the House of Magarac

Layoffs, strikes, and work stoppages were a fact of life in the steel valleys. Workers and their families were used to them. After the death of Dorothy Six, however, it was painfully apparent that the massive round of layoffs in the early 1980s was something other than a typical business cycle. The pride of US Steel's Duquesne Works, Dorothy Six was the world's largest blast furnace and the Mon Valley's most visible symbol of the dominance of steel. When her fires were banked in 1984, she became an equally strong symbol of steel's demise. A coalition mounted a grassroots "Save Dorothy" campaign to fend off the inevitable, but two years later the company demolished her, sending psychological shock waves up and down the valley.

Ironically, Dorothy Six did not die of old age. Built in the mid-1960s, she was comparatively young as blast furnaces go. Her ailment was a chronic case of technological and locational obsolescence, a cancerous industrial disease that turned the once powerful Pennsylvania steel industry into one of the more corroded spots in America's newly christened Rust Belt. In 1950, US Steel operated twenty-five blast furnaces in the Monongahela Valley. By 1988, there were only two left (figure 4.2).

The Monongahela and Ohio valleys functioned as giant assembly lines of steel. Regardless of the enormity of each station on the line—consisting of entire mills and their dependent towns—one could not be closed without shuttering others to which it was linked. Positive multiplier effects of primary metals and metal fabrication spun this interconnected industrial

FIG. 4.2. US Steel closed its Duquesne Works in 1984. Shown here are the remains of the furnace row and its ore pit bridge, 1984.

web. Set in reverse, each plant closing fostered yet another closing, putting the entire region into an inescapable downward spiral.

As late as 1979, US Steel employment in the Mon Valley was 28,000. By 1984, that number fell to 9,100. Over the same period, the total number of steelworkers in the Pittsburgh district declined by more than 50 percent (Hoerr 1988, 363–68). In some of the mill towns, the unemployment rate topped out at 25 percent. It was worse than the Great Depression. At least during the 1930s, the mills, although silent, still loomed over the towns. It was a matter of waiting for someone to throw the switch back on. In the 1980s, outside of a temporary job on one of the demolition crews, there was nothing to wait for. And many drifted away.

And what of Joe Magarac? Joe committed suicide by jumping into a ladle of molten steel when the mill shut down. By the sweat of his brow, the indefatigable Joe Magarac had stockpiled so many steel rails that the mill had to shut down early. Joe was rewarded for his hard work by being laid off. It was only from Thursday to Monday, but for a miracle Magarac made of steel the wait for work was too long. When the melter boss returned to the mill Monday morning he found Joe in the ladle up to his neck in molten steel.

"What the hells you do in dere, Joe Magarac? Better you gone crawl out dat ladle right 'way or I tink maybe for sure dat she gone melt you up."

"Dats fine. Dats good business, dats joost what I want. By Gods, I be sick dis time of mill what shut down on Thursday and no start 'em up again until Monday. What the hells I gone do all time mill is shut down anyway?" (Francis 1931).

Joe sacrificed his life to the mill, melting down his own body to make the world's best steel from which was constructed the world's greatest steel mill. And thousands of steelworkers followed in his footsteps.

The Spirit of Pittsburgh

By the early 1990s, the great unraveling was complete. The mill town blast furnaces had fallen, but the Golden Triangle downtown gleamed with a new crop of postmodern office towers. The West Mifflin slag dump had cooled, its nighttime glow now lit by the parking lot lights of the Century Three Mall. Across the Monongahela River, a mixed-income residential development called Summerset at Frick Park was built on the Nine Mile Run slag dump. The homes have a spectacular view of the broad meander that cups the site of the old Homestead Works, which has been rebuilt as a mixed-use development of retail stores, condominiums, and apartments known as the Waterfront. Its visual punctuation point is a row of brick smokestacks—all that is left of the one-hundred-foot plate mill—towering over the site as a postindustrial memorial to the new community's theme-sake. EchoStar manufactures television satellite dishes in McKeesport where National Tube once forged pipe, and the site of J&L's old Pittsburgh Works is now the home of the Pittsburgh Technology Center. It sits on a mere fraction of the site, and few of the steelworkers who worked there then work here now.

Steel is still being produced in the valley, and at a fraction of the labor costs, thanks to US Steel's new continuous caster at the Edgar Thompson plant in Braddock. A large blue sign spanning the main gate proclaims the "hot end" of the mill, including western Pennsylvania's last two operational blast furnaces, to be part of the "Mon Valley Works." Reading the word "works" as a verb, the sign is almost a cruel joke. But all of that steel stuff is getting to be so much ancient history, like the wreck of the Penn Central, or the Johnstown Flood, just another heritage tourism theme to be mined for the latest restaurant, mall, or museum with Joe Magarac stepping forward to tell the tale.

Places cannot go bankrupt. Economies come and economies go, but place is an identity forged by the collective consciousness of the people. The indomitable spirit of Pittsburgh—its work ethic, its heritage, its heroes and villains—lives on. Still operating high on a bluff overlooking the Monongahela River, locally famous Kennywood Amusement Park erected a fiberglass

FIG. 4.3. Joe Magarac, legendary Man of Steel.

image of Joe Magarac. He stands at the end of the Olde Kennywood Railroad ride within earshot of the valley's last operating steel mill. He shares the ground with other working-class legends of Pittsburgh's violent past: Homestead strikers forever poised in pitched battle against Pinkertons and scabs, and whiskey rebels in arms against ill-conceived federal tax schemes.

In 1915, beaux arts sculptor Charles Keck made a bronze relief of Joe Magarac and other images for the Manchester Bridge then being constructed over the Allegheny River between Downtown and the North Side (Toker 1986, 161). The bridge was demolished in 1970, but Joe was saved. He and other architectural relics rest in peace as a collection of cast-off memories located in a garden next to the Pittsburgh Children's Museum.

Down at the Point, the spiritual center of Pittsburgh overlooking the confluence of its three rivers, redevelopers molded mundane factory space into a showcase symbol of urban rebirth. As part of the city's Renaissance

Project in the 1950s, a public-private partnership cleared out wholesaling and light manufacturing space that had always crowded the Point. In its place arose the modernist expansion of the central business district. Point State Park was the crowning jewel crafted for the confluence, and at its very tip a symbol was needed, something that said Pittsburgh. Among the proposals was a giant statue of legendary patriarch and Hunkie hero, Joe Magarac (Toker 1986, 25). What better way to grace the front door of the foundry of the world than with a larger-than-life statue of Joe Jackass? A more amorphous fountain was chosen instead.

References

Botkin, B. A., ed. 1944. *A Treasury of American Folklore: Stories, Ballads, and Traditions of the People.* New York: Crown Publishers.

Bowen, Ezra. 1968. *The Middle States: Delaware, Maryland, Pennsylvania.* New York: Time-Life Books.

Byington, Margaret F. 1974. *Homestead: The Households of a Mill Town.* Russell Sage Foundation report, 1910. Reprint, Pittsburgh: University Center for International Studies, University of Pittsburgh Press.

Dicken, Peter. 1998. *Global Shift: Transforming the World Economy.* 3rd ed. New York: Guilford Press.

Francis, Owen. 1931. "The Saga of Joe Magarac: Steelman." *Scribner's Magazine,* November 1931.

Harvey, David. 1989. *The Condition of Postmodernity.* Cambridge, MA: Blackwell.

Hoerr, John P. 1988. *And the Wolf Finally Came: The Decline of the American Steel Industry.* Pittsburgh: University of Pittsburgh Press.

Lorant, Stefan. 1980. *Pittsburgh: The Story of an American City.* 3rd ed. Lenox, MA: Author's Edition.

Serrin, William.1992. *Homestead: The Glory and Tragedy of an American Steel Town.* New York: Random House.

Toker, F. 1986. *Pittsburgh: An Urban Portrait.* University Park: Pennsylvania State University Press.

FIVE

Pittsburgh's Strip District

FROM INDUSTRY AND WAREHOUSING TO ETHNIC CHIC

Joseph L. Scarpaci

"It would be cheaper to abandon it. . . ."
—*Frank Lloyd Wright, 1935, in a newspaper interview about redesigning downtown Pittsburgh*

Pittsburgh's restructuring from an industrial powerhouse to a service economy mirrors other Rust Belt cities (Bluestone and Harrison 1982). City planners are determined to make the city "grow and transform with the global economy" (City of Pittsburgh 1998). Long gone are the days when schoolchildren washed and changed clothes twice daily in an ongoing battle with the soot and ash from the city's steel mills (Graham 1991; Bell 1941). While the smokestack economy has taken a backseat to research and development, health care, and higher education, Pittsburgh continues to serve as a major warehouse and regional distribution center. Grocers in western Pennsylvania, eastern Ohio, most of West Virginia, and western Maryland still call on the city's produce yards or Strip District for wholesale items. This twenty-odd-block ribbon of warehouses and parking lots extends along the northwestern shore of Pittsburgh's celebrated Golden Triangle (figure 5.1). Wedged between a one-thousand-foot bluff to the southeast (Grant's Hill) and the Allegheny River to the northwest, the land use of the Strip reflects much about the city's social and economic history.

Land use patterns in the Strip are in a state of flux as this corner of the city actively transforms itself from Pittsburgh's premier wholesale produce center to a fashionable district of shops, restaurants, and nightclubs. Following a trend apparent in most waterfront cities, Pittsburgh's Strip District

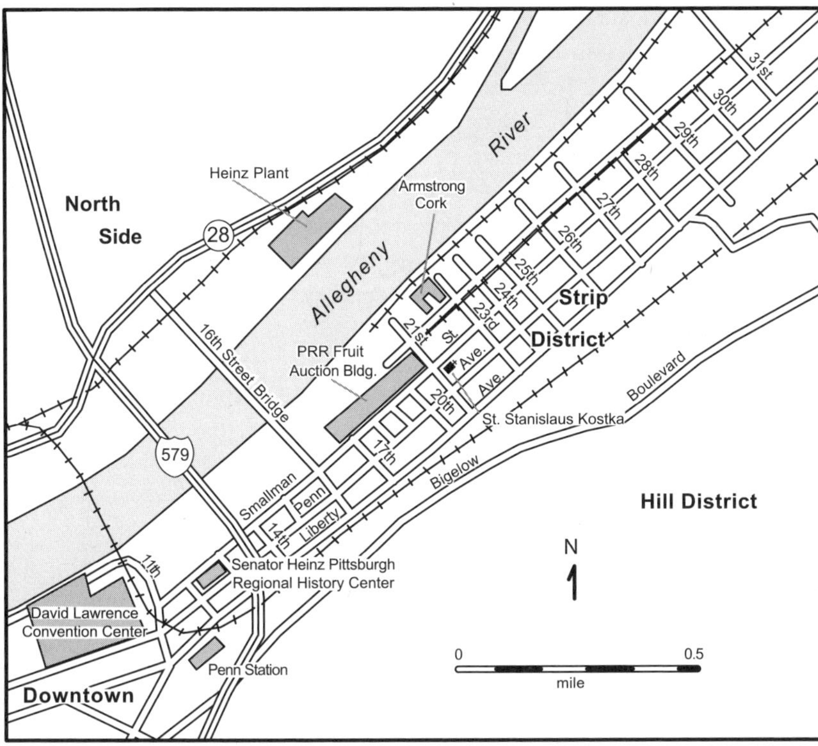

Fig. 5.1. Pittsburgh's Strip District.

represents the city's industrial past while adapting to current economic realities. To understand this transformation, we begin with highlights of the district's historical geography.

Riparian Farmland to Rail Yards

Before industrialization anchored itself there, the area known as the Strip was "a lovely wooded riverbank." The French settled near what today is the Point or the Golden Triangle, in downtown Pittsburgh, and built Fort Duquesne in 1754 to secure trade with the Delawares, Senecas, and Shawnees (Demorest 1958). Despite military victories against the British, the French abandoned the site shortly thereafter. In 1758, a new flag flew over the site as the British soldiers converted the garrison into Fort Pitt. Civilians settled the area in 1765. In 1804, Pennsylvania incorporated Pittsburgh as a borough, and in 1816 chartered it as a city (Glazier 1885).

North of the original fort at the Point lay the Strip District. Pittsburgh had not extended beyond its northeast border at Thirteenth Street by the mid-1700s. Historical records describe a small village of Delaware Indians—located at what is today Penn Avenue and Thirtieth Street—as the first permanent settlement in the area. It was called Shannopin's Town (Walther and Uhl 1995, 2). In 1773, Indian trader and settler James O'Hara arrived in Pittsburgh and purchased land from Thomas Smallman, who had "claimed" Shannopin's Town and the area that now occupies the Strip. O'Hara undertook farming and named his farmstead the Springfield Plantation. Periodic flooding of the Allegheny River enriched the alluvial soils of O'Hara's floodplain farm (NLC 1981, 88). Over the next century, several toponyms appeared on local maps: O'Haraville, Bayardstown, Denny's Bottoms, and Northern Liberties (Fanzo 1994, 13).

Pittsburgh's preeminent relative location at the confluence of three rivers and its access to abundant coalfields forever changed the area in the early nineteenth century. Boosterism touting industrial might came early to the city. In 1786, the *Pittsburgh Gazette* claimed that "this town must in future time be a place of great manufactory; indeed the greatest on the continent, or perhaps the world" (Walther and Uhl 1995, 1). Iron foundries forged artillery and bullets for the fledgling republic during the War of 1812 (Toker 1986, 189). The nation's canal boom also improved Pittsburgh's access to the Atlantic. Pittsburgh became a gateway for settlements along the Ohio, Mississippi, and Missouri rivers, stimulating a boat building and outfitting industry for westbound crafts (Demorest 1958). Eventually, the city lost its status as Gateway to the West to Cincinnati and later St. Louis (Heinz 1999).

Despite that shift in relative importance, Pittsburgh gained distinction as the largest inland port in the United States. A terminal for the Pennsylvania Main Line Canal erected in 1829 on Eleventh Street (now the southern end of the Strip) created demands for warehouses and light industry. The Pennsylvania Main Line opened in 1834, linking the city to Philadelphia.

Railroad construction, however, was not far behind. By the 1850s, the Allegheny Valley, Junction, and Pennsylvania railroads had rendered the canal obsolete. Settlers heading west could readily use trains. By 1854, Pittsburgh and Philadelphia were no more than fifteen hours apart by rail, which prompted the *Pittsburgh Gazette* to report jubilantly that such speed was "out to satisfy the fastest of this generation" (Handlin 1975, 121). To be sure, the steamship and canal eras left a clear imprint on wholesaling and industry.

The city of Pittsburgh annexed the Strip in 1837. An increasingly congested downtown area in the early 1800s nudged business to new locations. In addition, the Great Fire of 1845 laid waste to sixty acres that included businesses and fifteen hundred homes. The tragedy allowed the business community to untangle the industrial and residential quarters. Significantly, not just any place could accommodate industry and manufacturing. Allegheny County's hilly topography—part of the mature and dissected Allegheny Plateau—made bottomland both scarce and highly coveted as a place for heavy industry.

From the 1820s until around 1870, workers in the district's rolling mills produced charcoal pig iron and bloomery iron that they later turned into finished bars and plates (Walther and Uhl 1995, 7). When the Bessemer steel process was developed in 1856, Pittsburgh aggressively exploited coal from its hinterland as well as iron ore from the western part of the country. These raw materials reached the city through elaborate networks of rivers and canals. Although the Strip benefited from its relative location and new technology, it never cultivated a highly skilled labor force among its residents. By 1850, just under half of the residential labor force in the Strip was unskilled. Nonetheless, steel and iron unions grew steadily between 1862 and 1892. Iron puddlers engaged in a strike in 1867 to demand fair wages based on a sliding scale, and tried to normalize union rules (Glazier 1885; Demorest 1958).

Perhaps because of both its human and physical resources, industrial capitalism flourished in the Strip. Over the nineteenth and early twentieth centuries, a renowned cast of captains of industry acquired property in the Strip. Fuel taken from the four-to-twelve-foot-thick Pittsburgh coal seam powered large industrial enterprises. Coal also fouled the water and air but became the mainstay of the economy. A mixed blessing, one New York journalist observed, "It is interesting to hear a Pittsburgh discourse [that smoke] . . . far from being evil, is a blessing" (Parton 1864, 21). During the Civil War, the Union cast the famous sixty-ton Rodman cannons, which could hurl cannon balls three miles, in the Strip. John S. McCormick purchased the Pittsburgh Blacking Mill and shifted production from downtown to the Strip District in order to be closer to the metal casting and foundries around Twenty-fifth Street and the Allegheny Valley Railroad. Carnegie-Phipps and Company Union Mills launched operations at Twenty-ninth and Thirtieth streets. George Westinghouse began his Westinghouse Machine Company at Twenty-fourth and Twenty-fifth streets. Later, Westinghouse and Charles Martin Hall would combine the inventions of air brakes and aluminum here. The latter entrepreneur founded ALCOA, which evolved from the Pittsburgh Reduction Company, and built the first commercial aluminum factory at Thirty-third and Smallman streets (NLC 1991, 88; Toker 1986, 189; Denny 1973, 33–34). The nineteenth century also witnessed Thomas Armstrong corner the world cork market. His factory was erected at Twenty-third and Railroad Street. Willard Glazier described Pittsburgh's industrial landscape in 1885 this way: "Pittsburg[h] is a smoky, dismal city at her best. At her worst, nothing darker, dingier or more dispiriting can be imagined. . . . But her inhabitants do not seem to mind it. . . . Pittsburg[h] is not a beautiful city. . . . Down by the banks of the swift-flowing Allegheny most of the great foundries are to be discovered" (Glazier 1885). Indeed, James Parton's well-known remark that Pittsburgh was "hell with the lid off" was coined while he looked out over the Strip from Cliff Street on Grant's Hill (Toker 1986, 189).

By the end of the century, 62 glass factories, 350 coal mines, 25 steel mills and hundreds of small industrial sites had lined the Monongahela River alone (Heinz 1999). However, changing technology and zoning ordinances would shape the location of Pittsburgh's industry and produce yards. They would also erase most evidence of the smokestack past of the Strip District. Heavy industry dispersed along the floodplains of the three rivers and freed up space in the Strip. Wholesale produce merchants, originally concentrated along the 600 and 900 blocks of Liberty Avenue (not far from the site of the David Lawrence Convention Center), took advantage of railroad tracks running along Liberty Avenue. Laid in 1854 to move freight, these tracks linked Liberty Avenue with a freight depot close to the Point. Laborers then transferred goods onto boats and barges (Demorest 1958). Produce merchants would unload produce directly into their produce carts and wagons from railroad cars at the uptown Liberty Avenue location. By 1900, this section of Liberty Avenue had become highly congested, and the city wished to take advantage of the original industrial sites that were abandoned or reconditioned as warehousing.

In 1906, the city removed the railroad tracks from Liberty Avenue (figure 5.2). Produce vendors, in turn, relocated to the Strip District, where the Pennsylvania Railroad yards dispensed produce to grocers and ambulant peddlers who had established delivery routes throughout the city and Allegheny County. Produce vendors with horse-drawn carts worked the produce yards until World War II (figure 5.3). Working-class homes arose in this part of Pittsburgh, called Lawrenceville. The Pittsburgh Survey of 1907, a major study of the city's social conditions financed by the Russell Sage Foundation, described this part of Pittsburgh as "long swales of small, thickly built houses" (Kellogg 1909). Few of those houses (row houses, actually) stand today in the Strip District because demand for warehouses and light industry mounted, especially between Eleventh and Twenty-third streets.

By World War I, the Strip had tipped the scales from heavy industry to produce wholesaling, and whatever residential charms it had quickly faded. A rough-and-tumble blue-collar place, it had 133 saloons in its twenty blocks,

FIG. 5.2. Laying rail lines and cobblestones on Smallman Street, looking north, at St. Stanislaus Kosta Church, April 16, 1909. Courtesy of the Pennsylvania Department, Carnegie Library of Pittsburgh.

FIG. 5.3. "Carters: Trucks and drays circle the platform each morning, run produce to retailers, out-of-town wholesalers, keep 600 loaders busy." Looking south on Smallman Street. *Bulletin Index*, June 2, 1938. Courtesy of the Pennsylvania Department, Carnegie Library of Pittsburgh.

according to a 1915 survey, or 5 percent of the city's total. Not surprisingly, population loss has characterized the Strip every decade since the 1920s. At that time, it was a dirty and crowded place. Children played in the sooty alleys and dodged trains and trolleys. Outbreaks of diphtheria, typhoid, and scarlet fever were common. Families shared water coming from rear yard pumps. Yet, most wholesale produce men who worked in the Strip did not live there. Jewish and Italian dealers in the early twentieth century dominated the industry. Most Jewish merchants lived east of the Strip in the Hill District (today largely African American). A funicular railway (called the incline) carried them from the high bluff down to the floodplain. Most Italian merchants resided to the north of the Strip in the Bloomfield section of Pittsburgh (Walther and Uhl 1995).

Small and medium-sized wholesale produce firms proliferated in the Strip during the first half of the twentieth century. In 1926, the five-block-long Pennsylvania Railroad Fruit Auction Building—still standing along Smallman Street from Sixteenth to Twenty-first streets—cemented the produce industry's presence in the Strip. Smallman Street contained the larger wholesalers and auction houses, while smaller dealers concentrated on Penn Avenue; a pattern that remains today.

First- and second-generation non-English immigrant families dominated the produce business. Families of Italian, Central and Eastern European, Jewish, and Arabic origins found a niche there (table 5.1). While the produce industry increased its presence during the first part of the century, residential stock in the Strip declined. Pressures imposed by the Great Depression compounded the losses from the great St. Patrick's Day flood of 1936. Con-

TABLE 5.1. Common Surnames in Pittsburgh's Wholesale Produce Industry, by Ethnicity, Twentieth Century

Italian					
Ballestieri	Cassilli	Demma	Imperitori	Pusateri	Tamburie
Barsotti	Catalano	Dentisi	LoPresti	Ragu	Teresi
Bevelaqua	Colosimo	Folino	Machi	Raspanti	Tivoli
Bolla	Corso	Fortuna	Manna	Salpietro	Vivirita
Calderone	Dattilo	Galluze	Merlino	Scalise	
Camo	Degrasia	Gariotta	Porchia	Scarpaci	
Carcionie	Demaria	Gullo	Purpura	Sunseri	
Central and Eastern European, Jewish, Arabic					
Ayoob	Brecnkle	Haddad	Levy	Paskoff	Zeidemstein
Benatovich	Cohen	Haudenshield	Mallinger	Rhad	
Borowitz	Goldstein	Kleban	Nassar	Walling	
English, Irish, Scottish					
Dugan	Fisher	Miller	Queens	Shawnasee	Taylor

sequently, small produce businesses suffered, and many closed. When the Bureau of Building Inspection demolished more than one hundred homes over the next decade, it also eliminated the bandbox house: a three-story structure with a single large room on each floor. Between 1940 and 1970, the number of residential units in the Strip dropped from 851 to 359 (Walther and Uhl 1995, 33–34).

Just as the canal era yielded to railroads, technology and rapidly changing styles of grocery retailing in America would alter the economic geography of the produce yards. If produce wholesaling during the first half of the century linked America's farmlands to the Strip, the latter half of the century witnessed the expansion of interstate trucking. Pittsburgh's peak years of produce distribution were in the 1950s, when 141 wholesale distributors, half of whom clustered in the Strip, serviced thirty-one surrounding counties. Today, about a half dozen produce companies operate out of the Strip.

Two factors, though, undermined Pittsburgh's produce yards. First, national supermarket strategies and franchises had shifted in the 1970s, reflecting broader changes in American retailing. Not only did the national chains increasingly challenge the neighborhood grocer, but also A&P Company (nicknamed the gray lady of food retailing) watched its market share fall from 17.6 percent to 8 percent. In Pittsburgh and Altoona, it closed forty-four of its eighty-eight stores. Failure to aggressively merchandise its products, coupled with management turmoil, allowed the Safeway chain of supermarkets to surpass A&P as the leading food retailer in 1973 (*Business Week* 1975). The wholesale produce industry in Pittsburgh changed as well. In the 1970s, a number of wholesale produce companies folded, and smaller firms consolidated to form larger ones. Only two dozen dealers occupied the produce terminal building by the late 1970s (Historical Society of Western Pennsylvania, n.d.).

Second, wholesalers increasingly opted for newer, larger buildings near interstates. Trucks could deliver produce from the West Coast in two to three days, while railroads took five or six days (Walther and Uhl 1995, 35–36). Plans to relocate the produce district to a suburban warehouse complex south of the city (near Interstate 79 in Chartiers Valley), created a flurry of revitalization plans to turn the Strip into an office and residential riverfront complex (figure 5.4).

Although this Le Corbusier-like approach to reconfiguring the Strip failed, little produce reaches Pittsburgh by rail today. In 1999, the leading products and commodities carried into the Strip were, in order of decreasing quantity, corn syrup; plastic; scrap paper; pulp board and packaging material; food products, mostly soft drinks and beer; and produce (mainly less perishable and unrefrigerated items such as potatoes and onions). The Strip District

Fig. 5.4. Artistic rendering of a redevelopment plan in the Strip District, Eleventh to Twenty-first streets, ca. 1969, Penn Central Park. Courtesy of Pittsburgh Landmark Commission.

receives by rail only one-tenth of the freight that it did thirty years ago (Rus Peterson, personal communication).

The Strip District Today: Warehouses, Eateries, and Ethnic Vestiges

The Strip was home to immigrants who were neither English nor Scotch-Irish. Catholic Irish came to the city in large numbers in the early 1800s, and in 1808, they erected St. Patrick's Church, Pittsburgh's first non-Protestant church, at the corner of Seventeenth Street and Liberty Avenue. Today, four places of worship remain in the Strip, although the adjacent row houses of Slovak, Polish, and German immigrant parishioners are gone. St. Stanislaus Kostka (founded in 1875 and built in 1892) originally served Polish immigrants. St. Elizabeth of Hungary Church welcomed Slovak immigrants. These few churches added an element of grace to the Strip (Toker 1986, 189).

In the mid-1970s, a few produce distributors opened for business on Saturday mornings so they could discount merchandise that had not been sold during the week. Gradually, street vendors, antique stores, flea marketers, restaurants, and bars opened on the weekends to accommodate this latest retailing trend. By the early 1980s, several nontraditional businesses had taken

FIG. 5.5. The Strip District, October 1999.

FIG. 5.6. Smallman Street in the Strip, April 2001.

advantage of the large redbrick buildings that had previously been leased by the Pennsylvania Railroad or independent owners, but at that time stood vacant. Tapping into low commercial rental and property values, nightclubs, engineering and architectural firms, microbreweries, and eateries began moving back into the Strip. Because the residential population of the Strip fell to fewer than three hundred by the mid-1980s, down from a peak of 18,000 in 1915 (Walther and Uhl 1995, 13), there was little neighborhood opposition to these changes. Flexible office space and the possibility to rehabilitate warehouses into lofts attracted speculators (Muller 1999, 22). Greengrocers opened on both Saturdays and Sundays, and city and suburban families began shopping and eating along the old cobblestone streets. Nontraditional retailing (tapes and CDs, used items) became entwined amongst the traditional land uses. This breathed life into the Strip as the district reinvented itself. Today, commercial activity prevails twenty-four hours a day as trailers carrying vegetables and fruit unload during the evening and early mornings.

Contemporary Land Uses in the Strip

What is the land use profile of the Strip? To answer this question, I examined a large segment of the most recognizable core of the Strip, "the stores and sidewalks of Penn Avenue and Smallman Street between 16th and 22nd streets [where] people shop for everyday groceries and exotic foods" (Muller 1999, 1). In July 1999, I identified the 205 buildings and lots between Eleventh and Twenty-second streets, flanked by Smallman and Liberty, which constituted the core of the Strip. I included three variables. The unit of analysis was building entrances or lots, the latter used in instances where there were no buildings. Using doorways allowed multiple land uses to be assessed for each building. For example, at ground level there are often several ways to enter a building. Some entrances lead to apartments, others lead to retailing, or to both. The methodology allowed for counting these multiple land uses. I used this same approach in a published study of land uses in older sections of nine cities (Scarpaci 2005) and it has proven to be a useful way of understanding urban geography.

The three variables were measured this way. First, land use included eight attributes, assessed on a Likert scale ranging from the least to most noxious: (1) residential; (2) park or recreational/leisure open space; (3) restaurant or bar; (4) institutional (church or public facility such as government building, fire/police house, or school); (5) retailing or offices; (6) wholesale and light industry (the latter consisting of a single microbrewery); (7) parking; and (8) abandoned or under construction.

Two caveats must be made about the survey instrument. First, attributes

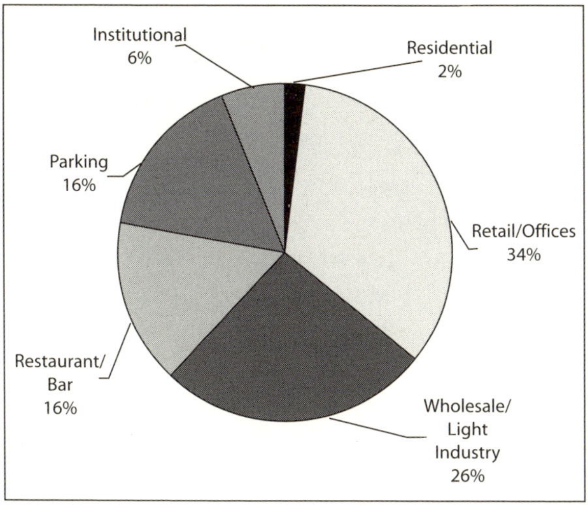

FIG. 5.7. Land uses in Pittsburgh's Strip District, July 1999.

two (park or recreation/leisure open space) and eight (abandoned or under construction) were not apparent at the street level. Second, no account of the surface area covered by parking lots was included. Instead, only the entrances to parking lots were coded. However, at least a quarter of the survey area (only a portion of the Strip District) is covered by parking lots. Thus, the reported value of 16 percent of land use devoted to parking underrepresents the importance of this variable (figure 5.7). A second variable assessed the condition of the building facade as poor, fair, or good. Variable three was building height as measured by the number of floors.

Land Uses

Wholesaling and light industry no longer dominate the Strip. Instead, retailing outlets and private business offices (34 percent) are the main land uses. The Strip's "rediscovery" as a place of ethnic eateries and after-hours revelry (Muller 1999) is evidenced by the 16 percent of the units classified that way. Most of the institutional land uses (6 percent) reflect the presence of county and city offices along Penn Avenue, as well a few churches. Significantly, only 2 percent of the doorways led to residences.

Building Condition

A street-level assessment of building facades provided a quick measure of aesthetic appeal and physical integrity of the structure. The study included a qualitative interpretation of the soundness of the mainly brick facades. Did they require structural repairs? What was the overall attraction of the building or lot (weeds growing, flaking paint, broken windows)? Nearly six out of ten sites (57 percent) were in good condition. Thirty-nine percent were in fair condition, while just 4 percent were in bad shape.

Building Height

Perhaps one of the most charming features of the Strip is the low-density, uniform redbrick appearance. It is a decidedly low-lying district, with a mean building height of just 2.6 stories. The mode statistic for building height is two stories, while four out of five buildings (81 percent) are four stories tall or less. Ninety-five percent of all buildings do not exceed five stories.

The Strip Reinvented

The social and economic history of the Strip mirrors that of the city, western Pennsylvania, and indeed the nation. Cities in the manufacturing belt are reinventing themselves in a post-smokestack era (Beauregard 1989; Wilson and Huff 1994). Around the country, firms compete fiercely in the global marketplace for talented workers. As part of that allure, the Strip offers Pittsburgh special amenities. Often misunderstood and stereotyped because of its gritty past, "If Pittsburgh were situated somewhere in the heart of Europe, tourists would eagerly journey hundreds of miles out of their way to visit" (Gill 1989, 74).

The Strip is evolving beyond a traditional warehouse district that characterizes the concentric zone or sector land use models of urban ecology. Competition from suburban wholesaling centers near interstate highways underscores the relevance of the Multiple Nuclei model. In the year 2006, the Strip has become a trendy, mixed-use pocket of the city with land uses that invite street activity twenty-four hours a day, seven days a week. (Outdoor markets serve as a unique place where Pittsburgh's social dialect ("Pittsburghese") can be heard in the sidewalks, cafes, and warehouses (Scarpaci 1999).

While a reduced produce district still operates, a growing weekend and evening service sector caters to a new clientele. Greengrocers, discount merchandise vendors, and discotheques welcome customers. Parking is abundant, though that will change. Seagate Technology, Inc., the world's largest maker of computer hard disk drives, built a $40 million, six-story laboratory and office building (figure 5.9) on what was a parking lot along the Allegheny riverfront at Thirteenth Street (Barnes 1999). Elsewhere in the Strip, old warehouses, flanked by the central business district to the south, and the bluffs that define the Hill District to the east, provide a distinct environment for niche retailers and consumers in search of chic, urban heritage spaces. Moreover, an elevated rail line demarcates the Strip from the central busi-

FIG. 5.8. Penn Avenue in the Strip, April 2003.

ness district and its adjacent cultural district. It has garnered a reputation as a center for live music. However, in January 2004, the Rosebud dinner club closed its doors, a fact that may signal a new trend in the area's investment. As one analyst remarked: "The death of a nightclub is never a good thing for a town obsessed for retaining young people and entertaining middle-aged residents who are young at heart." In October 2003, a nearby club, Metropol, was sold, leaving the 300-seat Rex Theater in the city's South Side as the only comparable venue. But in early 2004, nine out of thirteen bars had closed in the Strip. There is some evidence that enforcement of laws prohibiting driving while intoxicated (DWI) and higher prices for parking are also reasons for the Strip's changing retail makeup. Another observer of the Strip hoped that the club "closing[s aren't] a harbinger of more sour notes" (*Pittsburgh Post-Gazette* 2004).

These and other notable landmarks give this corner of Pittsburgh a strong sense of place. Its contemporary profile masks the district's industrial history. Changes in technology since the early 1800s have made the area a barge destination, a railroad terminal, a tractor-trailer-supplied warehouse district, and a parking lot for commuters and retailers. Restaurants and nightclubs infuse the Strip with a comparative advantage because they deliver "industrial strength" partying without disturbing residents. In the evenings, some establishments run a free shuttle service for patrons reveling in the South

FIG. 5.9. Allegheny riverfront before (1999) and after Seagate occupied the site (2004).

Side of Pittsburgh (two miles away on the Monongahela River). This link lets customers barhop without driving under the influence of alcohol.

Loft and warehouse conversion will remain a huge potential real estate market over the next decade or so. A major locus of these efforts is the Armstrong Cork Building on Railroad Street and Twenty-third Street. Residential development will likely ensue north of the core Strip District, between Twenty-third and Thirty-second streets flanked by Smallman and Liberty (City of Pittsburgh 1998, c-ii). Should revitalization continue, it is unlikely that problems of residential displacement that often accompany gentrification will appear (Holcomb and Beauregard 1981; Smith and Williams 1986) if only because the residential population is not large. The Lawrenceville Redevelopment Corporation actively promotes the adaptation of old warehouses to new businesses or condominiums (LDC 1999). A lack of public schools in the immediate area will be a disadvantage for some new homesteaders. City planners expect that dual-income no-children types (DINCS) and young urban professionals (yuppies) will find the area appealing because of the "niche opportunities for young singles, and empty nesters" (City of Pittsburgh 1998). The authenticity of the Strip's ethnic flavor and its seasoned charm will no doubt be challenged, commodified, and tainted as national chain establishments such as Starbucks, the Olive Garden, and McDonalds establish a foothold in the district.

In conventional economic development terms, the future tax base looks promising. The Strip contributes to the visual charm of the city's three rivers. Riverfront attractions include several miles of bicycle and walking trails that will skirt the riverbanks of the Strip. Already Pittsburgh's comparative advantage (8.58 miles) of waterfront looms large compared to other Rust Belt cities: Cleveland, with its Rock and Roll Hall of Fame and Museum and new

Browns Stadium on Lake Erie, has 5.6 miles of it; Baltimore claims 4.1 miles, including its celebrated Harborplace. Potential for historic preservation and adaptive reuse of old buildings is now assured because tourism shoulders the local economy as wholesaling once did. Students from the University of Pittsburgh as well as others from Carnegie Mellon University, Point Park College, Carlow College, Chatham College, and the Allegheny County Community College number 20,000 strong in the downtown area daily (City of Pittsburgh 1998). With abundant and cheap parking, the Strip offers students a unique, non-mall shopping experience. City boosters in the new millennium will tout these amenities.

Note

I wish to thank Kevin Patrick, Lauren Uhl, Darlene S. Violetta, and Joseph L. Scarpaci Sr. for comments on an earlier version of this paper. I am, however, solely responsible for any errors.

References

Barnes, T. 1999. Computer Firm Picks Strip for $40 Million Building. *Pittsburgh Post Gazette*, November 24.

Beauregard, R., ed. 1989. *Atop the Urban Hierarchy.* Totowa, NJ: Rowman and Littlefield.

Bell, T. 1941. *Out of This Furnace.* Repr., Pittsburgh: University of Pittsburgh Press, 1976.

Bluestone, B., and B. Harrison. 1982. *The Deindustrialization of America: Plant Closings, Community Abandonment and the Dismantling of Basic Industry.* New York: Basic Books.

Business Week. 1975. *Can Jonathan Scott Save A&P?* May 19, 128.

City of Pittsburgh. 1998. The Riverfront Development Plan: A Comprehensive Plan for the Three Rivers. Pittsburgh: City of Pittsburgh, Office of Mayor Tom Murphy.

DCP (Department of Planning). 1988. Investors' Prospectus, The Pittsburgh Downtown Plan: A Blueprint for the 21st Century. Pittsburgh: City of Pittsburgh Department of Planning.

Demorest, R. 1958. *Pittsburgh: A Bicentennial Tribute, 1758–1958.* Pittsburgh: Carnegie Library of Pittsburgh.

Denny, James O'Hara. 1973. The Strip. *Carnegie Magazine*, January, 29.

Fanzo, M. 1994. 24 hours in "The Strip." *Eastside Observer* (Pittsburgh), August, 13.

Glazier, W. 1885. Pittsburgh. In *Peculiarities of American Cities.* Philadelphia: Hubbard Brothers Publishers.

Graham, M. 1991. *Martha Graham: Blood Memory.* New York: Doubleday.

Handlin, O. 1975. The City Grows. In *Pittsburgh: The Story of an American City*, ed. S. Lorant, 81–128. Lenox, MA: Authors Edition.

Heinz, T. 1999. At River's Edge. *Pittsburgh Post-Gazette*, September 1.

Historical Society of Western Pennsylvania. n.d. Wholesale Produce Business. In *Walking Map of the Strip District* (brochure).
Holcomb, H. B., and R. A. Beauregard. 1981. *Revitalizing Cities*. Washington, DC: Association of American Geographers.
Kellogg, Paul U. 1909. In *Charities and the Commons*, January 2. Reproduced in "What was the Pittsburgh Survey?"
LDC (Lawrenceville Development Corporation). 1999, http://www.ldc-pgh.org.
Muller, T. 1999. Pittsburgh's Strip District. *AAG Newsletter* 43 (9).
NLC (Neighborhoods for Living Center). 1981. Pittsburgh Neighborhoods. Pittsburgh: City of Pittsburgh.
Parton, J. 1864. Pittsburgh. *Atlantic Monthly* 21, 21.
Pittsburgh Post Gazette. 2004. Sour Note: Rosebud Ends a Lively Run in the Strip. February 7.
Scarpaci, J. L. 1999. See Yunz Guyz Dahntahn. *AAG Newsletter* 43 (10).
———. 2005. *Plazas and Barrios: Heritage Tourism and Globalization in the Latin American Centro Histórico*. Tucson: University of Arizona Press.
Smith, N., and P. Williams, eds. 1986. *Gentrification of the City*. Boston: Allen and Unwin.
Toker, F. 1986. *Pittsburgh: An Urban Portrait*. University Park, PA: Pennsylvania State University Press.
Walther, T., and L. Uhl. 1995. Strip District History. Historical Society of Western Pennsylvania (mimeo.).
Wilson, D., and J. O. Huff, eds. 1994. *Marginalized Places and Populations: A Structurationist Agenda*. Westport, CT: Praeger.
Wright, F. L. 1935. City Target of Architect. *Pittsburgh Post-Gazette*, July 1.

SIX

Pittsburgh, City of Bridges

Kevin J. Patrick

Pittsburgh nicknames have come and gone: Gateway to the West, the Smoky City, City of Champions, even the venerable Steel City. One moniker, however, is as appropriate now as it was a hundred years ago, and will be a hundred years hence: Pittsburgh, City of Bridges. Bridges are not just one aspect of Pittsburgh's geography, they are the essence of Pittsburgh's cityscape, the representative form that comes from the layering of physical geography, historical development, cultural landscapes, civic art, economic geography, urban space, and place perceptions.

Pittsburgh is replete with bridge lore. George Washington nearly drowned in a half-frozen Allegheny River for lack of a bridge. The city once built a Bridge to Nowhere (the Ft. Duquesne Bridge) that it did not open for eight years, and closed a bridge to somewhere (the Point Bridge) that was not torn down for eleven years. Oakmont is renowned for its lavender bridge. The West End Bridge goes to the North Side, and in some years locals call the Monaca-Rochester Bridge the Rochester-Monaca Bridge, depending on which high school wins the annual football game (Gangewere 2001, 31). The Bellefield Bridge was buried in Oakland, and the Hot Metal Bridge was resurrected to carry cars rather than molten iron to the South Side. A Pittsburgh purgatory is to be forever crossing a bridge over some river while looking at the bridge you *really* want to be on, and realizing you can't get there from here. Pittsburgh is all about bridges.

The hydrology of the region set about shaping the city's spatial extent eons before the first Pittsburgher set foot on the Point. The Allegheny and

Monongahela rivers flow together to form the Ohio. All three have dual identities as blessings to waterborne commerce and barriers to overland transportation. All three act as transportation corridors through real estate that is steep-sided and hilly. All three attract a vast network of lesser tributaries that have dissected the uplifted Allegheny Plateau into an irregular landscape of hilltops and ravines on which no straight, level road can be built. The settlers who chose to inhabit this physical environment had no choices but to build bridges.

The earliest spans were private toll bridges built in an age of wood. Long, multiple-span covered bridges were first thrown across the Monongahela and Allegheny rivers in 1818 and 1819 respectively (Lorant 1980, 559–600). The bridges accommodated the pedestrians and wagons that used them. Roofs protected the bridge superstructure from the elements. Wood was also used for the more substantial canal aqueducts. In 1829, the Western Division Canal of the trans-Appalachian Main Line of Public Works entered the city over a covered aqueduct that crossed the Allegheny River at Eleventh Street.

The Great Fire of 1845 destroyed the Monongahela Bridge at Smithfield Street. A year later, the authorities pulled down the Allegheny aqueduct, which inspectors had proclaimed unsafe. John A. Roebling, pioneer wire cable manufacturer and bridge engineer, replaced both bridges with multiple-span suspension bridges in 1846–1847. These transitional structures signaled the end of the age of wood, despite the fact that the Forty-third Street Bridge across the Allegheny River would stand as Pittsburgh's last large-span covered bridge until 1924 (Gangewere 2001, 3). From the mid-nineteenth century through the opening decades of the twentieth, the metal truss bridge would reign supreme, most of them being built by the railroad.

Pittsburgh's Railroad Bridges

Unsung and ignored, invariably black and steel ribbed, Pittsburgh's railroad bridges are the silent industrial workhorses of the three rivers. In most cases, they are through trusses that emerged in the nineteenth century and then were adapted to heavier design specifications during the early twentieth century. The first train from Philadelphia steamed into Pittsburgh in 1852 over the Pennsylvania Railroad, commonly known as the Pennsy. Six years later trains rolled across the Allegheny River from Union Station over the city's first major railroad span. The bridge sat just downstream from the old canal aqueduct to connect the Pennsylvania Railroad with its subsidiary, the Pittsburgh, Ft. Wayne and Chicago Railway. To this day, the Ft. Wayne Bridge carries the name of this connection. The original Ft. Wayne Bridge

Fig. 6.1. This view of the Ft. Wayne Bridge shows the concrete pier extensions that were inserted when the bridge was raised in 1917–1919.

was actually a wooden truss span, replaced by a wrought iron lattice truss in 1868. Builders completed the current double-deck through truss at this location in 1904 (figure 6.1). Opened during the height of the railroad era, this span supported two main line tracks on the upper deck and two freight tracks on the lower, which once served freight terminals on either side of the river. Those freight terminals have long since been replaced by the commercial development of an expanding central business district, facilitating the abandonment of the lower deck.

The city's second railroad bridge opened in 1863 as part of the Steubenville Extension of the Pennsylvania Railroad. Built south from Union Station (predecessor to Penn Station at Grant Street and Liberty Avenue), the line crossed the Monongahela River before turning west toward Ohio via the panhandle of Virginia (now West Virginia). Officially called the Pittsburgh, Cincinnati, Chicago and St. Louis Railroad, the line and the bridge was more commonly known as the Panhandle (Kobus and Consoli 1997, 60–61). Engineers modified the original bridge in 1881 and replaced it in 1903 with the current bridge, which includes three main-span through trusses. Since 1985, it has been used to carry Pittsburgh Area Transit's relocated South Hills trolley line from the Mt. Washington Transit Tunnel (holed through in 1904) into downtown.

Around the turn of the twentieth century, the Pennsylvania Railroad was moving hundreds of trains a day through its Pittsburgh Terminal Yard, which stretched for twenty blocks behind Union Station. To reduce the congestion at this bottleneck, the Pennsy built a bypass network of tracks that required bridges over each of the city's three rivers. Although now belonging to the Norfolk Southern Railroad, these bridges continue to carry through-routed freight trains (Patrick 2002, 44). Eastbound trains entering the city from the expansive Conway Yard flow through the Ohio Connecting Railway Bridge to the south shore of the Ohio and Monongahela rivers, and then back over the Monongahela River via the Port Perry Bridge (opened in 1877) to reconnect with the Main Line at Turtle Creek. The lengthy Ohio Connecting Railway Bridge uses a series of deck trusses to step across Brunot's Island in conjunction with two through trusses to span the Ohio River's Main and Back channels. Built in 1890, the increased traffic necessitated the addition of a second track in 1915. To accommodate the extra width, builders erected a larger span around the smaller, original through trusses without stopping rail traffic. The older trusses were then dismantled from inside the newer bridge (Korus and Consoli 1997, 66).

In 1904, the Pennsy opened the Brilliant Branch from a Main Line junction in East Liberty, north down Negley Run Hollow, over the massive masonry arches of the Silver Lake Bridge, to a three-span through truss across the Allegheny River at Aspinwall. The link provided through-routed trains direct access to the Allegheny Valley Railroad and the Pennsy's Conemaugh Division (West Penn Railroad) along the north shore of the Allegheny River, without the need to pass through Union Station. Diminished rail traffic led to the closing of this bridge.

The Baltimore and Ohio (B&O) Railroad rivaled the Pennsylvania for traffic between Chicago and the Atlantic seaboard with a line through Pittsburgh opened in the 1870s. After crossing the Allegheny Mountains, the road (now run by CSX) followed the right bank of the Youghiogheny and Monongahela rivers to a downtown terminal at the north end of the Smithfield Street Bridge. Completed in 1884, its link to the Midwest split from this line at Junction Hollow and passed through a tunnel beneath the streets of Oakland and over the Allegheny River at Herr's Island (Washington's Landing) before continuing to Ohio by way of Butler. The current two-span through truss replaced the original bridge in 1921. In the same year, the B&O also erected the Glenwood Bridge over the Monongahela to access the lower Midwest via a main line junction at Wheeling, West Virginia. Upgraded in 1915, the three Pratt through trusses are a now familiar site to the patrons of Sandcastle water park, which was constructed just upstream.

Several other railroad bridges were built as critical links in the ceaseless

FIG. 6.2. One of the largest railroad bridges in the region, the Pittsburgh and Lake Erie's 1910 cantilever over the Ohio River at Beaver is still in use.

movement of iron ore, coal, coke, and limestone to and from area mills and mines. When the source of iron ore feeding Pittsburgh steel mills shifted to the Superior Upland of Minnesota in the late nineteenth century, two railroads carried the bulk of it into the city from Lake Erie ports. The Pittsburgh and Lake Erie Railroad (P&LE) operated as the link between the Connellsville coalfields and the ore docks on Lake Erie. The line was opened from Connellsville in 1883 and crossed the Monongahela River on a three-span through truss between Rankin and Munhall before running to its Pittsburgh terminal at the south end of the Smithfield Street Bridge. In 1889, the P&LE constructed a large through truss to carry its tracks across the Ohio River at Beaver. The current gargantuan cantilever span replaced the bridge in 1910 (figure 6.2).

The first ore boat arrived at Conneaut, Ohio, in 1892, stimulating Andrew Carnegie to form the Bessemer and Lake Erie Railroad (B&LE) to bring the ore to his Edgar Thompson plant in Braddock over a line completed five years later. The line included the high, six-span deck truss that stretched for more than a half mile across the Allegheny Valley at Harmarville. In 1918, a completely rebuilt bridge emerged that used a similar deck truss design and the same piers to accommodate a double set of tracks. Absorbed into US Steel in 1901, the B&LE has been a part of Great Lakes Transportation since 2001, which the Canadian National acquired three years later. Ore trains loaded with taconite still cross the span heading for the US Steel's Edgar Thompson plant, now the last mill in the valley.

US Steel also owned the Union Railroad, a terminal switching road serving the company's steel mills throughout the Monongahela Valley. In 1898, the Union Railroad constructed a bridge at Port Perry with two through trusses and three deck trusses to bring ore to the blast furnaces at Duquesne, McKeesport, and Clairton. The bridge was constructed immediately downstream from the Pennsylvania Railroad's Port Perry Bridge, and also crossed the B&O and P&LE tracks on the north bank. Heavy traffic on these four roads devoted to bulk materials needed by the steel industry once gave Port Perry the distinction of being the place with the highest freight traffic density in the world, measured as tons moved past a single point per day (Kobus and Consoli 1997, 71). The need for even greater rail capacity caused the Pennsylvania Railroad to rebuild its Port Perry Bridge with a double set of tracks in 1903.

The Union Railroad also used its Port Perry span as a hot metal bridge, carrying molten metal from Braddock to processing facilities on the other side of the river. This was a typical arrangement in the Mon Valley where few floodplains were copious enough to accommodate a full size integrated steel mill, so some of the mills had to sprawl over both banks. Typically, the "hot end" of the mill, including the blast furnaces, gas stoves, casting houses, and raw materials pit operated on one side of the river, and the "cold end," with its rolling mills and fabricating shops, was on the other. In this arrangement, the open-hearth furnaces, which converted the pig iron from the blast furnaces into steel, were on the cold end side. Steel mills railed hot metal from the blast furnaces, either cast or molten, across the river to the other end of the mill, and over what came to be known as "hot metal bridges." The mills are all gone and their sites redeveloped, but the four hot metal bridges still exist.

Downstream from Port Perry, the Union Railroad's Rankin Hot Metal Bridge stands unused in the isolated splendor of deindustrialization. The bridge opened with its two Pratt through trusses in 1900 to connect US Steel's Carrie Furnaces in Rankin with the Homestead works across the river. The Carrie Furnaces were closed in 1982, followed by the entire Homestead plant four years later. The Homestead property has been cleared and rebuilt as a mixed-use development called the Waterfront. A remnant of the Carrie Furnace complex still stands awaiting restoration as a heritage museum that would include the rehabilitation of the Hot Metal Bridge to reconnect the site with Homestead. The Union Railroad eventually used the McKeesport Connecting Railroad Bridge built in 1890 with two through trusses and two deck

FIG. 6.3. In this view of the rehabilitated Hot Metal Bridge, the Monongahela Connecting Bridge that carries the roadway is to the right. The original J&L hot metal bridge is to the left.

trusses. It functioned as another hot metal bridge connecting Duquesne's Dorothy Six blast furnace with the National Tube works in McKeesport.

Rival steel manufacturer Jones and Laughlin (J&L, later LTV) erected its sprawling Pittsburgh Works on both sides of the Monongahela beginning in the 1850s. In 1887, a double-tracked, multiple through truss bridge was constructed by the Monongahela Connecting Railroad to link to two sites. In 1900, Jones and Laughlin extended the bridge's five masonry piers on their downstream side to accommodate a second, single-track multiple through truss to be used exclusively as a hot metal bridge between J&L's Eliza Furnace and its South Side mills. The mill closed in 1985 and both parcels were cleared for redevelopment, leaving only the bridges. The Pittsburgh Technology Center rose from the ashes of the north shore furnaces, and a mixed-use development christened the South Side Works opened on the south shore in 2004. The Monongahela Connecting Bridge was rehabilitated in 2000 as a two-lane vehicular bridge confusingly named the Hot Metal Bridge, implying that there is only one bridge, which is how most people think of it. The actual hot metal bridge, the narrower of the two, stands on the downstream side disconnected from its now-demolished approach spans awaiting rehabilitation as a pedestrian/bike way (figure 6.3).

Of all the large-span railroad bridges built in Pittsburgh during the early twentieth century, only one was ever demolished without replacement. The Wabash Bridge opened over the Monongahela River in 1905 as part of the Wabash-Pittsburgh Terminal Railroad, a link in George Gould's ill-fated transcontinental railroad, which later became the Pittsburgh and West Virginia (P&WV) Railroad. The bridge linked the downtown Wabash Terminal at Ferry Street and Liberty Avenue with the Wabash Tunnel beneath Mount Washington. The line continued west to cross the Ohio River at Mingo Junction over a cantilever span that is still in service. During the Depression, passenger traffic on the P&WV dwindled to the point of abandonment, and the Wabash Bridge became scrap metal during World War II (Plowden 1974, 176). All that remains of this 1,504-foot cantilevered span are two stone bridge piers standing on opposite banks of the river. The Wabash Tunnel, however, is currently being readapted for a Pittsburgh Area Transit busway.

Re-bridging the Point

In 1899, the US War Department declared the six lower-most bridges over the Allegheny River—the ones connecting downtown Pittsburgh to Allegheny City (later merged into Pittsburgh)—to be hazards to navigation (Kuncio 1999, 62). A variety of engineering techniques highlight these bridges. Mid-river piers supported them all, but they did not line up evenly. River craft therefore threaded a sinuous course of low bridge clearances to access and exit the Allegheny River. The Army Corps of Engineers proposed a lock and dam on the Ohio River that would raise the pool level enough to cause these bridges to effectively barricade the Allegheny at its mouth. The desired improvement to river navigation condemned all but one of these spans, and ushered in a new generation of bridge building. By 1929, water was pooling behind the finished Emsworth Lock and Dam, and rising beneath five new bridges over the lower Allegheny.

The Union Bridge was the first to span the mouth of the Allegheny at the Point. Built in 1874 with barely forty feet of vertical clearance, it was a five-span, wooden covered bridge that put four piers in the river. For these reasons, it was the primary culprit in the river's navigability problems. Nonetheless, it held the title as the longest surviving covered bridge in the state when it was dismantled in 1907. Its replacement, the two-span through truss Manchester Bridge, was finished in 1913 but not opened until 1915 due to a dispute over the location of the North Side approach. The bridge was famous for its elaborate portal sculptures that included a flanking steel worker and coal miner at one end, references to mythical Joe Magarac and union advocate Jan Volkanik, and frontier guide Christopher Gist and Seneca chief Guyasuta at the other. When authorities demolished the Manchester Bridge they saved these decorative portals, which now reside at the Children's Museum garden on the North Side. Incongruously, the bridge's North Side pier survived as well and still stands as an unexplained wall at the water's edge near Heinz Field.

Farther upstream, the city pulled down the Federal, Seventh, and Ninth Street bridges between 1925 and 1927 as part of a grand replacement project that resulted in the Three Sisters Bridges. The two-span bowstring through truss at Federal Street had opened in 1893 as the replacement to John A. Roebling's 1859 Allegheny Suspension Bridge. Still retaining plenty of life, engineers unhinged the Federal Street Bridge from its piers, set it on barges, and floated it down to Coraopolis where it was put into service over the Back Channel to Neville Island for another sixty-seven years (Gangewere 2001, 26).

The Seventh Street Bridge was another pioneering suspension span. In 1884, Gustav Lindenthal designed the complex, double-span bridge to be supported by two sets of chain-linked eyebars set one above the other. The Ninth Street Bridge was an 1890 multiple-span through truss resting on a phalanx of five boat-threatening river piers. The four-span Mechanic Street (Sixteenth Street) Bridge dated to 1838. The covered bridge suffered several floods and fires; the most recent fire forced reconstruction as late as 1923. All of these bridges were sacrificed before the rising waters of the river.

A three-span, steel through arch replaced the old Mechanic Street Bridge. Opened in 1922, four entrance pylons topped with armillary spheres banded by signs of the zodiac and supported by winged horses flanked the new Sixteenth Street Bridge. This type of monumental ornamentation, although anathema to the increasingly popular modern movement, was commonplace on public works still being influenced by the neoclassical City Beautiful movement. The Washington Crossing Bridge, opened at Fortieth Street in 1924, was as much a monument to George Washington as it was a modern bridge. A pair of regal obelisks flanked an eastern approach plaza to the three-span, open-spandrel, steel deck arch, and the metal railings were festooned with the great seals of the thirteen original states. The bridge commemorates the place where George Washington and his guide, Christopher Gist, crossed the Allegheny River in December of 1753 on their return from French Fort Le Boeuf. George Washington was sent to tell the French to leave the upper Ohio Valley. They refused. If that wasn't bad enough, on the way back their raft fell apart in the Allegheny River, and both men spent a frigid night on a mid-river island (Lorant 1980, 595).

Of the six lower Allegheny River bridges, only the Pennsylvania Railroad's Ft. Wayne Bridge was deemed too important to demolish. The entire bridge was gradually jacked up between 1917 and 1919 to gain the necessary clearance without disrupting its heavy train traffic (Kobus and Consoli 1997, 40). The concrete extensions capping the original masonry bridge piers record this elevating event.

To minimize disruption and property damage, the city required that the new Sixth, Seventh, and Ninth Street bridge locations and approaches be left the same as before. At the same time, the influential Pittsburgh City Art Commission rejected the original plan for three cantilevered bridges in favor of three identical suspension bridges, which were considered more aesthetically pleasing (Kuncio 1999, 66). The requirements of the city, however, precluded the construction of massive anchorage piers needed for the main cables. The solution was to support the spans with pinned eyebars anchored to the ends of stiffening girders that support the roadway (figure 6.4). Completed in 1926 (Seventh Street), 1927 (Ninth Street), and 1928 (Sixth Street), the canary yellow bridges were the first American bridges to use self-anchoring suspension technology. They are also the country's only identical bridge triplets, and are the largest remaining suspension bridges held up with eyebar chains instead of steel cables. The upper Ohio Valley was the center of chain-link suspension bridge technology in nineteenth and early twentieth centuries. The suspension system was discredited in 1967 after forty-six people were killed in the catastrophic failure of the Silver Bridge, an eyebar suspension bridge spanning the Ohio River at Point Pleasant, West Virginia.

The Monongahela bridges were not as low as the ones spanning the Allegheny. The original Point Bridge at the mouth of the Monongahela was an iron, chain-link suspension bridge built in 1877 with one long span having more than twice the vertical clearance as the nearby Union Bridge. It remained serviceable throughout its useful life, but its narrow cart way crowded with trolley tracks caused the bridge to suffer from a functional obsolescence at the dawn of the auto age. It was dismantled soon after a beefier cantilever through truss replacement was opened immediately upstream in 1927 (figure 6.5). Although both bridges are history, their stone-faced south abutments still stand like forgotten battlements hidden within the neglected vegetation of the riverbank.

The Smithfield Street Bridge is arguably the most historic span in the city. It stands in the location of the Monongahela Bridge, the city's first major river span, and replaced John Roebling's first Pittsburgh suspension bridge. Opened in 1883, the double lenticular truss bridge is the work of Gustav Lindenthal. It is the oldest major span in the city and the largest lenticular truss bridge in North America. Pittsburghers of the recent past knew this as the trolley bridge, because it was the last bridge to carry streetcars into the Golden Triangle. The trolleys actually crossed on an expansion span built

FIG. 6.4. Lowermost of the Three Sisters, the Sixth Street Bridge was recently renamed the Roberto Clemente Bridge, emphasizing its link between downtown and the Pittsburgh Pirates' new stadium, PNC Park.

FIG. 6.5. This 1927 W. L. Coffman photograph was taken just before the new cantilever Point Bridge was opened, when traffic was still crossing the old 1877 suspension bridge.

in 1890–1891 when another set of lenticular trusses was added to the bridge (PHMC and PennDOT 1986, 129). In 1985, the South Hills trolley line was removed from the Smithfield Street Bridge and relocated to the abandoned Panhandle Bridge just upstream.

The South Side mill town of Birmingham was linked to Pittsburgh in 1861 with a covered bridge at South Tenth Street. The old Monongahela Lock and Dam #1 was constructed upstream from this bridge, which was replaced by a four-span through truss in 1904. The old lock and dam was removed after the rising waters of the much larger Emsworth Lock and Dam downstream on the Ohio made its lift unnecessary.

Pittsburgh Bridges in the Early Auto Age

Simultaneous with the struggle to untangle the bridge-river knot was a shift in bridge-building responsibility toward the public sector. Illustrating this shift was a 1910 report produced for the Pittsburgh Civic Commission by no less a personage than Frederick Law Olmstead. Entitled *Pittsburgh Main Thoroughfares and the Downtown District*, it contained recommended improvements for riverfronts, bridges, and dozens of streets throughout the Pittsburgh area. Although the report contained a few gritty Pittsburgh photos of unkempt streets and coal-laden wharves partially obscured by smoke, most of its photos were of refined public works in European cities, implying what Pittsburgh *could* be.

Allegheny County had entered its Golden Age of bridge building. Charged with a heightened sense of civic responsibility during a time of unprecedented economic prosperity, the county erected approximately one hundred bridges between 1920 and 1935, forty-three of them major spans. After 1924, most bridge construction was done under the aegis of the Allegheny County Department of Public Works, whose massive operating budget exceeded that of many states (Kuncio 1999, 63). By this time, the automobile had become the most significant factor influencing everything from bridge design to bridge location within a regional highway network, which the county set out to build. New boulevards were constructed along the banks of all three rivers and crisscrossed the city from bridge to bridge.

Opened with much fanfare on March 27, 1928, the Liberty Bridge was the epitome of the modern highway links being built for automobile age Pittsburgh. Unlike the other downtown bridges of its day, Liberty Bridge soared over Mon riverfront communities instead of connecting them and was devoid of streetcar tracks. The multiple-span deck truss was designed in conjunction with the mile-long Liberty Tubes (opened four years earlier) as part of a regional highway plan to link the Golden Triangle with its burgeoning South Hills suburbs. Like a World's Fair vision of the future, commuting motorists could zip off to the urban fringe by gliding high over the traffic of the South Side surface streets and beneath the crowded streetcar suburbs of Mt. Washington.

Automobile use also left its mark on the lower-level replacement of the 1904 South Tenth Street Bridge. Construction crews holed through the vaulted, dual-tube Armstrong Tunnel in 1927 to carry vehicular traffic beneath the Monongahela Bluff between downtown and a new suspension bridge to the South Side completed in 1933. The elegant bridge incorporated muted Art Deco detailing, and remains the only major cable suspension bridge in western Pennsylvania.

Over a mile in length (5,800 feet), the 1931 McKees Rock Bridge is still the longest bridge in Allegheny County. Built essentially as an elevated highway with a modern traffic circle, it connected the northern approach to the recently completed Ohio River Boulevard. Inspired by New York's Hell Gate Bridge, the McKees Rocks Bridge has a number of steel deck arch spans supporting the approaches to the main 750-foot through arch with a reverse-curve top chord flanked by a set of four massive ashlar pylons rising 180 feet above the Ohio River.

The West End Bridge opened at the head of the Ohio River a year later, linking Ohio River Boulevard and the North Side to Carson Street and Saw Mill Run Boulevard, the newest automobile thoroughfare to the South Hills suburbs. Before the bridge, communication between the North Side and the West End had to first go through the downtown Point. Exhibiting the latest bridge-building technology, the West End's 780-foot main span stood as the nation's longest tied arch bridge for nearly forty years (figure 6.6). The arch ends of a tied arch bridge are "tied" by the lower chord that runs beneath the roadway. The thrust of the arch is therefore taken up by the tension of the bottom chord so the bridge abutments need not be so massive (PHMC and PennDOT 1986, 97).

The cantilever deck truss was another new bridge type introduced to the river valleys of Allegheny County during the 1930s. Like the tied arch, the cantilever span has a long reach, minimizing the need for mid-river piers. Ornamentation was a thing of the past. With its clean lines, efficient use of materials, and unobstructed views from the deck, the cantilever deck span exuded modernity.

The cantilever deck truss first soared across the Mon Valley in 1937 with the opening of the Homestead High Level Bridge. It replaced Brown's Bridge, a five-span through truss dating to 1897. Brown's was typical of pre-auto bridges, narrow, low, and oriented toward river town surface streets, allowing easy access for horse-drawn wagons, streetcars, and pedestrians. By comparison, the High Level Bridge reflects motor vehicle traffic and an

FIG. 6.6. The 1932 West End Bridge showing its Warren pony truss approach spans.

FIG. 6.7. The cantilever deck truss, like the 1938 Highland Park Bridge, was a popular type of river span in the Pittsburgh area from the 1930s through the 1960s.

orientation to the regional road network. The bridge sweeps upward to a north end anchorage on the plateau surface where it ties into the early auto suburbs built along Beechwood Boulevard in Squirrel Hill.

The same was true for the Highland Park Bridge, a cantilever deck truss built over the Allegheny River a year later (figure 6.7). The old Highland Park Bridge was a cantilever through truss built from Sharpsburg's Nineteenth Street in 1902. Like Homestead's Brown's Bridge, this bridge was narrow, low, and carried a considerable live load of pedestrians and streetcars. The new Highland Park Bridge came into operation just upstream in conjunction with Allegheny Lock and Dam #2 (complete in 1934). The lock, dam, and bridge project illustrates the complex level of regional transportation planning that had been achieved by the 1920s and 1930s. The bridge approaches intersected Freeport Road and Allegheny River Boulevard using grade-separated trumpet interchanges similar to the ones then being designed for the Pennsylvania Turnpike.

The high-level, auto-oriented, cantilever deck truss became the standard river crossing into the postwar era. Numerous examples were constructed throughout the county, including the Rankin Bridge (1951), the Pennsylvania Turnpike's Allegheny River Bridge (1951), the Senator Robert D. Fleming Bridge at Sixty-second Street (1962), and the Glenwood Bridge (1966). In every case, trolley tracks—a standard necessity for bridges after 1890—were not included.

Hollow-Hopping Spans

In addition to the challenge Pittsburgh's three rivers present to overland transportation are the barriers created by a labyrinth of steep-sided ravines and hollows carved by the rivers' tributaries dissecting into the plateau surface. The spatial extent and character of many Pittsburgh neighborhoods have been influenced by the nature of this irregular topography. Spanning these hollows and connecting the hilltops was not a concern until the establishment of city-wide, then regional, transportation networks starting in the late nineteenth century.

The earliest builders of neighborhood-connecting, hollow-hopping spans were the electric streetcar companies in the 1890s. Conforming to a radial design centered on downtown Pittsburgh, this was the first city-wide transportation system built as a network. Frequently, communities on a particular line had to be linked together with deck trusses or trestles that carried trolleys over intervening ravines, such as the bridges still in service on Pittsburgh Area Transit's South Hills "T" Line. Streetcar suburbs on the Ohio River bluffs in Bellevue, Avalon, and Ben Avon at the turn of the twentieth century were dependent on a trolley line that leapt across three deep ravines atop high trestles. The Pittsburgh neighborhoods of Bloomfield and Schenley Heights were similarly linked.

Around the turn of the century, the city of Pittsburgh and Allegheny County's Department of Public Works started building its own hollow-hopping spans as part of public streets improvement projects. Invariably, these bridges were graceful, single-span deck arches made of steel or reinforced concrete with classical lines and architectural detailing inspired by the City Beautiful movement. The Panther Hollow (1897) and Schenley Park (1898) bridges are the oldest surviving hollow-hopping spans in the city. Both were constructed as steel deck arches on the sinuous main drive through the romantically landscaped Schenley Park (Schmidlapp 1986).

Other steel deck arches were constructed elsewhere, such as the McAfee Bridge (1927) and East Street Bridge (1930) on the North Side, but the material of choice for this type of bridge was reinforced concrete in the early twentieth century. Built in 1912 to open the hilltop Lincoln District for development, the open-spandrel Larimer Avenue Bridge literally soars across Negley Run Hollow in one stunning rainbow leap of reinforced concrete. Classical ornamentation on these bridges peaked in the 1920s, exemplified best by the eagle-topped obelisks that guard the entrances to Bellevue's Jack's Run Bridge, the open-spandrel concrete arch that replaced the former trolley trestle in 1924.

By the 1930s, the concrete arches began to reflect the unadorned principles of modernism encouraged by the utilitarian requirements of the automobile, although muted art deco and streamlined modern detailing was not uncommon. The building of Ohio River Boulevard as the main thoroughfare down the Ohio Valley from the Point illustrates the supremacy of modern technology over romantic beauty. The cliff-side highway required six reinforced concrete arches to cross hollows opening toward the Ohio River. Completed in 1930, the builders used the same falsework to systematically erect the six bridges (Kuncio 1999, 67).

In the wake of Ohio River Boulevard, the Department of Public Works moved on to its greatest challenge, the bridging of Turtle Creek Valley. In 1931, the George Westinghouse Bridge opened as the world's largest reinforced concrete arch bridge (figure 6.8). Five titanic arches, the largest spanning a gulf of 460 feet, supported a four-lane highway two hundred feet above the valley floor. A masterpiece in bridge-building technology, the Westinghouse Bridge was also the most impressive example of the ongoing modernization of the Lincoln Highway (US Route 30), then the nation's premier transcontinental road. The progressive optimism of the span is reflected in the heroic,

FIG. 6.8. Opened in 1932 as the world's largest reinforced concrete vehicular arch span, the George Westinghouse Bridge was celebrated as an engineering wonder.

bas-relief figures representing man's command of electrical power sculpted onto the entrance pylons, which constitute the best art deco ornamentation of any bridge in the county.

Pittsburgh's era of the reinforced concrete arches extended into the 1950s, when they were used in the construction of the Penn-Lincoln Parkway, most notably, the multiple-span Nine Mile Run Viaduct. The bridge type began to lose favor, however, with technological advancements in the construction of longer beam spans using steel girders or prestressed concrete. Some of the earlier concrete arches were prone to spalling, and by the 1970s they were shedding hunks of concrete onto the streets below. The arches of the 1921 Greenfield Bridge are wrapped in netting to prevent spalled concrete from plummeting onto parkway traffic passing beneath the span. This potentially deadly hazard to traffic was so great that engineers constructed a canopy beneath the Greenfield Bridge and over the parkway to catch the debris falling from the arch.

Interstate Highway Spans

After the passage of the Interstate and Defense Highway Act of 1956, highway planning and construction occurred at a national scale, 90 percent of it being funded by the federal government. Interstate highways and their associated bridges were the triumph of the automobile, dictating designs that emphasized vehicular speed and volume and excluded all other forms of transportation.

Like most large cities, Pittsburgh's network of limited-access expressways was under construction by the time Congress passed the Interstate Highway Act. Begun in the early 1950s, the Penn-Lincoln Parkway was the city's east-west, limited-access replacement of US Route 22 (William Penn Highway) and US Route 30 (Lincoln Highway). The year 1959 marked completion of the final link in the parkway with the opening of the Ft. Pitt Bridge and Tunnel. The Ft. Pitt Bridge was also a key piece of infrastructure in a massive urban renewal project that cleared out the old trackage, freight stations, and warehouses of the Point to make way for Gateway Center and Point State Park. A short section of freeway separated the park from downtown Pittsburgh and linked the Ft. Pitt Bridge with the Ft. Duquesne Bridge, its sister span over the Allegheny River. Both were double-deck, tied arch through spans built to replace the two bridges at the Point.

Authorities condemned the old Point Bridge across the Monongahela River as soon as the Ft. Pitt Bridge opened in 1959, but left it standing for another eleven years. Although construction for the Ft. Duquesne Bridge ended in 1961, it stood unused for the next seven years while a controversy raged over where the North Side approaches would go. Ironically, a similar contention had delayed the opening of its predecessor, the Manchester Bridge, which continued to carry North Side traffic until 1968.

Throughout the 1960s, locals derided the Ft. Duquesne Bridge as the "Bridge to Nowhere," gaining infamy in 1964 when a disoriented University of Pittsburgh student drove his car off the bridge's unfinished north end. The student survived the sixty-foot plummet, and eventually the bridge connected with Interstate 279, an elevated expressway through the North Side. In 1970, public authorities demolished the Manchester and Point bridges.

With 130,000 vehicle crossings per day, the Ft. Pitt Bridge is now the busiest bridge in the city. The tied arch constructed with stronger, lighter steel became a favorite for long-span interstate highway bridges. A tied arch constituted I-79's 1976 Neville Island Bridge across the Ohio River and a year later formed the Birmingham Bridge replacement of the old Brady Street Bridge to the South Side.

Opened across the Allegheny River in 1987, the Veterans Memorial Bridge (I-579) represents the staid efficiencies now afforded by high-tensile-strength steel forged into extremely long plate girders. The bridge is a simple, understated, and underwhelming beam bridge. Its completion was the final link in a belt of limited-access highways that circles the Golden Triangle, fulfilling a proposal presented to the city in the 1930s by none other than New York City's power broker and preeminent bridge and highway builder, Robert Moses.

Many of Allegheny County's major spans are second- and even third-generation bridges. They stand as engineering monuments to the technology of the time period as influenced by the geography of their settings. They represent the ongoing interplay between human landscapes, technological innovation, civic art, and the physical environments that makes Pittsburgh distinct. In time, they will all need to be replaced, rehabilitated, or relocated, assuring the future of Pittsburgh as the City of Bridges.

References

Gangewere, Robert J. 2001. *The Bridges of Pittsburgh and Allegheny County.* Pittsburgh: Carnegie Library of Pittsburgh.

Kobus, Ken, and Jack Consoli. 1997. *The Pennsy in the Steel City: 150 Years of the Pennsylvania Railroad in Pittsburgh.* Publication of the Pennsylvania Railroad Technical and Historical Society. Kutztown, PA: Kutztown Publishing.

Kuncio, Gerald M. 1999. Golden Age in the City of Bridges. *Western Pennsylvania History* 82 (2).

Lorant, Stephen. 1980. *Pittsburgh: The Story of an American City.* 3rd ed. Lenox, MA: Authors Edition.

Olmstead, Frederick L. 1911. *Pittsburgh Main Thoroughfares and the Downtown District.* Pittsburgh: Pittsburgh Civic Commission.

Patrick, Kevin J. 2002. Triangle Tracks. *Western Pennsylvania History* 85 (1): 35–49.

Pennsylvania Historic Museum Commission (PHMC) and Pennsylvania Department of Transportation (PennDOT). 1986. *Historic Highway Bridges in Pennsylvania.* Harrisburg: PHMC and PennDOT.

Plowden, David. 1974. *Bridges: The Spans of North America.* New York: W. W. Norton and Company.

Schmidlapp, Christina M. 1986. Pittsburgh's Park of the Century. *Pennsylvania Heritage* (Spring 1986): 32–37.

SEVEN

Chatham Village

THE ENDURING LEGACY OF COLLABORATIVE GENIUS

Christopher Cusack and George Pomeroy

Tucked within Pittsburgh's Mt. Washington neighborhood and located a mere two miles from the Golden Triangle, Chatham Village is among the most attractive communities in Pittsburgh and in the United States at large. Set on a hillside and consisting of fewer than two hundred row house units ringed by a greenbelt, it has all of the quaint charm the word "village" implies. The calm and appealing appearance of this small-scale multifamily housing development, however, belies its significance among planned communities. Chatham Village, along with Radburn, New Jersey; Sunnyside, New York; and Baldwin Hills, California, embody the Garden City movement in the United States. These planned communities represent a twin legacy of architectural design and social thought that grew out of the partnership of Clarence Stein and Henry Wright. The significance of this legacy resonates anew with the recent popular attention given to New Urbanism, which promotes the development of pedestrian-friendly neighborhoods and strives to minimize automobile use through small lots, dense development, and mixed retail and residential land uses (Kunstler 1996; Duany et al. 2000; Congress for the New Urbanism). This essay presents the tradition upon which Chatham Village was conceived and the history of the community and describes its geographic layout and urban design. A final thought is given to the collaborative genius of Chatham's designers, Clarence Stein and Henry Wright, and their enduring legacy in geography and planning (Parsons 1998).

Roots of the Garden City Tradition

Chatham Village lies squarely within the Garden City tradition. The Garden City idea first came together coherently in the mind and work of Ebenezer Howard and was popularized through his book *Garden Cities of Tomorrow,* published in 1902 (Hall 1988). This new settlement form would remedy a number of ills. It would be a solution to urban overcrowding, the proliferation of slums, encroachment of urban land use onto agriculturally productive rural land, the lack of employment opportunities (both for rural migrants and urban slum dwellers), and problems of health in cities. Strangely, planners and designers propose garden cities today as remedies for urban sprawl—quite the opposite of the urban crowding which so captivated the attention of early planners. Garden cities also provided the best of both the rural and urban life (Hall 1988). Howard's famous Three Magnets Diagram well captures these ideas. Peter Hall notes that this diagram not only implies a physical ideal but also a social one, as indicated by the words "freedom" and "cooperation." Howard developed the first two garden cities, Letchworth (1902) and Welwyn (1919), in Britain. Of a practical mind, Howard intended his planned community to be a profit-making or at least financially self-sustaining concern. This was a thought not lost upon the Buhl Foundation in planning for Chatham Village several years later.

Earning the interest and appreciation of American planners, the seed of Garden City ideals required some cultivation in order to germinate in the United States. According to Lewis Mumford, it was Clarence Stein who "did more than any other single person in America to realize in practice the ideas that Ebenezer Howard first set forth" (Parsons 1998, 129).

Stein and Wright introduced Howard's ideals to the United States through Sunnyside, New York, a seventy-acre plot in Queens that was developed as America's first Garden City suburb. Undertaking a far more ambitious project, the duo then endeavored to build Radburn, New Jersey, as a "truly self-sufficient community" (Roth 1979, 267). Though prospects for Radburn were good, its timing could not have been worse. Shortly after the first of three planned neighborhood areas was built, the stock market crashed. Also, America's love affair with the automobile during the balance of the century could not have been anticipated. These forces severely impeded the development of Radburn (Roth 1979, 267).

Genesis of Chatham Village

While restricting the Radburn project, the Depression also exacerbated the nation's existing housing crisis, jeopardizing the future of many urban communities. As the housing crisis escalated, so too did conflict over solutions to the problem. In Pittsburgh, the Pittsburgh Housing Association advocated greater government involvement. However, social orthodoxy in Pittsburgh dictated that housing reform be directed under the auspices of business and professional leaders and executed by voluntary agencies (Lubove 1969, 64) in what today would be labeled a public-private partnership.

Charles F. Lewis, executive director of the philanthropic Buhl Foundation, led efforts to prove that additional government involvement was unnecessary. Lewis examined Stein and Wright's experiments at Sunnyside and Radburn and concluded that "limited-dividend companies demonstrated that income groups avoided by commercial companies could be housed at a profit" (Lubove 1969, 72). Stein and Wright signed on as consultants after Lewis convinced the Buhl Foundation to sponsor "a demonstration of good housing as an example to the nation" (Vater 1998, 8.2). The name chosen for this demonstration project was Chatham Village, in honor of William Pitt, Earl of Chatham.

Following a thorough examination of potential low-cost sites, the Bigham Estate in the Mt. Washington neighborhood was revealed to be most advantageous (figure 7.1). "The Bigham Estate site was selected because it provided a largely undeveloped property, of single ownership, in close proximity to downtown Pittsburgh, and because Mt. Washington rose above the smog line, offering the desirability of clean air" (Vater 1998, 8.3). A likely no less important factor was the conservative middle-class community surrounding the estate (Lubove 1969, 75). In keeping with the Garden City tradition, Chatham Village was also enclosed by a parklike greenbelt (Richert and Lapping 1998). Twenty-five acres of steep, wooded hillside, known as Chatham Wood, serve to "buffer the community and preserve views from the residential area" (Vater 1998, 7.4). Preserving the area's natural habitat of native flora and fauna, the woods shelter both deer and fox. Two miles of walking trails threading the greenbelt also make the woods a year-round recreational resource. As surrounding areas continue to be developed for commercial and industrial activity, the benefits of this far-sighted contribution of the Garden City movement have grown with time.

Despite its many good qualities, the site also posed a considerable challenge for Stein and Wright. The land was steep and rough, and only half the acreage appeared to have potential for development (Newton 1971, 496). Yet the challenges posed by the hilly terrain also generated Chatham Village's greatest acclaim, as each aspect of design was successfully customized to the slope of the land. For instance, the roads at Chatham Village are not laid out in a grid, but rather they follow the contours of the hillside in a curvilinear fashion. Additionally, the foundations of the two- and three-bedroom houses

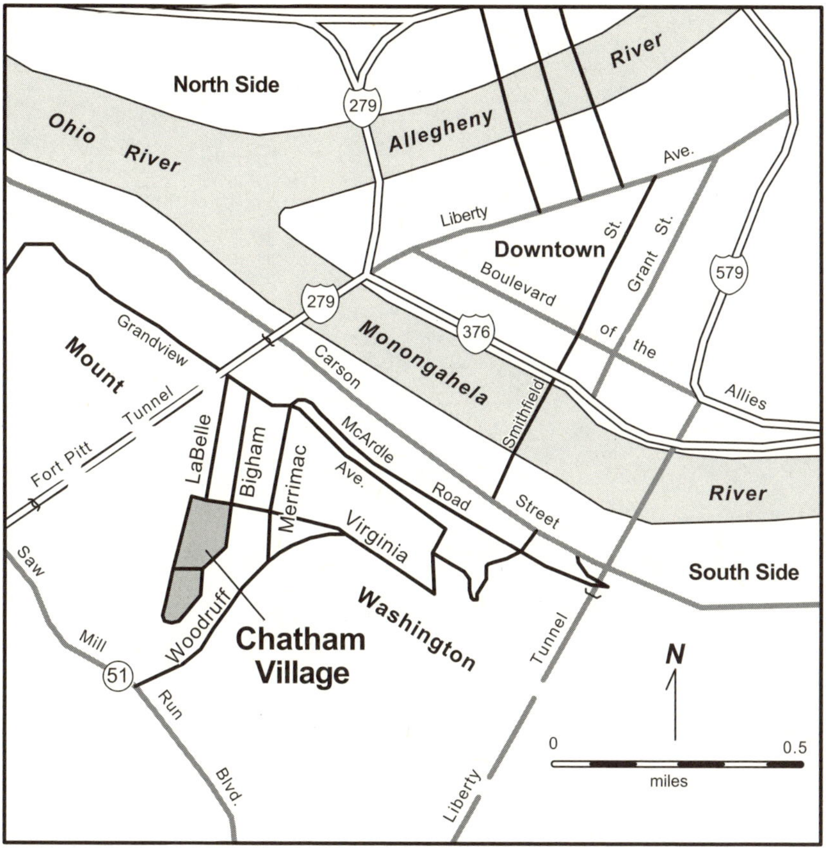

FIG. 7.1. Relative location of Chatham Village.

drop to follow the contours of the land. As a result, "The fall of the land, instead of being a hindrance, is availed of to contribute both visually and operationally to the excellence of Chatham Village" (Newton 1971, 497).

The hilly terrain, coupled with the desire for affordable housing, resulted in the construction of row housing as opposed to the single-family detached housing originally envisioned by Lewis. Stein and Wright applied the same concepts that they pioneered at Radburn to their plans for Chatham Village (figure 7.2). These included: "'superblock' subdivision; separation of pedestrian and vehicular traffic; houses fronting on park-like inner courts; generous provision for recreation and leisure (the houses occupied only 16 of 45 acres, another 25 consisted of woods and pedestrian trails, and 4 were used for playgrounds)" (Lubove 1969, 77). Also included in the development were a market building and a communal clubhouse.

FIG. 7.2. Pedestrian walkway in Chatham Village.

Within a year of the project's 1931 commencement, the first 129 units had been completed. Success of the initial phase resulted in the construction of a second section of 68 homes in 1935–1936 (figure 7.3). The second section complemented the original units and maintained the continuity of the development. "The two units of Chatham Village are entirely harmonious; the project is without question a single work and is so to be judged" (Newton 1971, 497). A third phase, undertaken in 1956, consisted of a three-story apartment building and a separate garage compound. Constructed in three phases, the singular product of Chatham Village is testament to the potential of town planning and has been universally accepted as one of America's most charming and successful housing projects (Newton 1971, 496–97).

Less successful, however, was the intention of the development to serve as a sanctuary of affordable housing, with rents set as low as $9 per month per room. Although the Buhl Foundation supported Chatham Village as a project for people of limited means, it did not, in the end, accommodate such a population. While the Buhl Foundation claimed that no "arbitrary standards" were set for acceptance of potential residents, it never disclosed its selection criteria nor its reasons for acceptance or rejection of applicants. Rather, it simply pointed to the long waiting list as proving Chatham's ability to attract "alert, thoughtful, energetic, intelligent American families" (Buhl Foundation 1932, 7).

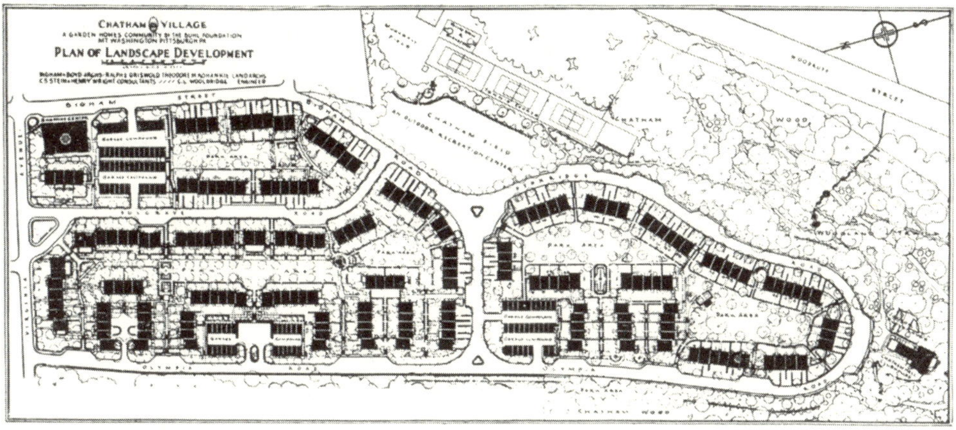

FIG. 7.3. General plan for the final development of Chatham Village.

Although originally planned for those people truly disadvantaged by the housing crisis, the desire of the Buhl Foundation to make a profit availed Chatham Village to white-collar professionals. In fact, to ensure that the village met the needs of such professionals, the foundation sponsored an investigation of their housing preferences. This policy shift manifested itself decades later when a representative sample of the village included four lawyers, two doctors, two engineers, a dentist, a salesman, a banker, a railroad executive, and a planning executive (Jacobs 1961, 64). By placing economic objectives ahead of housing goals, the Chatham Village demonstration project exposed "the bankruptcy of voluntarism as a strategy for mass housing betterment" (Lubove 1969, 82).

Ensuring homogeneity through careful tenant selection from a pool of professionals was only one of the lasting policies of Chatham Village. Indeed, most managerial policies remained intact even after ownership of the village changed hands. In 1960, the Buhl Foundation sold the property to Chatham Village Homes, Inc., a residents' cooperative. Since that time, residents purchase memberships and pay a monthly fee for upkeep and expenses. In keeping with the tradition established by the Buhl Foundation, the cooperative mandates adherence to a number of regulations. For example, bylaws prohibit exterior alterations, and interior improvements are subject to review and approval by the cooperative. Also, in accord with the meticulous maintenance of the grounds, older children and teenagers cannot play in the courtyards (Vater 1998, 7.3; Jacobs 1961, 80).

Mandatory adherence to policies set by members of the cooperative's governing board signifies Chatham Village as a precursor to the current generation of homeowner associations. However, while policies at Chatham curtail certain activities, they remain less invasive than those of the more recently formed associations. "Originating in Stein and Wright's Sunnyside, Radburn, Chatham Village, and Baldwin Hills, community ownership has now taken on socially restrictive forms—gated communities and collectively owned golf courses" (Parsons 1998, 130). Social insularity, however, does render Chatham akin to the recently developed upper-echelon communities. In antithesis to its original intent, Chatham Village is an exclusive community instead of a model of affordable housing.

A Legacy That Endures

Ultimately, Chatham Village failed to realize its original ideal: the provision of affordable housing for people of limited means. In nearly every other facet, however, the village is a tremendous accomplishment. Successful as a profit-making venture, Chatham Village enabled the Buhl Foundation to trumpet capitalism as the antidote to the nation's housing problem. While that goal paled in the face of the Great Society and rising federal programs decades later, it is in step with the national fiscal climate of the new century. As representative of Stein and Wright's late collaborations, Chatham is also one of the duo's most aesthetically rewarding. As a place to live, the village's exceptionally low tenant turnover and traditionally long waiting lists affirm its popularity (Arendt 1994, 358; Newton 1971, 500).

Despite Chatham Village's success and warranted recognition in scholarly books and journals, many local planning boards and commissions remain unaware of the lessons to be learned from the project. But awareness may be growing of the linkages between current planning efforts and the planning and design principles originally applied by Stein and Wright. In particular, a strong nexus exists between the currently popular New Urbanism movement and the application of Garden City ideals by Stein and Wright. New Urbanism shapes public perception through popular mediums, including a May 1995 issue of *Newsweek*, and a July 1998 edition of the television news show *Nightline* with Ted Koppel, and it is generally associated with two broad goals: to create a greater sense of community by accommodating a greater diversity of land uses and social interaction in neighborhoods, and to rethink the public realm, especially public spaces and the typical streetscape. In accomplishing this is it is important to reorient the typical community toward a pedestrian- and transit-friendly environment, while also minimizing negative traffic and environmental effects (Fulton 1996, 3).

Though receiving much attention as a new planning approach, these objectives are not unlike those implemented in Chatham Village decades earlier. In fact, the very impetus behind New Urbanism weighed heavily in the work of Stein and Wright. Hailed by some as a fresh approach to suburban sprawl, New Urbanism seeks to counter the inefficiencies of automobile-based housing development. Likewise, Chatham Village was also built to address the motor age. "The work of planners Stein and Wright, based directly on the English Garden City concepts, was a significant development in opposition to the trend toward suburban growth" (Vater 1998, 8.4). Additional similarities between the approaches include the "neighborhood unit" concept, which involves a layout of a large suburban block oriented around green space; a curvilinear or modified-grid street network; and design principles aimed at engendering community spirit (Fulton 1996; Newton 1971). As a result, among the primary critics of the movement are those who simply see too many similarities between New Urbanism and the Garden City ideals of Stein and Wright. As posited by John Kaliski, "Questioning the 'new' in New Urbanism is perhaps what is really at the root of any criticism of the movement" (Fulton 1996, 8).

Despite parallels between New Urbanist designs and the plans for Chatham Village and Radburn, several distinctions remain. For example, Stein's implementation of cul-de-sacs is criticized by some New Urbanists because it leads to pockets of seclusion. Additionally, many New Urbanist designs focus on streets, whereas Stein and Wright utilized design principles to distinguish between pedestrian and automobile traffic (Fulton 1996, 8). In one important aspect, however, a greater distinction exists between Chatham Village and Radburn than between Radburn and the New Urbanist developments. Consistent with the intention for Radburn, New Urbanist communities are designed to function as potentially self-contained units of mixed-use development. There was no such plan for Chatham Village, which has no industry, schools, churches, or library (Newton 1971, 499).

New Urbanist designs are by no means intended as replicas of Stein and Wright's Garden City. However, notable similarities between the movements reveal the persistence of urban problems and consistency of planning responses. Communities throughout the United States are currently striving to address such disparate needs as the provision of affordable housing, preservation of open spaces, and restoration of communal pride. Yet neither these issues nor responses to them are unique to the present day. The planning and design principles applied at Chatham Village warrant a fresh review. Successful on multiple fronts, Chatham Village reveals the potential for a multifamily housing development that also preserves open space and fosters a communal attitude.

References

Arendt, Randall. 1994. *Rural by Design: Maintaining Small Town Character.* Chicago: American Planning Association.

Buhl Foundation. 1932. *Chatham Village: A Modern Community of Garden Homes Combining Architectural Charm with Security and Cultured Living.* Pittsburgh: Eddy Press Corporation.

Congress for the New Urbanism. www.cnu.org.

Duany, Andres, Elizabeth Plater-Zyberk, and Jeff Speck. 2000. *Suburban Nation: The Rise of Sprawl and the Decline of the American Dream.* New York: North Point Press.

Fulton, William B. 1996. *The New Urbanism: Hope of Hype for American Communities?* Cambridge: Lincoln Institute of Land Policy.

Hall, Peter. 1988. *Cities of Tomorrow: An Intellectual History of Urban Planning and Design in the Twentieth Century.* New York: Blackwell.

Jacobs, Jane. 1961. *The Death and Life of Great American Cities.* New York: Random House.

Kunstler, James Howard. 1996. *Home from Nowhere.* New York: Simon and Schuster.

Lubove, Roy. 1969. *Twentieth-Century Pittsburgh: Government, Business, and Environmental Change.* New York: John Wiley and Sons.

Newton, Norman T. 1971. *Design on the Land: The Development of Landscape Architecture.* Cambridge: Belknap Press of Harvard University Press.

Parsons, Kermit. 1998. Clarence Stein's Variations on the Garden City Theme by Ebenezer Howard. *Journal of the American Planning Association* 64 (2): 129–30.

Richert, Evan D., and Mark B. Lapping. 1998. Ebenezer Howard and the Garden City. *Journal of the American Planning Association* 64 (2): 125–27.

Roth, Leland M. 1979. *A Concise History of American Architecture.* Boulder: Westview Press.

Vater, David J. 1998. *National Register of Historic Places Registration Form: Chatham Village Historic District.* Washington, DC: United States Department of the Interior, National Park Service.

EIGHT

A Community's Struggle

LITTLE ALLEGHENY WEST TAKES ON THE PROS

John Canning

The debate surrounding the building of sports complexes is a complicated one, shrouded in emotions, urban boosterism, and politics. Globally, cities compete to attract strong athletic teams and franchises in what has become a huge market in urban promotion. Snagging a regional or international soccer tournament, housing a major franchise, or showcasing a state-of-the-art sports complex "puts cities on the map" (Berg 2002). But Mauricio Ortiz's (2002) econometric analysis of US cities between 1979 and 1999 revealed that building a new football stadium actually had a negative impact on a city's employment growth rate. Loyal sports fans, however, are apt to dismiss such projections (Shropshire 1995), opting instead for the local pride that comes with being a fan. While the debate surrounding the political, economic, and emotional benefits of new stadiums will likely continue for years, one aspect that is not discussed concerns the local impacts on neighborhoods adjoining these facilities. In some cases, like Cleveland's Jacobs Field and Browns Stadium, displacing residences never became much of a problem because residential areas simply did not exist there. But what about cases where neighborhoods do exist in the vicinity of proposed complexes?

In recent years, Pittsburgh has built two state-of-the-art sports stadiums at the edge of several long-standing neighborhoods, particularly Allegheny West. Most of Allegheny West is within an eight-to-ten-minute walk from the heart of the sports complex district (figure 8.1) and will have access to light-rail that can transport residents downtown. The North Side is already well served with bus transportation. At the same time, Allegheny West will

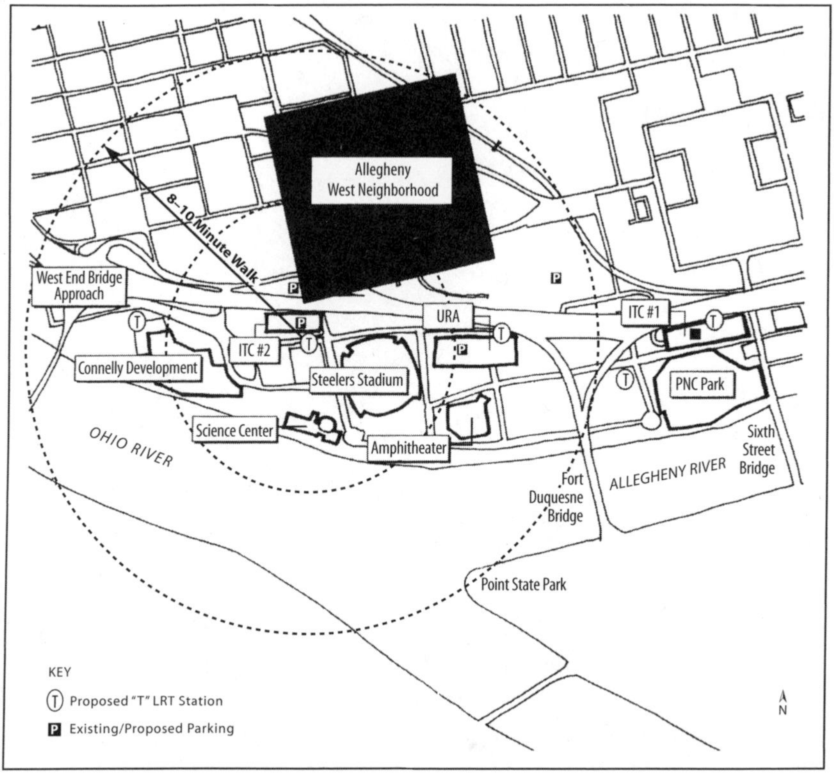

FIG. 8.1. Allegheny West neighborhoods with walking-time radii shown. Courtesy of Urban Design Associates.

be more accessible to sports fans, and that bodes well for local shops, taverns, and restaurants. Much of this advantage is premised on use of the light-rail system by sports fans.

Heinz Field is for football and PNC Park is for baseball. Building two stadiums is increasingly common in US cities to encourage optimal seating, team loyalty, and economic development. The reasoning behind imploding Pittsburgh's thirty-year-old Three Rivers Stadium in 2000 to make way for the new construction is that baseball fans need no longer watch a baseball game on a football field, and football spectators need not be constrained by seating around a baseball diamond. Building these facilities—especially in the US manufacturing belt—is made difficult because of deindustrialization and the resulting challenge of finding fiscal support. Once planners, citizens, and politicians address the problem of funding, an unanswered question lingers: What about the effects of crowding, street parking, and other disamenities that tens of thousands of fans impose on a neighborhood?

This chapter explores that question in the setting of Pittsburgh's North Side. It traces proposals put forth by local neighborhood organizations and the Pittsburgh mayor's office prior to the construction of these two fields. The chapter begins by reviewing an important design and planning proposal and then documents the to-and-fro that ensued between the locals and city authorities. It begins by assessing the so-called Plan B, which was designed to accommodate two large stadiums. The chapter then teases out the local geography of North Side—a long-established section of Pittsburgh with neighborhoods, hospitals, and shopping—with the North Shore district, a new planning region targeted to segregate riverfront properties such as the science museum, the two sports complexes, and lots of parking. The main section of the chapter reviews how a compromise was reached and how residents negotiated the conditions for the project approval.

The Evolution of Plan B

Tom Murphy's election to a second term as mayor of the city of Pittsburgh in November 1997 gave considerable impetus to plans for the construction of two new sports facilities on the north bank of the Allegheny River. This area, called the North Shore, lies directly across from the city's central business district (figure 8.2). A previous attempt to fund these stadiums through an increase in the local sales tax failed in a regional referendum. The Murphy administration, working with the Pittsburgh Pirates and the Pittsburgh Steelers organizations, began crafting a new approach, Plan B, for funding the construction of a new baseball park, a new football stadium, and a major expansion of the David L. Lawrence Convention Center. By October 1998 the planning process expanded to include a variety of public and private stakeholders. These representatives came from the city's Sports and Exhibition Authority, the Riverlife Task Force (an organization created to develop plans for public parklike use along the shorelines of Pittsburgh's three rivers), Pennsylvania's Department of Transportation (PennDOT), the Pittsburgh Port Authority (public transportation), and two major property holders along the northern shoreline of the Ohio River at the westernmost section of the property under consideration for development—the Carnegie Science Center and the Connelly Property Group (North Shore Consensus Plan and Design Guidelines 2001, 2)

These stakeholder groups participated in a series of intense planning sessions coordinated by the prestigious Pittsburgh firm Urban Design Associates during the winter months of 1998–1999. In February 1999 legislation known as the Regional Destination Financing Plan was passed by the Pennsylvania General Assembly in Harrisburg. This provided the additional

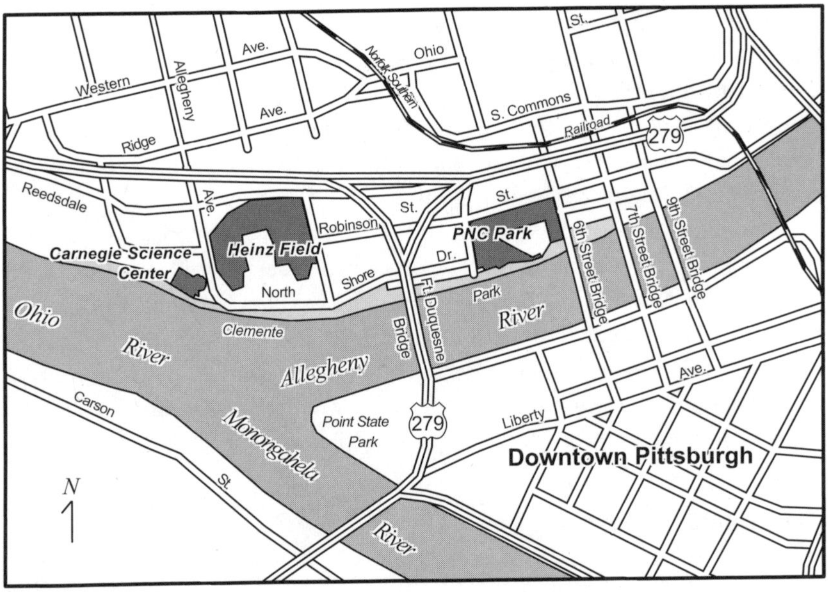

FIG. 8.2. North Shore district.

financing necessary to fund the construction of two new sports facilities as well as the expansion of the convention center. Plan B now moved from a planning process to one of implementation. This implementation included the creation of a new community on Pittsburgh's North Side to be known as the North Shore.

The North Side and the North Shore

Figure 8.2 shows that the northern border of the North Shore is a complex of highways (six lanes in most cases) and the spine line of the Norfolk and Western Railroad connecting Pittsburgh with Chicago. This barrier of concrete and iron rails separate the North Shore from the long-standing and adjacent North Side communities of Manchester, Allegheny West, Central North Side, and East Allegheny. Surface parking separates Heinz Field and PNC Park.

Each of the nearby neighborhoods host community-based organizations (CBOs) with substantial and successful track records in the areas of neighborhood revitalization, community advocacy, and housing development. In the 1970s these CBOs of the North Side came together to form the North Side Leadership Conference (NSLC), an umbrella organization through which the separate neighborhoods could act with more unified political and economic strength. Under the leadership of NSLC executive director Ed Brandt, a process was initiated at the outset of Plan B implementation to have regular monthly meetings in which representatives of the communities adjacent to the North Shore could examine and discuss with city officials and North Shore stakeholders the beneficial as well as detrimental impacts that Plan B developments might have on their neighborhoods. Of the four residential communities adjacent to the North Shore, Allegheny West was closest to the development area. As the scope of Plan B became clearer to the public, the residents of Allegheny West began to express great concern about how the major developments along the neighborhood's southern border would impact their community. The Allegheny West Civic Council (AWCC), a CBO with a thirty-year history of advocacy and development, began taking steps in the summer of 1998 to seek professional guidance in planning for the future relationships between the eight-block community of Allegheny West and the massive developments planned for the nearby North Shore.

Mary Means Comes to Town

To assist the neighbors of Allegheny West in responding to Plan B, the AWCC retained the services of Mary Means and Associates (MMA) of Alexandria, Virginia, a nationally recognized firm in the area of community strategic planning. Mary Means and her staff came to Allegheny West in November 1998 to study the neighborhood and meet with as many residents as possible in a community-wide discussion. Over the course of the following months, members of the MMA staff returned to the community and conducted an intensive strategic planning process. Along with Allegheny West residents and business owners, the MMA consultants met with city officials, transportation experts, and representatives of the North Shore stakeholders group. A key component of the latter was the Steelers organization, with which discussions ensued about plans, issues, and concerns relative to the various impacts that Plan B might have on Allegheny West. The objective of the process was clearly stated in the final MMA report to the AWCC: "The intent of this [Allegheny West] plan is not to halt or stall development along the North Shore, but rather to help the neighborhood think strategically and to better understand the potential opportunities and obstacles associated with North Shore developments" (Mary Means and Associates 1999, 2).

Not surprisingly, the report identified the following impacts the development might have on the Allegheny West neighborhood: parking along the residential streets and in empty lots, traffic patterns that would bring many more vehicles into the community, trash and litter left in the community after major sports events, and uncivil behavior of some tailgaters before and after stadium events (Mary Means and Associates 1999, 2). In turn, the MMA staff identified several strategies to "mitigate the potential negative impacts of Plan B developments on the [Allegheny West] neighborhood" (Mary Means and Associates 1999, 19). Such strategies included "the establishment of a broader North Side Impact Mitigation Group that would address the impact issues in a pro-active manner, the creation of a plan to manage access and parking for stadium events and everyday uses . . . to ensure easy access to the North Shore with minimal or no effect on the surrounding neighborhoods" (Mary Means and Associates 1999, 21); the development of a management plan for event days that would address both vehicular and pedestrian traffic, and a set of procedures to address the issues of safety, security, and post-event cleanup. The report called for "a commitment on the part of the city to strict code enforcement related to parking, tailgating, and open container regulations" (Mary Means and Associates 1999, 21).

As the Allegheny West representatives to the NSLC began to share information of the MMA planning process in their community with their counterparts from the other North Side neighborhoods adjacent to the North Shore, the request was made to expand the role of MMA to a broader area. In July 1999, the Department of City Planning agreed to retain MMA to "help city staff and neighborhood residents work with North Shore Stakeholders to develop mitigation and improvement strategies for the Near Northside neighborhoods (primarily Manchester, Allegheny West, Central Northside, and East Allegheny" (Mary Means and Associates 2000, 2). The broader study by MMA largely followed the pattern used in Allegheny West and suggested very similar strategies for addressing traffic, parking, aesthetic issues (litter and uncivil public behavior), and development issues (Mary Means and Associates 2000, 43–47).

Both MMA reports emphasized the importance of proactive planning to address potential problems as well as the need for building partnerships and understanding between the North Side neighborhoods and the North Shore stakeholders. Similarly, both MMA reports contained considerable discussion of "best practices," policy models that identified how other major American cities had addressed issues associated with large sports complexes and surrounding neighborhoods.

2001–2002, "The Year of the Shakedown Cruise"

Within a year after these reports were presented, the final construction work on the baseball field, PNC Park, was completed for the opening day of the Pittsburgh Pirates season in April 2001. By midsummer the new football stadium was being readied for the opening of the 2001 football season of the Pittsburgh Steelers and the University of Pittsburgh Panthers. The discussions, studies, and plans of the previous three years would be tested by the realities of North Shore events.

The opening game at PNC Park, as well as the whole 2001 season, was a success for the Pirate organization in terms of the sale of season tickets as well as the sale of tickets at the gate. It was also a success from the perspective of the residents in the adjacent communities. There were few traffic and parking problems because a new multistory parking facility was constructed near the baseball park, and the parking lots across the Allegheny River, in the central business district, were a relatively short walk for baseball fans. In an effort to encourage the connection between PNC Park and the heart of the Golden Triangle, city officials closed the Roberto Clemente Bridge (formerly the Sixth Street Bridge) to vehicular traffic to create a safe and spacious pedestrian walkway across the river. Moreover, much of the allure in getting to the North Shore sports complexes is walking across the bridges and gazing up at Mt. Washington, downtown, and the North Shore–North Side districts. Throughout the baseball season there were few if any problems of baseball fans parking along the residential streets north of the highway and railroad line. Within the stadium, the distributed sound system was designed to have little amplified sound projected beyond the park. The shops and restaurants located in the Federal Street side of PNC Park complex were a major catalyst in transforming what had been a dark and underdeveloped section of the lower North Side into a vibrant two-block commercial district. Prior to stadium construction, the lower North Side housed many shot-and-beer bars, abandoned storefronts, and a hodgepodge of small parking lots. At the AWCC meeting on April 10, 2001, Mike Coleman, one of the council's representatives to the NLC Plan B committee, reported that "everyone was pleased with how little [negative] impact the Pirate game had on the neighborhood" (AWCC minutes, April 10, 2001).

As the baseball season continued throughout the summer months of 2001, so did the final phases of the construction of the new football stadium. In late spring the H. J. Heinz Company, one of the oldest and most prestigious firms in Pittsburgh, purchased the naming rights for the football facility (figure 8.1). Thus was born Heinz Field with its characteristic mustard yellow seats and ketchup red signs and detailing. While many of the community concerns regarding PNC Park had been resolved by the summer of 2001, a number of issues related to the impact of events at Heinz Field on the nearby eight-block community of Allegheny West remained on the table. The MMA report to Department of City Planning had identified these concerns in July of 2000. Plans to address these issues—traffic patterns, parking on residential streets and in unlicensed surface lots in the Allegheny West and Manchester neighborhoods, unruly behavior of fans, and litter—had not been developed to the satisfaction of the communities. In their report the Mary Means consultants had identified this guiding principle: "Games and events on the North Shore should be managed as other major public events in the City—with resources to promote a safe quality experience for the participants, and to minimize or avoid [negative] impacts on the surrounding areas of the City" (Mean and Associates 2000, 26).

Several best practices were described in that report with the intent of encouraging the city officials to consider similar practices on the North Shore and adjacent neighborhoods. In Denver, the parking enforcement issue had been addressed in the following manner: "the police department tripled the number of ticket writers, coordinated with a local towing company to ensure that the necessary number of tow trucks would be available for towing, and increased parking fines from $25 to $200" (Mary Means and Associates 2000, 31).

Similarly, Denver's practices were cited as an effective approach to maintaining civil behavior at tailgating parties held before, during, and after stadium events. There "Community Resource Officers (not the Denver P.D.) on bike[s] patrol in surrounding neighborhoods. The officers patrol around the stadium three hours before and three hours after stadium events. In addition breathalyzer stations are set up at key intersections to discourage public intoxication" (Mary Means and Associates 2000, 32).

The MMA group identified a best practice in Seattle for dealing with the issue of litter and trash left in neighborhoods adjacent to Husky Stadium. There, "the Seahawks will establish several crews of staff to pick-up trash after events in the neighborhoods in the vicinity of the stadium" (Mary Means and Associates 2000, 35).

The issue of amplified sound spilling out of Heinz Field into the nearby communities, while not identified in the MMA report as a major problem for North Side residents as a whole, was a great concern to many people in Allegheny West who lived within three or four blocks of the stadium. While the distributed sound system in PNC Park kept most of the sound within the park, the sound system designed for Heinz Field was projected north through and beyond the stadium from a "jumbo board" located at the south end of the field. The design of Heinz Field left large open spaces on the north end thus preventing the containment of most amplified sound within the stadium.

David's Sling—The Law as Leverage

Developments on the North Shore had to conform to the code regulations established by the City Planning Commission. The codes include regulations related to signs and sound. In April 2001 the Zoning Board of Adjustment was to address issues related to the appropriateness of the signs to be placed on the exterior of Heinz Field. At the regular meeting of the AWCC on April 10, 2001, the council president urged members of the community to attend the zoning meeting to "turn up the heat so that there are no approvals [of the signs] until the sound, traffic and sign studies are complete" (AWCC minutes, April 10, 2001). A month later the sign issue became a major lever used by this small neighborhood association against the city and the Steelers organization. During the AWCC meeting on May 8, 2001, the members in attendance voted unanimously to "request the Zoning Board of Adjustment not to approve large signs for Heinz Field until all issues of parking, traffic studies, and noise are handled" (AWCC minutes, May 8, 2001). Discussions at the NSLC Plan B meetings with city officials and representatives of the Steelers in May and June seemed to be moving toward a resolution of the major issues. However, with the opening of the football season only a few weeks away, the hopefulness of these discussions gave way to quick and arbitrary decisions by city officials and administrators and a legal response by the AWCC.

In early July 2001 the City Planning Commission approved a request of the Steelers organization to remove regulations limiting the sound levels in Heinz Field. The response of the AWCC executive committee was to retain a highly regarded attorney to act for the community and to appeal the decision of the planning commission. At the AWCC meeting on July 10, 2001, the membership approved the action of the executive committee. At the same meeting the membership authorized the filing of a legal brief with the Zoning Board of Adjustment opposing any signs that were corporate logos of the Heinz or Coca-Cola companies. (The Coca-Cola sign was to identify that section of the Heinz Field complex known as the Coca-Cola Hall of Fame.) After considerable discussion of these actions the AWCC president stated: "our objective is to get concessions on the sound level and fan behavior. We are not really concerned about signage" (AWCC minutes, July 10, 2001). Within the month, AWCC also raised the issue of the sale of alcoholic beverages in Heinz Field at a hearing, requested by the AWCC, before the local administrator of the Pennsylvania Liquor Control Board. At this meeting the AWCC presented concerns about fan behavior resulting from uncontrolled sale of beer in the stadium (AWCC minutes, August 14, 2001).

Clearly, by the start of the football season in August, the multimillion-dollar Steelers organization and the city authorities were at loggerheads with the organization of the smallest community in Pittsburgh. Throughout the season little progress was made in the Plan B meetings, which the Steelers representative no longer attended, or in the courts. The issues, theoretical in

July, became quite real in October and November. At the monthly meetings of the AWCC residents regularly reported incidents of parking violations, lack of enforcement, traffic snarls, violation of open container laws, uncivil fan behavior, and excessive noise from the stadium. Pressure was being applied on city officials from all sides: residents, business owners, and local political leaders. The legal issues raised by the AWCC were still undecided and moving within the court system. With the uncertainty of how the courts would rule on these outstanding appeals, the Murphy administration wished to resolve issues of concern to the residents of Allegheny West.

The Citizens and Their Mayor

In late winter the mayor's office, acting through the NSLC, requested a meeting of a few Allegheny West residents, along with the AWCC representatives to the Plan B meeting and a number of city officials, to explore ways to resolve the major outstanding issues. After this long and candid meeting the mayor agreed to have the city act to meet the needs of most of the outstanding concerns with the exception of the noise issue. In return the AWCC would agree to drop all legal actions before the courts.

Although a memorandum of understanding between the AWCC and the mayor was not signed, the residents of Allegheny West who took part in the mayor's meeting reviewed with the community at the AWCC meeting on March 12, 2002, a number of actions the city officials agreed to take to address community concerns. These actions included a variety of measures to control problems of traffic, parking, and policing:

- An annual provision of $10,000 to AWCC for the hiring of police details to enhance the enforcement of parking regulations and regulations governing behavior in the Allegheny West community and the Allegheny Commons
- Aggressive enforcement of parking violations, including towing of vehicles parked in locations that threaten public safety
- Adjustments of the Heinz Field traffic management plan so as to encourage more patrons at Heinz Field events to park in the garages of the central business district
- Strict enforcement of residential permit parking violations and a substantial increase in fines for violations during Heinz Field events
- Sustained enforcement against improperly licensed surface parking lots north of the stadium
- Action by ordinance to prohibit tailgating on public sidewalks and rights of way north of the highway

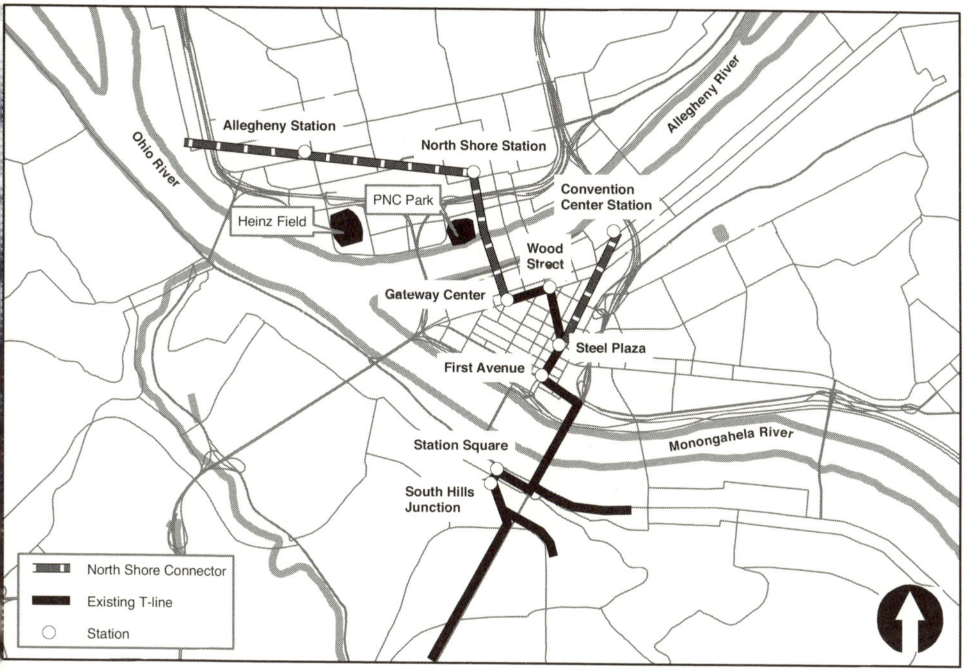

FIG. 8.3. North Shore Connector.

- Assured enforcement of no-alcohol laws within the Allegheny Commons and the prohibition of fires within the commons
- Enforcement of open container laws north of the highway
- Enforcement against acts of public urination, exposure, and disorderly conduct or brawling north of the highway
- Placement of twelve to fifteen permanent trash receptacles between Heinz Field and Western Avenue
- Placement of temporary trash receptacles between Heinz Field and Western Avenue on event days
- Street sweeping of Allegheny, Western, Ridge, and Galveston avenues on the mornings following events at Heinz Field

Another public works project—the North Shore Connector—will bring the city's light rail to the sports complexes (figure 8.3). It will also feed into the South Hills streetcar network from which suburban fans can travel. Construction began in 2004 amid a difficult fiscal climate for the study. Its completion should help to further mitigate street congestion problems for the communities of Manchester, Allegheny West, Central North Side, and East Allegheny.

Fighting the Good Fight

The action items listed above were included in a letter sent to Mayor Murphy from the leadership of AWCC (AWCC minutes, March 12, 2002). In return, the membership agreed to withdraw from all legal proceedings. A letter to the AWCC from the mayor's executive secretary in early April indicated the administration's agreement with those items. Except for the noise issue, most other substantive concerns seemed to have been addressed on paper. The real test occurred in August of 2002 when the football season resumed at Heinz Field. The battle was long and costly (well over $30,000 in legal fees); a considerable amount was borne by a small community organization. By late 2005, parking problems, rowdy fan behavior, litter, and related issues had not been eliminated, but were being significantly curtailed due to cooperative actions by city officials, the police, and several diligent residents of the Allegheny West community.

In the national rush for economic development, and motivated by urban boosterism, and the demands of sports fans (many of whom are voters and taxpayers), decision makers can overlook the interests of local communities living near these complexes. Efforts to build Heinz Field and PNC Park were not free of problems, as the filing of lawsuits attests. Nonetheless, most of the stakeholders in deciding where to locate the sports complexes achieved what they sought: balanced economic development, respect for long-standing residential communities, and a significant level of enforcement by the police. Contrary to criticisms leveled at city planners—that decision making about the sports arenas has been top-down and has deprived local neighborhoods of resources (Copeland 2004)—this case study suggests cause for optimism. As the AWCC president commented to a group of neighbors: "It is money well spent for twenty or thirty years of living the good life in Allegheny West" (J. DeSantis, interview by author, June 25, 2002). The good fight launched through local activism helped to mitigate the deleterious impact of large sports complexes on the North Side without compromising the city's larger economic development dreams. A secondary concern about which the local community has no control is whether the Pittsburgh Pirates and Steelers can perform well enough to sustain ticket sales in the many seasons ahead. The Steelers' 2006 Super Bowl victory, however, marked a step in that direction.

References

Allegheny West Civic Council. April 2001–March 2002. Minutes of Monthly Council Meetings.

Berg, Leo van den. 2002. *Sports and City Marketing in European Cities*. Aldershot and Burlington, VT: Ashgate.

Copeland, Dave. 2004. CMU's "Creative" Thinker Makes Creative Move. *Pittsburgh Tribune-Review*, March 13, http://www.pittsburghlive.com/x/search/s_184360.html (accessed November 29, 2004).

Mary Means and Associates. 1999. Allegheny West Neighborhood Strategic Plan. Alexandria, VA: Mary Means and Associates.

Mary Means and Associates. 2000. Northside Neighborhood Impact Study: Mitigation and Improvement Strategies for Pittsburgh's Near Northside Neighborhoods. Alexandria, VA: Mary Means and Associates.

North Shore Consensus Plan and Design Guidelines, September 2001, www.riverlifetaskforce.org/whatWeDo/AR2002text.pdf.

Ortiz, Mauricio. 2002. Do Professional Sports Franchises and Professional Sports Stadiums Have Any Effect on Employment in a City? M.A. thesis, Virginia Tech, Blacksburg, VA.

Riverlife Task Force. 2001. *A Vision Plan for Pittsburgh's Riverfront*, Pittsburgh, PA: Riverlife Task Force.

Shropshire, Kenneth L. 1995.*The Sports Franchise Game: Cities In Pursuit of Sports Franchises, Events, Stadiums, and Arenas*. Philadelphia: University of Pennsylvania Press.

Urban Design Associates. 2001. North Shore Consensus Plan and Design Guidelines. Pittsburgh, PA: Urban Design Associates.

III PITTSBURGH'S SUBURBS AND BEYOND

PART III SHEDS LIGHT on the relationship between Pittsburgh's central city population growth and that of its suburbs. Like most metropolitan areas, Pittsburgh's growth for the last half century has been greater in its suburban townships and municipalities than in the city itself. Pittsburgh began losing population to its suburbs between the 1950s and 1960s and has not yet recovered. Chapter 9 addresses these issues through a map analysis from 1950 to 2000. It also reviews city government's efforts to avoid bankruptcy. Whether the "hollowing out" of city population through suburban growth will continue is unclear, but Pittsburgh will need to make its cost of living competitive if it wishes to secure a sufficient taxpayer base for public services.

James T. Hathaway and James C. Hughes go beyond the suburbanization process in western Pennsylvania by focusing on regional shopping centers at the edge of the Pittsburgh and Beaver Falls metropolitan areas. Building on Scarpaci's conclusions in chapter 9, the authors show that interstate highway development helped to put small places on the map by making them relatively more accessible. In this case, the Prime Outlets mall at Grove City draws shoppers from a broad radius and has been a boon to the local economy. However, in America's unsatisfied quest for newer and bigger malls with high-end anchors, there is evidence that outlet malls are losing the competitive edge they once held. With only about one-tenth of the national $1.2-billion market in this form of retailing, both the outlet industry in general and Grove City in particular will need to reposition themselves in order to provide jobs. Grove City, like scores of cities across the United States with populations under ten thousand, will be facing this dilemma over the next few years.

NINE

Pittsburgh's Suburbs

HOLLOWING OUT THE CORE

Joseph L. Scarpaci

The image of Pittsburgh's smoky and industrial landscape will long endure. Historic records portray barge-choked rivers flanked by warehouses, steel mills, and rail yards where European immigrants toiled in hellish conditions. As a gritty industrial river town in the late nineteenth and early twentieth centuries, most factory workers commuted to work by walking over bridges or taking funiculars—called "inclines" locally—from the high tops of Mount Washington (figure 9.1). Like many US cities in the pre-automobile era, Pittsburgh's city limits failed to anticipate population growth and commercial expansion during the twentieth century.

Several "push" factors contributed to the city's spread and eventual population loss. James Parton's quip that Pittsburgh is "hell with the lid taken off," and Herbert Spencer's more dire remark, "six months residence here [in Pittsburgh] would justify suicide," contributed to a view of the Steel City as inhospitable. Residents knew all too well the environmental problems that plagued the smoky valleys and sought respite beyond the industrial corridors as income, opportunity, and land became available. The allure of the leafy suburbs was heightened by the ability to take trams and streetcars in the late nineteenth and early twentieth centuries, not just in Pittsburgh, but throughout the manufacturing states (Mills 1972; Levy 1997, 15). The electric streetcar accelerated Pittsburgh's suburban expansion. By 1920, more people were making the automobile commute from the city's South Hills because of widened roads and tunneling under Mt. Washington (Hoffman 1992a, 1992b). Suburbanization, or the flight to blue- and white-collar bedroom

FIG. 9.1. *Harper's* View of Pittsburgh from Mount Washington, 1872.

communities, caused an urban population decline from the 1960s onward. More residents of counties adjacent to Allegheny found their settings more desirable than Pittsburgh. This metropolitan growth pattern is common to other cities of the nation's manufacturing belt (Palen 1995; Garreau 1991; Safdie 1997; Vance 1962). To what extent was Pittsburgh's experience like other parts of the nation?

Less is know about Pittsburgh's suburban evolution than about the city's urban, economic, and historical geography. Drawing on county-level decennial census data from the tristate area (western Pennsylvania, eastern Ohio, and northern West Virginia), I analyze how suburbanization has unfolded over the past half century. I demonstrate that Pittsburgh's pattern of suburbanization reflects a process found in most North American metropolises: a gradual "hollowing out" of the city's population that was accompanied by suburban growth. The chapter argues that Pittsburgh's decline was at least as much the result of rigid city boundaries that failed to keep pace with the outward spread of population as it was of suburban growth in western Pennsylvania. This latter process was driven mainly by new lower-tax communities as well as the development of secondary roads and interstate highways that eased the commute. While suburban white-collar workers now form the mainstay of the city's labor force—especially in the management services, corporate, industrial, and medical-educational research sectors—the city and state governments in 2004 were considering the much-tried revenue technique of taxing suburban commuters who travel the tristate's clogged roads daily to downtown Pittsburgh. The city's accommodation with its suburban neighbors has not been an easy one, and the ability to work in the city without having wages taxed may have to change as mayors and legislators in Harrisburg devise strategies to reverse massive budget deficits in the early twenty-first century.

Suburbanization in the United States

If technological improvements in the form of high-rise buildings and highway construction promoted the densification of American downtown areas, it also ushered in a gradual depopulation of the city center. Manufacturing began to decentralize in the nineteenth century even though it retained an urban presence. Rail lines and streetcars eased commuting to the city center from adjacent suburbs. Rigid political boundaries drawn up in the nineteenth century failed to contain urban growth as residential housing spilled over old city limits into adjacent jurisdictions. Across the United States, these forces led to a decline of population density and total population in the city center. In addition, incomes were rising and workers could spend more on land, transportation, and housing. This allowed a growing middle class in the first half of the twentieth century to leave the tenements and slums of the industrial core behind and to set off for the promise of the suburbs (Levy 1997, 15).

The Early Years: Leaving the Three Rivers Behind

The thinning out of the downtown area of Pittsburgh was slow, but it began early. In 1859, horse-drawn trams were running through the city. By 1888, fifty-six miles of track spread through Pittsburgh and surrounding towns, carrying twenty-three million passengers that year (Muller and Tarr 2003, 24). This technology lent a hand in lowering central-city population and, as automobile and mass transportation came to Pittsburgh, it made it easier to leave the congested city behind. A tunnel under Mount Washington in 1899 opened up new white-collar "bedroom communities" to a shorter commute to downtown (Guerrieri 2000). The opening of the Liberty Bridge (1928) facilitated automobile travel out of the city. Communities that formed part of the old trolley suburbs of the South Hills (Mt. Lebanon, Dormont, Beechview, and Brookline) supported bridge construction for economic reasons. Automobile access from the South Hills to downtown Pittsburgh triggered suburbanization in West Mifflin, Pleasant Hills, Bethel Park, and Upper St.

Clair. Pittsburgh's expanse was similar to other cities where streetcar and rail development quickened during the interwar period (Jackson 1985).

Urban planner John Levy observed that the environmental movement of the 1960s and 1970s "had the effect of causing people to want to embrace what was left of the natural world and thus propelled them outward in search for a less synthetic living environment" (1985, 50). Nowhere is this truer than in Pittsburgh. City schoolchildren as late as the 1940s would change clothes or bathe at lunchtime to shed the dusty film that covered them. Although the air would become clean and Allegheny County's air standards would lead the nation (Tarr 2003), rising housing prices and new technologies that dispersed businesses (fax, Internet, teleconferencing) lent a hand in pushing residents into the suburbs. While only 15 percent of Americans lived in the suburbs in 1920, the 50 percent mark was passed a half a century later (Palen 1995). Counties adjacent to Allegheny deprived the city of Pittsburgh of a tax base in the late twentieth century, a problem that reached near-crisis proportions in the new millennium.

Population Change: The Tristate County Area, 1950–2000

One way to assess Pittsburgh and the Appalachians is to measure population change in the twenty-one-county area that I have identified within the tristate area of western Pennsylvania, southeastern Ohio, and northern West Virginia. Using decennial census data, I measured the standard deviation of population change that was above and below the regional mean, assessed by half standard deviation increments (figures 9.2, 9.3).

Between 1950 and 1960, the tristate area was in a strong growth phase. Except for Greene County, Pennsylvania, most counties witnessed above-average growth, especially the adjacent counties to the north (Beaver and Butler) and the west (Westmoreland) of Allegheny County (figure 9.2). The following decade revealed a continuation of that trend. By 1980, however, Allegheny County fell to <1.5 standard deviation for the first time in the study period (figure 9.3). Completion of the north-south Interstate 79 spurred growth in the counties south and north of Allegheny County (figures 9.4, 9.5, and 9.6). At that time, regions as far south as Morgantown, West Virginia, and north toward Erie, Pennsylvania, and Butler County fell into the commuting field for city workers.

By 1980, Allegheny County registered population decline in excess of 1.5 percent while Butler County to the north and Greene County to the south displayed strong growth. Counties surrounding Morgantown, West Virginia, displayed the strongest growth and underscored a modest revival in nonmetropolitan growth that characterized many counties in the United

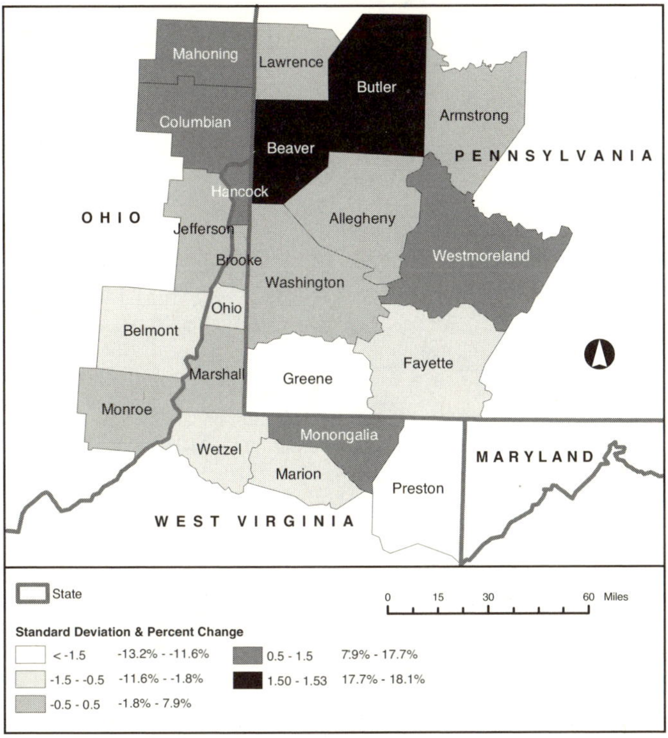

FIG. 9.2. Population Change, 1950–1960.

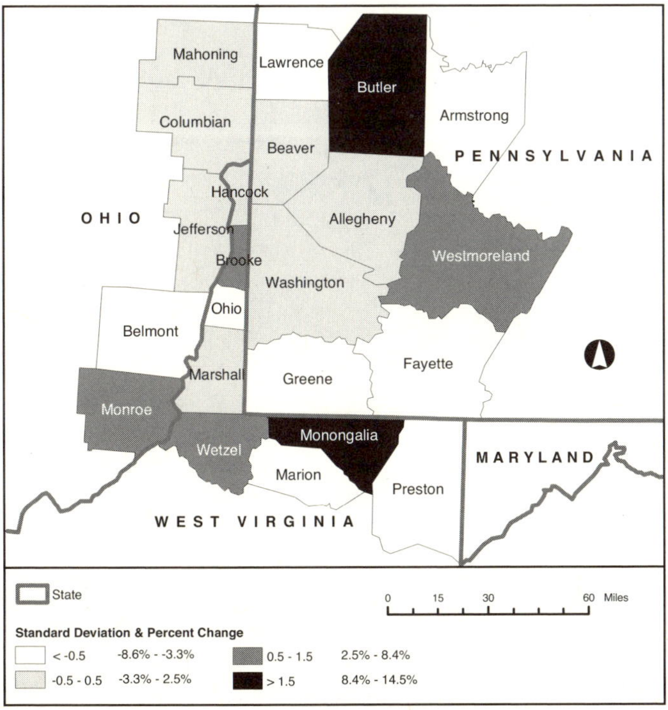

FIG. 9.3. Population Change, 1960–1970.

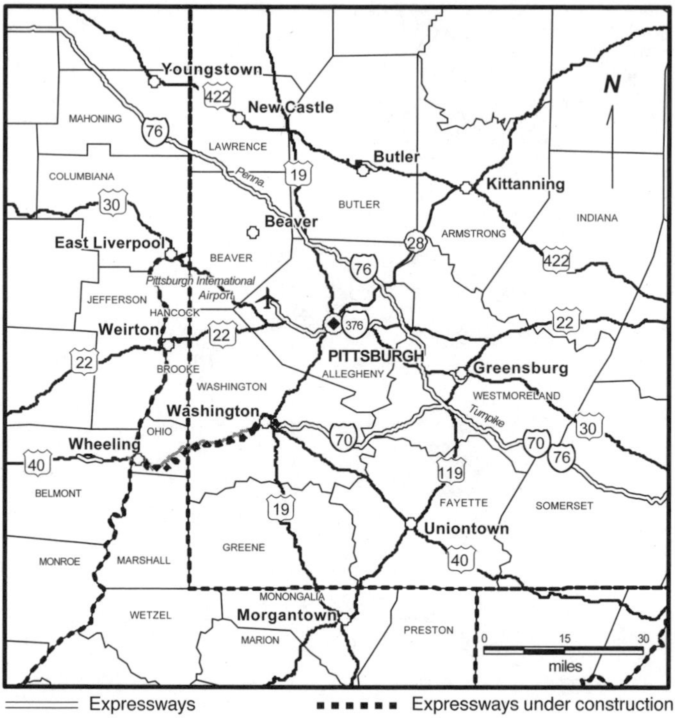

FIG. 9.4. Limited-Access Expressways in the Pittsburgh Metro Region, 1960.

For clarity and consistency, route numbers are marked as they are now, not as they were in 1960. In 1960, I-76 west of US 22 was I-80S and I-376 was part of I-76.

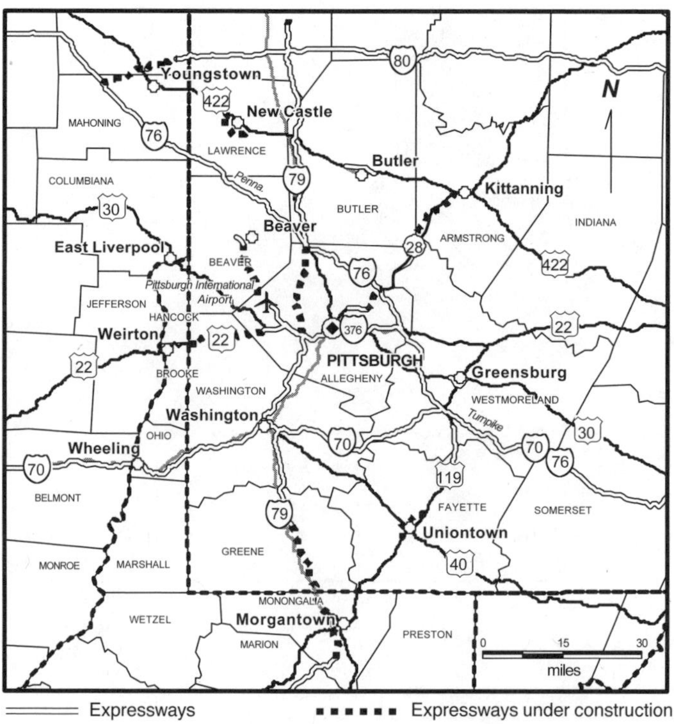

FIG. 9.5. Limited-Access Expressways in the Pittsburgh Metro Region, 1970.

For clarity and consistency, route numbers are marked as they are now, not as they were in 1970. In 1970, I-76 west of US 22 was I-80S, and I-376 was part of I-76.

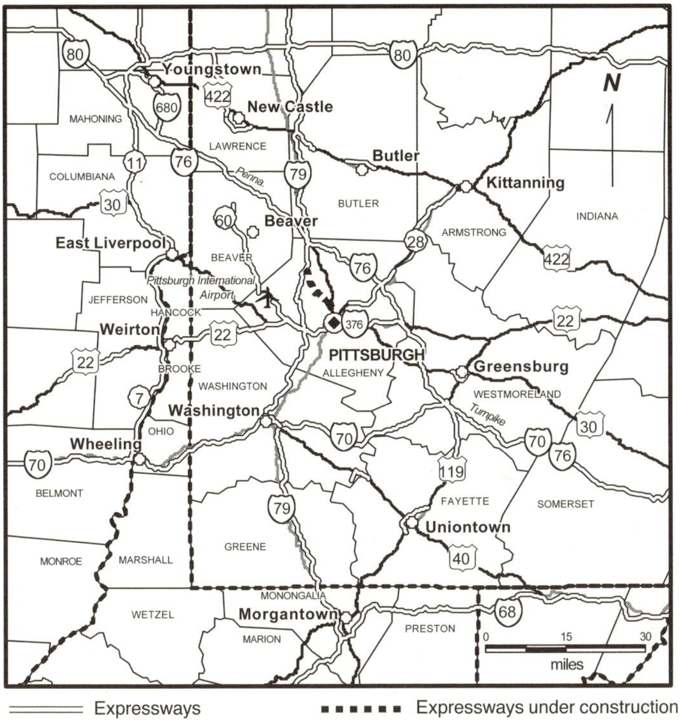

Fig. 9.6. Limited-Access Expressways in the Pittsburgh Metro Region, 1980.

For clarity and consistency, route numbers are marked as they are now, not as they were in 1980. In 1980, I-68 was US 48.

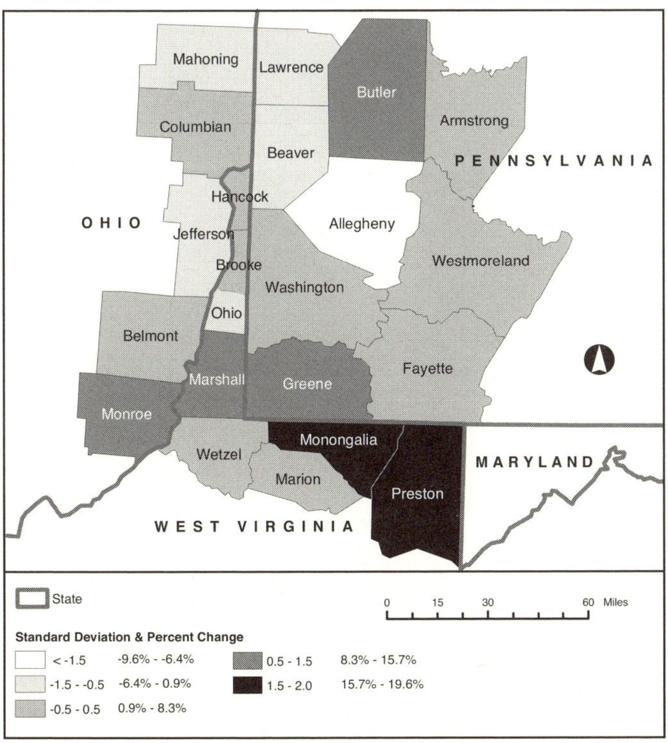

Fig. 9.7. Population Change, 1970–1980.

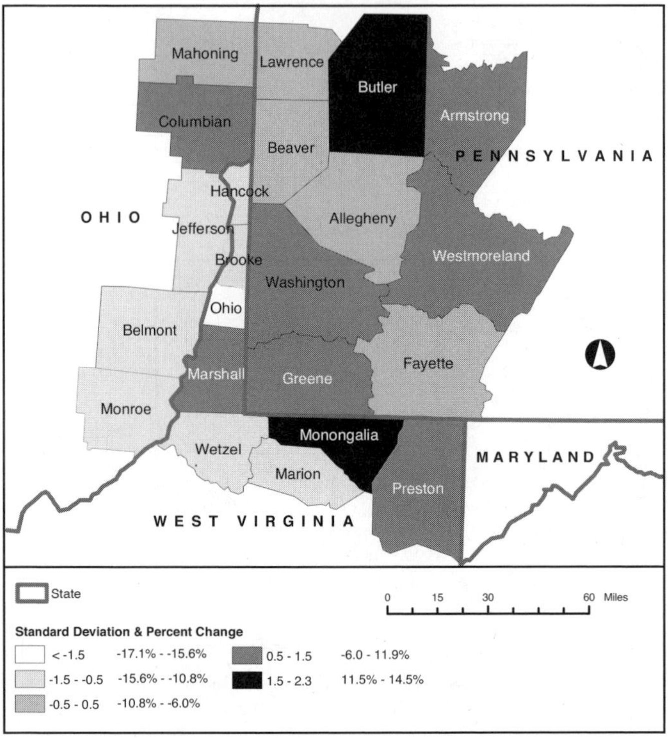

FIG. 9.8. Population Change, 1980–1990.

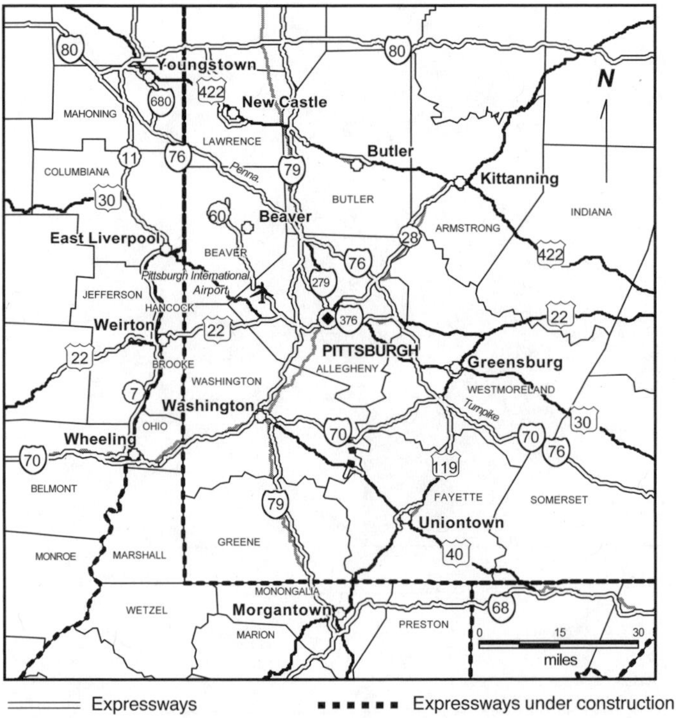

FIG. 9.9. Limited-Access Expressways in the Pittsburgh Metro Region, 1990.

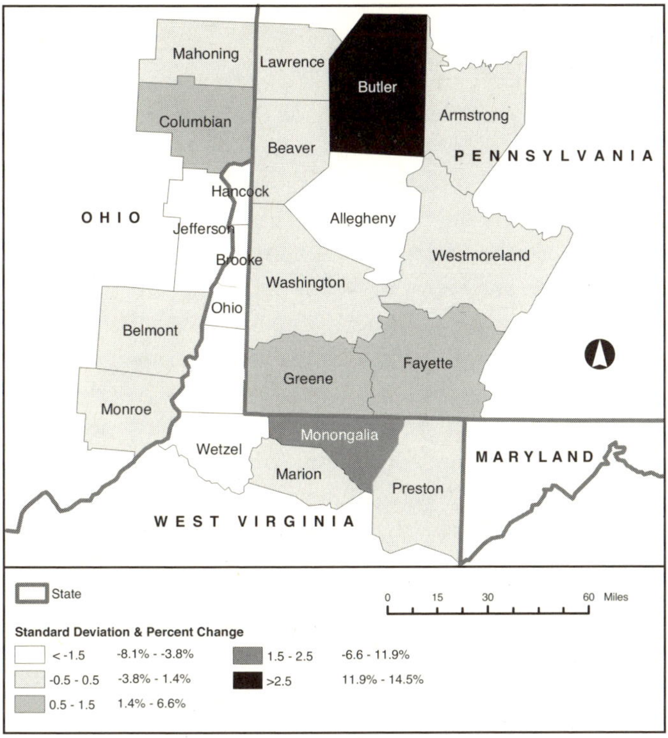

FIG. 9.10. Population Change, 1990–2000.

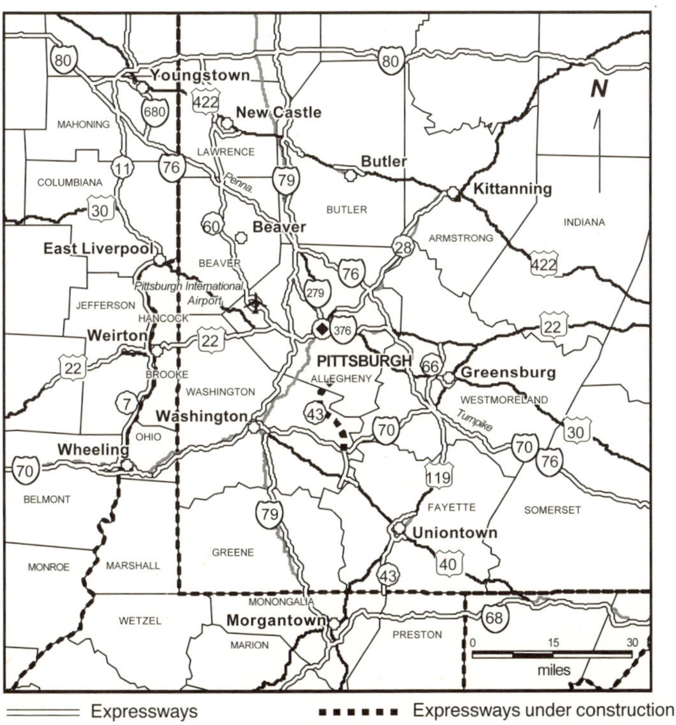

FIG. 9.11. Limited-Access Expressways in the Pittsburgh Metro Region, 2000.

States that grew as retirement communities and because of second-home lakeside communities. The year 1980 also marked the beginning of the hollowing out of the Pittsburgh metropolitan area (figure 9.7). A decade later, Pittsburgh's suburban counties displayed a modest rebound except for the distressed industrial counties of the West Virginia panhandle (Wheeling) and along the Ohio Valley between Ohio and West Virginia (the metropolitan areas of Youngstown, Ohio, and Weirton, West Virginia) (figure 9.8).

Lastly, the 2000 census repeated the 1980 pattern of below-average population growth for Allegheny County with the continuation of the 1990 pattern of sluggish growth along the Ohio River (figure 9.9). A series of office park establishments along the Interstate 79 corridor, both north and south of Pittsburgh, served as white-collar employment centers, especially in Washington County. Greater Pittsburgh International Airport in western Allegheny County opened a new airport just five miles from its existing airport in 1992 that included a large indoor shopping mall. New jobs there failed to lift the counties' relative rates of growth (US Airways employs eight thousand employees in the tristate area and, in 2004, was the region's largest employer). However, the Pittsburgh airport's role as a leading hub and employer for the tristate area is increasingly challenged by Philadelphia, which US Airways has identified as a gateway to European destinations. Moreover, post–September 11 security measures have made it more difficult for shoppers to frequent the airport shopping mall, although some progress was made in mid-2004 to allow nonticketed consumers to circulate in the airport's retail corridors.

Pittsburgh's population decline appears to be inextricably tied to its fiscal health. In absolute terms, the city's population fell by nearly half from 604,332 in 1960 to 327,898 in 2002. As David Cauchon describes it: "As taxpayers left, the city bled a little more financially every year. Pittsburgh has run an average annual deficit of at least $37 million every year since 1993" (Cauchon 2004). Understanding this fiscal hemorrhaging is essential if sound recommendations are to be put forth about how to solve this problem.

Fiscal Health and the City Suburbs

Suburban Pittsburgh's modest growth over the past half century underscores a perennial rift between central cities and their suburban neighborhoods. On the one hand, suburban amenities have long held a powerful allure to those wishing to leave the inner city behind. As noted earlier, the decentralization of manufacturing and jobs have pushed generations of urban residents to the suburbs. On the other hand, downtown revitalization has increased the quality of urban living. Pittsburgh's steel mill closings enhanced the city's rich cultural, sports, retailing, and university amenities. Nevertheless, Pittsburgh has been searching for a tax base to sustain city services. In doing so, it may have priced itself out of the residential market and lost potential taxpayers to jurisdictions in Allegheny, Washington, Fayette, and other adjacent counties.

Pittsburgh shares traits with other Rust Belt cities: it has an aging infrastructure (water, sewage, utilities) and well-paid public employees that must be supported through taxes. These revenues derive from property, commercial, and sales taxes, as well as parking fees and entertainment taxes on sporting events. Although its many universities and students contribute to the sales taxes, nonprofit organizations such as universities do not pay property taxes. Accordingly, Pittsburgh had the thirty-sixth highest tax rate among over two hundred cities analyzed in the City and County Data Book 2000 (US Census Bureau, County and City Data Book 2000, Table C-7). While its $737 per capita tax figure paled compared to twenty-four other cities with figures in excess of $1,000, there were over sixty cities that had half that tax rate (less than $350), and they were mostly in southern and western (Sunbelt) states.

One aspect of rising costs and declining tax base surfaced in the early 2000s when the city's fiscal position worsened greatly. Mayor Tom Murphy and the city council in 2002 and 2003 considered various revenue options such as raising parking fees and entertainment taxes or additional hotel and convention fees and surcharges. Budget deficits for the city of Pittsburgh 2004 budget were estimated in February 2004 to reach $50 million and were expected to climb to $79 million by 2005. What led to this deficit beyond the mismatch between city revenues and expenditures? Although the nuances of this fiscal crisis are beyond the scope of this discussion, two landmark events stand out.

First, the city launched a major public facilities construction project between 2000 and 2002. Three Rivers Stadium, built in 1970 at the cost of $33 million, was demolished in 2000 even though $3 million remained on the mortgage. Pittsburgh politicians and sports fans were swept up in the national fervor of showcasing state-of-the-art sports complexes dedicated to single sports. Nearby Cleveland set the regional example by building a baseball park (Jacobs Field, 1994) and football stadium (Cleveland Browns Stadium, 1999).

At first glance, it would seem that Pittsburgh Pirates and Steelers fans would not be outdone in their quest for new sports facilities. Pittsburgh and Allegheny bundled the sports complexes with a remodeled convention center back in the 1990s. Analysts from the Allegheny Institute for Public Policy argued that the city lost precious time in positioning itself in an ever-growing convention center market across the United States.

> Pittsburgh had an opportunity to get ahead of the flood of convention space. In 1997, the state authorized $145 million for construction of a new center (which was expected to cost $260 million) and permitted the county to increase the hotel tax from 5 percent to 7 percent to help with construction and operation costs. By insisting that the new convention center be part of a package that gave priority to stadium construction, Pittsburgh's decision-makers lost nearly two years when it could have been moving ahead of all the new space that will be coming on-line in the next couple of years. (Haulk and Montarti 2002)

When residents of seven counties surrounding Pittsburgh were asked about whether these stadiums and convention center should be financed partly on bond and tax revenues, voters soundly defeated the proposal. Not to be outdone, the state legislators found a way to circumvent the electorate's will and the stadium projects commenced at the cost of $281 million for a new state-of-the-art football complex (Heinz Field, 2001) and $216 million for a baseball park (PNC Park). Attendance in the first fifteen Pirate games at PNC Park averaged less than 18,000 spectators (Vasillarios 2003). Second, enthusiasm to enhance the David Lawrence Convention Center located on the banks of the Allegheny River next to the central business district grew under the mayoral term of Sophie Masloff (1988–1989), who replaced Richard S. Caliguiri (1977–1988). Mayor Tom Murphy (first elected in 1994) carried his enthusiasm and boosters to enhance the Steel City's sports and convention profile in the state capital of Harrisburg. He helped to negotiate an agreement to help fund the $332 million needed to remodel the convention center. Nonetheless, the city's Sports and Exhibition Authority (SEA), the city agency responsible for financing the $830 million sports arenas and convention center (80 percent of which comes from public funds), does not have enough money to pay the estimated $700 million balance for these projects (Gamrat 2002, 3). That has not dampened the public's enthusiasm for a new ice hockey arena to house the Pittsburgh Penguins.

Pittsburgh and Allegheny Country reassessed the valuation of land and buildings to help remedy its fiscal crisis. The city's total rose from $2,125,768 in 2000 (it had hovered around that figure since 1993) to $13,346,238 in 2001, and then $14,677,677 in 2002: a sevenfold increase in three years without a comparable increase in new construction. However, land millage fell from 184.5 to 10.8. Personal property tax was appealed in Pittsburgh as part of the Regional Asset District (RAD) tax in 1995. This reassessment of real property

TABLE 9.1. Principal Real-Estate Taxpayers, City of Pittsburgh, 2003

	Amount (in '000s)	*Percentage*
500 Grant Street Associates (One Mellon Center)	$517,850	3.53
600 Grant Street Associates (USX Building)	264,303	1.81
Market Associates (Subsidiary of PPG Industries)	205,076	1.40
Grant Liberty Development	146,661	1.00
Oxford Development	139,111	0.95
Pittsburgh National Corporation	138,117	0.95
Buncher Company	137,959	0.95
Total		10.59

Source: City of Pittsburgh 2003, Table 6, p. 111; percentage calculated by the author.

brought the ratio of total assessed value to total estimated value from 0.191 in 1999 and 2000, to 1.000 in 2001 and 2002 (City of Pittsburgh 2003, 109). By 2003, seven companies working mainly in real estate were contributing about 11 percent of the city's commercial property tax (table 9.1).

None of these measures offset Pittsburgh's mounting budgetary problems. Growing deficits and a declining bond rating caused the city to be placed into Pennsylvania Act 47, a kind of fiscal custodial relationship where the primary decisions to remedy the budget crisis were transferred to powers outside the city (Cauchon 2004). Teachers, police, and firefighters were laid off in an attempt to narrow the revenue shortfall. In February 2004, the state legislature was considering an alternative to Act 47 that would entail an independent control board to help the distressed city. Pennsylvania governor Edward G. Rendell supported the oversight board because it helped to restore financial health to Philadelphia in 1991–1992 (Barnes 2004). One strategy that Pittsburgh mayor Tom Murphy clung to was that the deficit could not be fully restored without help from 1.5 million residents who live in adjacent counties. On the one hand, it became abundantly clear in 2004 that the city could not keep pace with the rising cost of services. On the other hand, suburban residents were reluctant to pay more taxes or service fees, because they had voted against the sports complexes in the late 1990s. In a desperate search to narrow the deficit, Mayor Murphy and the city council were contemplating a controversial commuter tax. If history is any indicator, such efforts are rife with problems, as seen in Chicago mayor Richard J. Daley's (1955–1976) efforts to tax Chicago commuters in the 1970s, only to have the State Supreme Court strike down that mandate. In the meantime, city parking fees increased by 50 percent as a stopgap measure to shore up dwindling city revenues. However, there is some indication that higher parking fees may drive off those the city needs most: suburban workers and shoppers.

Juggling Jurisdictions in the New Millennium

When David Lawrence assumed the mayor's office in 1945 he found that the decline in property values through the Great Depression and World War II was yielding fewer revenues than in 1935. The Economy League, consisting of corporate advisors, recommended that the 1946 budget could only be enhanced if the efficiency of municipal operations was improved, costs were lowered, and revenues rose. Specifically, it argued for adding new revenues, extending the sources of revenues beyond the boundaries of Pittsburgh, transferring some city functions to the county, and increasing the return of state-collected revenues to the city. The same propositions were floated in 2004. The city has already increased the parking tax by 50 percent, and some proponents call for an increased merchant and sales tax. Still others "want more suburban tax support for the city, by hiking the $10 occupation tax or through a commuter income tax" (Delano 2004, 15).

Suburbanization has hollowed out Pittsburgh's core spatially and economically. Whether Pittsburgh makes up for lost revenues or not, it enters the new millennium with an uneasy association with its suburban counties, without which its economy cannot survive. However, should most suburbanites, concerned with quality schools, relocate to the city? Enrollment in the city's schools declined by a half percentage point annually between 1990 and 1997, and then quickened to two and a half points for the next thee years. City schoolchildren taking the SAT exam in 2000 averaged 904, which is 84 points lower than the state mean (Haulk and Rogel 2002, 2). What does all this suggest? "Whether this is because Pittsburgh families with school-aged children are sending their children to non-public schools or are moving away from the City in disproportionate numbers, the recent decline in enrollment suggests very strongly that the Pittsburgh School District is rapidly losing the confidence of parents" (Haulk and Rogel 2002, 2).

Without suburban cooperation or money, reversing the city's population, educational, and economic slide will not be easy. To be fair, however, Pittsburgh is not unlike other cities such as Cleveland and Philadelphia that are trying to court suburbanites by means of sports and entertainment complexes to live in or visit their downtowns. A more permanent fix to the problem might be jurisdictional reorganization between city and suburbs, a messy political geographic formula to which Americans have never warmed (Palen 1995). Pittsburgh writer Brian David (2004) proposed reorganizing the northern suburbs from forty-eight jurisdictions into eight municipalities (Wexford, Gibsonia, Springdale, Sewickley, Ben Avon, North Hills, Fox Chapel, and Natrona) as a way to combine resources and solve the city's budget woes. Another resident commented, "regionalism would help [Allegheny

County] as a whole survive as populations shift due to suburban sprawl" (David 2004). Jurisdictional cooperation may be the only way Pittsburgh can tolerate population loss but maintain its symbolic, cultural, and economic functions as the major city in the tristate area. How the city negotiates that alliance with suburban taxpayers will surely be as difficult in the twenty-first century as cleaning the air was in the last one.

References

Barnes, T. 2004. House OKs City Oversight. *Pittsburgh Post-Gazette,* February 5.

Cauchon, D. 2004. Pittsburgh's Renaissance in Jeopardy. *USA Today,* January 30.

City of Pittsburgh. 2003. Comprehensive Annual Financial Report for the Year Ended December 31, 2002. Pittsburgh: Office of the City Controller.

David, B. 2004. What North Municipalities Could Be. *Pittsburgh Post-Gazette,* February 4.

Delano, Jon. 2004. Roots of City's Financial Woes Go Back Decades. *Pittsburgh Business Times,* Jan. 30–Feb. 5.

Gamrat, F. 2002. Private Financing for a New Penguins Arena. Allegheny Institute Report #02–08. Mt. Lebanon, PA: Allegheny Institute for Public Policy.

Garreau, J. 1991. *Edge City.* New York: Doubleday.

Guerrieri, V. 2004. Trundling through Trolley History. *Pittsburgh Tribune-Review,* February 5.

Haulk, J., and E. Montarti. 2002. Midweek Perspectives: The New David L. Lawrence Convention Center Will Find the Competition Tough. *Pittsburgh Post-Gazette,* March 13, post-gazette.com http://www.post-gazette.com/forum/comm/20020313edmont13p3.asp (accessed November 15, 2004).

Haulk, J., and W. Rogel. 2002. Undeserved Award for Pittsburgh Teachers' Union. *Policy Brief* 2 (45). Mt. Lebanon, PA: Allegheny Institute for Public Policy.

Hoffman, S. J. 1992a. "A Plan of Quality": The Development of Mt. Lebanon, a 1920s Automobile Suburb. *Journal of Urban History* 18:141–81.

———. 1992b. The Saga of Pittsburgh's Liberty Tubes: Geographical Partisanship on the Urban Fringe. *Pittsburgh History* 75:128–41.

Jackson, K. T. 1985. *Crabgrass Frontier: The Suburbanization of the United States.* New York: Oxford University Press.

Levy, J. M. 1985. *Urban and Metropolitan Economics.* New York: McGraw-Hill.

———. 1997. *Contemporary Urban Planning.* Upper Saddle River, NJ: Prentice Hall.

Mills, E. S. *Studies in the Structure of the Urban Economy.* Baltimore: Johns Hopkins University Press.

Muller, E. K., and J. A. Tarr. 2003. The Interaction of the Natural and Built Environments in the Pittsburgh Landscape. In *Devastation and Renewal: An Environmental History of Pittsburgh and Its Region,* ed. J. A. Tarr, 11–40. Pittsburgh: University of Pittsburgh Press.

Palen, J. J. 1995. *The Suburbs.* New York: McGraw-Hill.

Safdie, M. 1997. *The City after the Automobile.* Boulder, CO: Westview Press.

Tarr, J. A. 2003. *Devastation and Renewal: An Environmental History of Pittsburgh and Its Region.* Pittsburgh: University of Pittsburgh Press.

Vance, J. 1962. Emerging Patterns of Commercial Structure in American Cities. In *Proceedings of the I.G.U. Symposium in Urban Geography*, ed. K. Norborg, 485–518. Lund, Sweden: Gleerup.

Vassilaros, D. 2003. PNC Park: They Built It, But No One Came. *Pittsburgh Tribune-Review*, April 29, http://livesite.pittsburghlive.com/x/tribune-review/columnists/vassilaros/s_131671.html.

TEN

Factory Outlet Malls

PRIME OUTLETS AT GROVE CITY

James T. Hathaway and James C. Hughes

Industrial restructuring in the Pittsburgh area reverberates well beyond the confines of the Monongahela, Ohio, and Allegheny river valleys. While much has been written about the city of Pittsburgh's dramatic shift from a steel, refractory, and manufacturing powerhouse to a city of services, less is known about the changing location of services in the tristate area. Indeed, the development of a fine web of interstate highways in western Pennsylvania has transformed the nature of retailing, especially regional shopping centers.

The purpose of this chapter is to examine the phenomenon of factory outlet malls and to place them in the context of larger issues that economic geographers study, including economic restructuring. Market analysts and locational analysts define an outlet center as one in which 50 percent or more of the tenants are manufacturer's outlets. We focus on Prime Outlets at Grove City, Pennsylvania, while placing it against the development of the outlet mall industry.

Outlet malls are an important part of the new retail landscape. They combine producer-owned stores offering name brand goods at reduced prices with no-frills designs and locations in what we call the "metropolitan shadow." The first multi-tenant factory outlet center opened in Reading, Pennsylvania, in 1974. A relatively new development, factory outlet malls were the fastest-growing segment of shopping center retailing in the 1990s. However, growth has slowed. The number of centers has decreased, while total floor space and sales have increased. In 1998, there were 312 factory outlet malls nationwide, with $12.2 billion in annual sales. By 2002, the number had dropped to 260, but sales were $15 billion (Prime Retail 2005). Outlet malls are a small portion of shopping center retailing, with total shopping center sales totaling $1.23 trillion in 2002 (International Council of Shopping Centers 2004).

Theoretical Context

The development of the outlet mall industry exemplifies capitalism's continuous struggle to adapt to changing conditions. We use factory outlet malls as an example of retail restructuring, that is, change in or between the constituent parts of the retail economy. We draw from literature in three overlapping areas: the geography of services, the new retail geography, and the geography of consumption.

Consumer services provide most of the new jobs in America (U.S. Department of Commerce 2002, 385). As the service sector continues to expand its share of the national economy, geographers are researching the impact of this expansion on local economies. Outlet malls illustrate the flexible and gendered nature of contemporary service employment. Unlike the traditional forty-hour workweek associated with industrial manufacturing, many service workers find that employers have made work hours flexible. Service jobs also tend to be gendered, with a particular job dominated by one sex or the other. For example, 67.5 percent of all U.S. sales workers in retail and personal services were female in 2001 (U.S. Department of Commerce 2002, 382).

A revitalized retail geography would look at local retail phenomena in the larger context of national and global economies. Topics that the new retail geography may investigate include new forms of retailing, changes in labor markets and work organization, movements of retail capital, and reconfigured consumption spaces (Blomley 2000). We will show how each of these topics is manifested in the outlet mall phenomenon.

Academic interest in consumption has been growing rapidly (Miller et al. 1998). Geographers have shown only intermittent interest until recently in the study of consumption of commodities despite the ubiquity of consumption in everyday life, its immense economic importance, and the interest it has stimulated in other social sciences (Thrift 2000). Economic geography has been dominated by studies of production, but a new focus on consumption has helped provide a more complete rendering of the nature of changes in the economy. Factory outlet malls are an important and relatively new component of America's landscapes of consumption.

Why Factory Outlet Malls?

Factory outlet malls are a response to the changing needs of retail, producer, and investment capital. Retail capital is nervous, with competition intensifying and consumers spending less on apparel. The American retail market is increasingly saturated. Americans are spending more on cars, dining out, and entertainment, and less on clothing and home furnishings (Steinhauer 1997). Competition is especially fierce in retail clothing, with discounters, revitalized department stores, mass merchandisers, and mail order and online retailers all after the same market.

Factory outlet malls reflect the struggle between producers and retailers. Producers lost ground to retailers in recent decades as retailing became increasingly concentrated in the hands of fewer and larger retailers (Wrigley and Lowe 2002, 21). Retailers could increasingly dictate terms in scheduling production and negotiating prices and delivery dates (Jones 1995, 25). Producers are trying to get control and profit back by using factory outlet malls. In fact, in a factory outlet mall, retailers and producers are largely the same. Outlets have become new profit generators for the manufacturers. Prices are kept down by acquiring merchandise in increasing proportion from overseas plants: in the 1990s from Mexico and the Caribbean Basin (Jones 1995, 25–26), and more recently from China.

Factory outlet malls are also a response to consumer demand. Customers accept the notion of designer label desirability. Designer labels are the prime feature of an outlet mall; virtually all stores are named after a brand. A few examples are Ann Taylor, Reebok, Mikasa, Brooks Brothers, J. Crew, and Sony. The $15 billion in annual sales suggest that many consumers are buying the factory outlet concept.

Investment capital is looking for new investment opportunities. The funding for outlet malls is often complex. Prime Retail, a Baltimore-based publicly traded company, put up money originally for the Prime Outlets at Grove City, as did FruCon, a private company in Germany, and some other real estate investment trusts. In 1996, Prime Outlets at Grove City became fully owned by Prime Retail (PR Newswire 1997). Then, Prime Retail expanded too quickly, and in the late 1990s was heavily in debt. Since December 2003, Prime Retail has been owned by the Lightstone Group LLC of Lakewood, New Jersey. The changes in ownership underscore both the uneven investment patterns that characterize the industry nationally and portend changes in the years to come.

Prime Outlets at Grove City

A recent expression of these trends is the proliferation of outlet malls. An example is Prime Outlets at Grove City, which began as a $40 million development along I-79 fifty miles north of Pittsburgh. The development opened in August 1994 and hosted 4.6 million visitors in 2001. The mall has expanded three times, and there are presently 137 stores and restaurants and 532,705 square feet of floor space. The industry average was 50 stores in 2000. In 2001, factory outlet malls averaged 211,715 square feet of floor space (Value Retail 2004). Prime Outlets ranks as the seventh largest outlet mall (in terms of number of stores) in the nation (Outlet Bound 1999). One feature that sets this factory outlet mall apart from many others is the fact that it serves both tourists and an unusually large proportion of regional shoppers because of lack of competition. The Mall of America in Bloomington, Minnesota, has lots of "shoppertainment" (theme parks, movie theaters, nightclubs), while Prime Outlets at Grove City has no more than a food court.

Location is carefully considered by factory outlet mall developers. Prime Outlets at Grove City and other outlet malls are located near interstate highways in the rural metropolitan shadow. A major firm in the industry (Prime Retail) strives to have metropolitan areas totaling 2.5 million within 100 miles of a site, and a daily traffic count of at least 30,000 on nearby interstate highways. The Prime Outlets at Grove City have 8.1 million people living within a 100-mile radius, and are easily accessible to two major interstate highways: I-79 and I-80.

A further locational criterion is a distance of more than 20 miles to existing shopping centers. The Grove City Shops' nearest competitors are a declining, older mall 25 miles away near Sharon, Pennsylvania, a small enclosed mall 20 miles away near Butler, and the nearest super-regional mall in the Pittsburgh area, which is 46 miles away. In fact, the Pittsburgh region as a whole has been reported to be relatively "under-retailed" (Hazel 1994a). Seventy-eight percent of visitors to the Prime Outlets at Grove City come from seven nearby counties, and over 90 percent come from either western Pennsylvania or eastern Ohio (figure 10.1). The average travel time of visitors was 57 minutes in 1999 (Prime Outlets 2004). Finally, the factory outlet mall's developer wants at least 3 million tourists annually within the trade area. The Prime Outlets at Grove City' trade area has 8 million tourists. Nevertheless, only 24 percent of customers in 1999 were tourists, a figure that is close to the average for the owners of Prime Outlets.

A less tangible locational aspect of factory outlet malls is perceived safety, which may be related to their rural settings. Fear of crime influences shopping patterns (Cockerham 1994, Halverson 1996, Nicholls 1994). Only

25 percent of Americans in a survey said they feel that malls provided a safe and secure environment (Underwood 1994). This perception is reinforced by articles in the popular press such as "Danger at the Mall" in *Good Housekeeping* (Kiger 1998). Non-store retail formats (e.g., television shopping networks) have begun playing on customers' fears for their safety (Forseter 1994, *Chain Store Executive with Shopping Center Age* 1995). The typical enclosed shopping mall is seen as a microcosm of society that includes "criminals, gangs, drug dealers, and transients" (Johnson and Warchol 1997, 87). For better of worse, the shopping mall has become the village green of America. Crime seems out of place at the rural bucolic settings of Prime Outlets at Grove City and similar outlet malls. A comment from a Slippery Rock University exam paper may be representative: "When shopping at the Grove City outlets you don't have to worry about getting mugged, you just have to worry about getting the best deal."

Developers carefully consider mall design. A mall manager told us that they want prestige brand names to be visible from the interstate (A. M. Ackerman, interview by author, 1995). Factory outlet malls typically have a simpler design than traditional regional shopping centers. The Prime Outlets at Grove City are unenclosed, one-story in height, anchorless, and relatively small in terms of square footage, considering their draw. By and large, factory outlet malls may be described as no-frills. This may reinforce shoppers' perceptions of bargain pricing, and the Prime Outlets at Grove City fit this profile.

Prime Retail designs its malls to be at the upper end of the no-frills category. Prime Retail describes its Grove City mall as follows: "Nestled in the countryside like a village, its architecture suggests an elegant, rural main street and creates a pleasant shopping environment" (Prime Retail 1999). This description contains themes of nostalgia and nature that are attractive to affluent American consumers. The village-like setting helps distinguish it from what may be seen as chaotic and dirty downtown shopping areas and from the placeless aura of generic suburban shopping malls. A component of the nostalgia theme at Prime Outlets at Grove City is the Victorian appearance of the stores. Goss notes that much of America's retail built environment evokes the Victorian era, and that this time is "associated with the simple virtues, stable identity, and sense of purpose of America's halcyon days" (1999, 68). The reference to the countryside in the Prime Outlets at Grove City self description calls attention to "nature." In fact, this outlet mall has gone a step further by preserving and incorporating a wetland area into its design. These features are part of a recent trend in American shopping center design. For Price (1995, 195), "developers install nature like a sign to affluent middle-class shoppers, saying this place is a real place, and it's for you."

Outlet mall customers tend to be relatively well-off. The median household income of customers in 1999 at the Prime Outlets at Grove City was $49,901, about $8,000 above the national average (Prime Outlets 2004). The typical Grove City shopper is white (95%), female (78%), owns a home (77%), and is married (67%). The median age is 48.3. Twenty-nine percent of shoppers have children under 18, and 23 percent are retired (A. M. Ackerman, interview by author, 1995). The overwhelming proportion of female shoppers is consistent with patterns at all shopping centers (Underhill 2004, 15).

The employees tend not to be affluent. Most factory outlet mall jobs are typical of the new flexible service economy. There are now 1,500 full- and part-time employees, but according to an information sheet distributed by the mall, Prime Outlets at Grove City's estimated 1995 payroll was $10,500,000 for one thousand employees. That works out to an average of $10,500 a year. Some employers pay $1.50 more than the minimum wage (*Allied News* 1998). Sony, for example, starts its employees at eight dollars an hour. However, most mall employees are employed part-time and do not receive benefits. We estimate, based on numerous visits, that well over three-quarters of employees are women.

Consequences for the area surrounding Prime Outlets at Grove City are mixed, although we believe that most people within a few miles have a somewhat positive view of the mall. Like some other factory outlet malls, it has generated a profusion of businesses, including four gasoline/convenience stores, four motels, and six restaurants. The largest new facility is a sports complex that offers summer sports camps, tournaments, and league play, although it recently went bankrupt and is now in receivership. Development makes some residents feel that the rural tranquility they value is quickly disappearing. Traffic volumes began to overwhelm capacities and a third lane was added to the bridge over I-79, but local municipalities do not yet have the resources to cope. For example, the Springfield Township Volunteer Fire Department is concerned about its ability to respond to an emergency, and there are police, sewer, and water concerns (Adams 1999). On the other hand, the mall has brought shopping opportunities, new tax revenues, and jobs to a relatively rural area with few other job prospects.

Beyond the immediate environs of the outlet mall, the consequences are again mixed. Many residents appreciate the convenience of having many more shops and restaurants within easy driving distance. Millions of people know about Prime Outlets at Grove City; this helps put the area "on the map." On the negative side, the mall has led to several store closings in the two main shopping districts of Grove City, about five miles away.

Outlet Malls: How Successful in the Future?

Factory outlet malls reflect broad trends in retailing and the Grove City center is no exception. These trends include the rapidly changing nature and institutions of capitalism, including the appearance of a unique producer-retailer combination, the diverse strategies of the apparel sector, and the increasingly flexible and gender-based nature of employment.

The sites selected by factory outlet malls depart from prevailing post–World War II locational patterns. With an increased willingness of consumers to travel, and retail saturation in urban and suburban areas, the industry has chosen once seemingly remote locations. Locations in the metropolitan shadow have been accessible to millions of customers because of expanded interstate highways and cheap fuel costs. The $15 billion outlet mall industry seems to reverse the traditional rural to urban flow of retail dollars, to disaggregate services, and to disperse development.

Factory outlet malls are a relatively new and successful form of consumption space. Consumers perceive factory outlet malls to be price-competitive, crime-free sources of name brand merchandise. Investors perceive the malls as attractive destinations for their money. Outlet malls are a product of investors seeking profitable opportunities in the turbulent retail industry, producers fighting back, and consumers perceiving branded goods to be superior. Overall, Prime Outlets at Grove City has been exceptionally successful so far. But how long will it last?

As in most forms of retail, not all factory outlet malls have remained successful. For example, the Shops at Georgian Place, which are fifty miles east of Pittsburgh in Somerset, Pennsylvania, may have had much of their trade area captured by Prime Outlets at Grove City. In 2001, the complex had only about twenty tenants even though the capacity is for approximately sixty (Gannon 2001). Even at Prime Outlets at Grove City, considered one of the top twenty outlet malls in the United States, there has been tremendous turnover. Although occupancy remains near capacity, thirty-eight stores have closed in the last five years.

Competition will get tougher as additional factory outlet centers and other retailing opportunities—including online shopping—develop. Prime Retail has built another outlet mall 105 miles away in Lodi, Ohio, near Cleveland, that has cut into Prime Outlets at Grove City's trade area. Factory outlets may be losing their price edge over regular stores (Forest 1995), and the factory outlet industry itself has reached saturation. The success of new developments comes largely at the expense of existing market share. This intensified in the 1990s because most builders insisted that others would not be able to build, while saying that they themselves had ambitious construction schedules (Hazel 1994b). A huge 1.1-million-square-foot factory outlet mall called Pittsburgh Mills was completed in summer 2005 just thirty-five miles southeast of Grove City. However the trends play out, we believe that Prime Outlets at Grove City and the retail development it has spawned will remain an important part of the Pittsburgh region's postindustrial economic landscape.

Note

We thank the editors for their helpful comments.

References

Adams, N. 1999. Springfield's Top Spot Grows with Township. *Allied News* (Grove City, PA), May 12, 8.

Allied News (Grove City, PA). 1998. Springfield Development Only Answer. October 7, 17.

Chain Store Age Executive with Shopping Center Age. 1995. Keeping Centers Safe: Managing Security Needs. *Chain Store Age Executive with Shopping Center Age,* April, AM14–AM16.

Blomley, N. 2000. Retailing, Geography of. In *The Dictionary of Human Geography,* ed. R. J. Johnson, D. Gregory, G. Pratt, and M. Watts. 4th ed. Oxford: Blackwell.

Cockerham, P. W. 1994. Safe Shopping. *Stores Magazine,* June, 38–39.

Forest, S. 1995. I Can Get It for You Retail. *Business Week,* September 18, 84–88.

Forseter, M. 1994. Fear and Loathing in Retailing. *Chain Store Age Executive with Shopping Center Age,* April, 70.

Gannon, J. 2001. Tale of Two Outlets. *Pittsburgh Post-Gazette,* October 10.

Goss, J. 1999. Once-upon-a-Time in the Commodity World: An Unofficial Guide to Mall of America. *Annals of the Association of American Geographers* 89:45–75.

Halverson, R. 1996. Crime Steal Shoppers' Confidence. *Discount Store News,* May 6, 70.

Hazel, D. 1994a. Where to Put Them in Pittsburgh? *Chain Store Age Executive with Shopping Center Age,* February, 69–71.

———. 1994b. Can Outlets Keep Expanding? *Chain Store Age Executive with Shopping Center Age,* March, 184–85.

International Council of Shopping Centers. 2004. Retail Sales in Shopping Centers Increase in 2002, http://www.icsc.org/srch/about/impactofshoppingcenters/PRRetail Sales.pdf (accessed March 10, 2004).

Johnson, B., and G. Warchol. 1997. Giving Security Space at the Mall. *Security Management,* June, 87–91.

Jones, J. 1995. Forces behind Restructuring in U.S. Apparel Retailing and its Effect on the U.S. Apparel Industry. *Industry, Trade, and Technology Review,* March, 23–27.

Kiger, P. 1998. Danger at the Mall. *Good Housekeeping,* February, 82.

Miller, D., P. Jackson, N. Thrift, B. Holbrook, and M. Rowlands. 1998. *Shopping, Place and Identity.* London: Routledge.

Nicholls, J. 1994. Feelings of Safety Based on When, Why Shoppers Visit Mall. *Marketing News,* August 15, 13.

Outlet Bound. 1999. Search Outlet Centers by Location, http://www.outletbound.com/searchbyloc.html (accessed August 27, 1999).

Price, J. 1995. Looking for Nature at the Mall: A Field Guide to the Nature Company. In *Uncommon Ground,* ed. W. Cronon. Cambridge, MA: Harvard University Press.

PR Newswire. 1997. Prime Retail, http://www.prnewswire.com (accessed October 25, 1997).

Prime Retail. 1999. Prime Outlets: Grove City, http://www.primeoutlets.com/GroveCity/index.html (accessed September 4, 1999).

———. 2005. Prime Outlets: Industry Overview, http://www.primeoutlets.com/corporate/iofacts.asp (accessed October 12, 2005).

Steinhauer, Jennifer. 1997. Stores Look to Rest of Year as December Sales Flatten. *New York Times,* October 27.

Thrift, N. J. 2000. Consumption, Geography of. In *The Dictionary of Human Geography,* ed. R. J. Johnson, D. Gregory, G. Pratt, and M. Watts. 4th ed. Oxford: Blackwell.

Underhill, Paco. 2004. *Call of the Mall.* New York: Simon and Schuster.

Underwood, E. 1994. Mall Busters, Like Crime, a Boon for Home Shopping. *Brandweek.* January 17.

U.S. Department of Commerce. 2002. *Statistical Abstract of United States,* 2002, Washington, DC.

Value Retail. 2004. VRN Research Data, http://www.valueretailnews.com/research/research_index.htm (accessed March 10, 2004).

Wrigley, N., and M. Lowe. 2002. *Reading Retail.* London: Arnold.

IV APPALACHIAN CULTURAL AND NATURAL RESOURCES

PITTSBURGH IS INEXTRICABLY woven into the fabric of Appalachia. The hills and incised valleys that give the city few straight or level roads continue well beyond the last suburban housing plan into a forest-cloaked hinterland of long commutes, whitewater rapids, deer camps, and rural poverty. Our examination of Pittsburgh's mountainous backyard begins with an examination of access to Internet technology in Appalachia by a group of researchers from Virginia Tech, James Bohland, Anita Puckett, and Jean Plymale. As employment in the coal industry dwindles because of mechanization and corporatization in the mining sector, alternative industries based on information technologies gain importance. The authors identify a variety of cultural, class, and gender barriers, as well as limits of physical infrastructure, that impede the diffusion and adoption of Internet usage throughout the region. The largely rural nature of Appalachia imposes special challenges in adopting new technologies to bridge the digital divide between Appalachia and the rest of the nation, and within the region itself. If, as they contend, "place counts in Appalachia," then the physical infrastructure for Internet access will have to come in line with the rest of the nation. Moreover, transferring Internet knowledge in Appalachia means more than bringing in instructors from outside the region; sensitivity to place, language, and local culture remains paramount in Appalachia.

In chapter 12, geographers Risa Whitson, Lawrence E. Wood, Kurt Fuellhart, and Amy K. Glasmeier take a sweeping review of Appalachia's economic development over the past forty years or so. The region's history of resource exploitation and ensuing federal regional development programs had only partial success in alleviating poverty. Long-term regional dependence on natural resource exploitation has produced enduring hardship, especially for the region's most vulnerable citizens. More than one-third of the counties that were economically distressed in 1960 remained so in 2000. Despite efforts by the Appalachian Regional Commission to yank the region out of poverty, penury continues, especially in the southern Appalachians. Building roads, water lines, and sewage facilities characterized the development strategies of the past. In the future, the authors contend that such an approach will not launch Appalachia on the road to economic recovery unless the necessary political will and a deconcentration of corporate power takes hold. In this regard, both Pittsburgh and the Appalachians face new resource needs that break tradition with the bricks-and-mortar and smokestack infrastructure of the last century.

Chapter 13 by Geoffrey L. Buckley, Timothy G. Anderson, and Nancy R. Bain examines the fringe region of southeastern Ohio. The area is remotely at the edge of Pittsburgh's metropolitan area, different from the rest of Ohio, but perhaps most closely similar to Appalachia. Like the chapter before it, the role of the Appalachian Regional Commission forms a lens through which recent economic development can be assessed. The authors argue that three factors explain why southeastern Ohio does not fit neatly into any North American region. First, its distinctive historical settlement geography sets it apart from Appalachia. Second, while mining has been important, the region's orientation and hinterland relationships make it distinct. Third, it is poorer than the rest of the state and possesses an aging physical infrastructure. Its small towns and cities, coupled with the lack of whitewater amenities that mountainous Appalachia has, conspire to make its postindustrial restructuring especially challenging.

The next three chapters assess growing recreational industries throughout Appalachia. In chapter 14, Lizbeth A. Pyle highlights the growth in central Appalachia's whitewater industry and takes a more positive assessment of community development than the previous chapter. Pyle details how the local economies and small towns near the Gauley, New, and Cheat rivers in West Virginia are actively promoting this outdoor sport. As outfitters, communities, and states more aggressively market whitewater rafting and related tourism activities, economic multipliers will continue to increase. Seasonal usage will always be a constraint in the whitewater industry, but new product development and improved entrepreneurial skills will strengthen the industry. Millions of potential users living in cities like Columbus, Cleveland, Roanoke, Charlotte, Winston-Salem, Greensboro, Richmond, Pittsburgh, Washington DC, Louisville, and other cities are a just a few hours away from the Appalachian whitewater industry.

Deborah Che turns her sights northward to understand yet another outdoor activity: deer hunting. She traces the history of deer hunting in the mountains of north-central Pennsylvania and links it with the heritage of the region surrounding the Allegheny National Forest. Long a seasonal destination for city dwellers in Cleveland, Erie, Pittsburgh, and Youngstown, hunting camps still dot the landscape and form an important part of the local economy. However, changing leisure patterns and a rise in the deer populations in previously deer-poor regions of southern Pennsylvania threaten hunting tourism in the region. Nonetheless, Che argues that the deer camp experience retains an allure more powerful than hunting in one's "suburban backyard" and has been a persistent feature of the region's outdoor and leisure geography.

Part IV concludes with Richard A. Roth's case study of watershed planning. He explains how a local nonprofit organization, New River Community Partners, responded to President Clinton's American Heritage Rivers Initiative that identified fourteen rivers, including the New River, for their unique aesthetic and watershed features. Implicit in the initiative was a mandate that the local community have a say in how this special designation will be handled on the New River. In this case, however, the "local communities" include residents living far apart from each other and in three states. Findings show that the predominantly volunteer planning programs led to a series of outcomes that did not require the creation of any new government agencies. Unlike the top-down actions of the Tennessee Valley Authority, the case of volunteer community planning programs in the New River watershed shows that grassroots input can meaningfully steer broad government mandates without either co-opting the agendas of local residents or requiring huge amounts of federal funding. If chapter 12 suggests that Appalachia is rich in natural resources but poor in human capital, this chapter suggests otherwise. These findings are especially promising given the scaled-back role of federal programs in the region during the second administration of George W. Bush, as well as the growth of the whitewater industry that will continue to employ workers in a sustainable industry that distinguishes Appalachia.

ELEVEN

The Decline of Space and the Ascent of Place

INTERNET TECHNOLOGY IN APPALACHIA

James Bohland, Anita Puckett, and Jean Plymale

The "death of distance," "the incredible shrinking world," and "the elimination of isolation" are common phrases describing the geography of the information age. The ability to move information, capital, and innovations at higher speeds than previously possible is the driving force in this new economy. Regions marginalized in the old economy are poised to participate in the new one. The death of distance offers economically distressed counties in Appalachia the prospect of becoming fuller partners in the new economy. The Internet is viewed as a positive force for community development, as Internet use can create new networks of interaction at both commercial and personal levels.

Juxtaposed to the euphoria spun by the apostles of the information age, evidence is accumulating that the potential for community and personal development through information technology in general, and the Internet in particular, depends on place. Zook (2000) claims that much of the growth of the Internet has concentrated in a relatively small number of urban areas within the United States. Just eight cities—San Francisco, New York, Los Angeles, Washington DC, Chicago, Boston, Miami, and Dallas—dominate Internet expansion within the United States, reflecting and reinforcing an old physical geography of economic growth. Moss and Townsend (1998) document significant variations in regional connectivity to the Internet. This variability in integration to the network has long-term consequences for those unable to participate in the new economy, who will continue to be marginalized (Kitchin 1998; Castells 2000; Mitchell 2000).

The presence and persistence of a "digital divide" separating population groups (by class, gender, race, and education) and places (rural versus metropolitan and inner city versus suburb) provides evidence that not all regions or groups benefit from this new technology. The National Telecommunications and Information Agency (NTIA) concluded that "regardless of income level, Americans living in rural areas are lagging behind in Internet access. Indeed, at the lower income level, those in urban areas are more than twice as likely to have Internet access than those earning the same income in rural areas" (NTIA 1999, xiii).

Moreover, the divide has been increasing rather than decreasing over time (NTIA 1995, 1998, 2000; Castells 2000). In Virginia, for example, rural communities with lower income and educational levels are the least able to take advantage of the benefits of information technology (Bohland et al. 2001). What, then, does the Internet and its promise for community development hold for Appalachian communities, particularly for those rural communities historically associated with extraction economies?

Oden and Strover (2002) have recently documented telecommunication penetration and utilization within the Appalachian region. Their comprehensive data, along with other case studies, data on national Internet geographies, and national or state surveys, enable us to understand better the joint futures of the Internet and Appalachia. We argue that although Internet technology offers Appalachian communities the potential for economic renaissance and community development, the obstacles to full or even moderate integration into the new information economy are formidable. Moreover, we believe, as do others (Anderson et al. 1995; Wresch 1996; Andrew and Petkov 2003), that the principal barriers are not technological but are associated with the cultural, political, and social contexts of the communities. The structures, symbols, and values that help give meaning to Appalachian places can be powerful barriers to integration into the information economy. Unless we understand how the context of place intersects with the information highway, the ability of Internet technology to serve as a catalyst for a new economy in Appalachia is limited.

Space: The Long Last Mile

Our focus on social and cultural aspects does not presuppose the existence of a well-developed telecommunications infrastructure in Appalachia. The physical infrastructure for sustainable Internet utilization, particularly for community development, is insufficient in many communities. ("Sustainable" here refers to the maintenance of Internet services over an extended time period and regular use of those services by organizations and individuals.) In Appalachia, the "last mile"—the significant barriers still existing to connecting international, national, and regional networks to household or community users—may have shrunk, but it has not been eliminated.

Patterson (1997) argues that sustainable Internet communities occur when at least 20 percent of the population within a community uses the Internet. He and others (Martin 1997; Ward 1997) argue that the evolution of sustained Internet occurs in three interdependent stages. First, physical access to Internet grade computer technology for individuals and industry-competitive technologies for commercial users is available to large numbers within a community. Second, a demand for Internet services exists so that a substantial user base is present to support the creation of the physical telecommunication infrastructure. And third, the user base grows to a level that can sustain usage and promote future growth and development of Internet technology and services within a community. Few communities within Appalachia have achieved stage three, some are in stage two, but significant portions are in stage one (Puckett 1997).

The principal technological barriers in Appalachian communities are the persistence of older telephone systems in many counties within the region and the small, albeit growing, number of local Internet Service Providers (ISPs). Until these barriers are addressed, rural Appalachian communities will remain marginalized, even within the new geography of the information age.

Although approximately 95 percent of US households have telephone connections, Internet availability via dial-up connections are still a constraint in many rural communities. The Department of Commerce reported that "while rural areas are generally as connected as urban areas, those groups (*lower income*) that are less likely to own phones have especially low penetration rates in rural areas" (NTIA 1999, 2). According to the Rural Task Force of the Federal Communications Commission, the disadvantaged in rural areas rank "at the bottom of the scale with respect to telephone penetration" (Rural Task Force 2000). Appalachian states generally have phone connectivity rates comparable to national statistics (table 11.1), and Internet access rates at the state level have been increasing (Oden and Stover 2002). State rates, however, can be misleading. In some Appalachian communities, for example, 20 percent of residents may still lack direct phone access (Puckett 1997). Quality of phone services and the condition of the physical telephone infrastructure represent further technical barriers. In some cases local and cooperative phone networks are technically inadequate to ensure reasonable Internet connections.

Wireless technologies offer opportunity for increased speeds and quality of connection. In some instances, industries have used satellite connections

TABLE 11.1. Internet Access and Telephones

State	*Percent of Households with Internet Access* 1998	2000	*% Change*	*Percent of Households with Telephone* 1998	2000	*% Change*
AL	21.6	35.5	64.4	93.3	91.9	-1.5
GA	23.9	38.3	60.3	91.4	91.1	-0.3
KY	21.1	36.6	73.5	93.3	93.3	0.0
MD	*31.0**	*43.8**	41.3	*96.5**	*95.0**	-1.6
MS	13.6	26.3	93.4	89.5	89.2	-0.3
NY	23.7	39.8	67.9	*94.8**	*95.1**	0.3
NC	19.9	35.3	77.4	93.1	93.9	0.9
OH	24.6	40.7	65.4	*95.6**	*94.8**	-0.8
PA	24.9	40.1	61.0	96.8	96.6	-0.2
SC	21.4	32.0	49.5	92.9	93.2	0.3
TN	21.3	36.3	70.4	*94.6**	*95.5**	1.0
VA	*27.9**	*44.3**	58.8	93.9	*95.4**	1.6
WV	17.6	34.3	94.9	93.8	94.0	0.2
US	26.2	41.5	58.4	94.1	94.4	0.3

Italics and *: above national average

Sources: Appalachian Regional Commission, Links to the Future: The Role of Information and Telecommunications Technology in Appalachian Economic Development, section 4, Telecommunications Infrastructure in the ARC Region, http://www.arc.gov/index.do?nodeId=1013; NTIA (July 1999) *Falling Through the Net: Defining the Digital Divide*; NTIA (October 2000) *Falling Through the Net: Toward Digital Inclusion*; FCC, Telephone Subscribership in the US (February 1999 and March 2001).

for their information and data transfer needs. The expansion of wireless to individual residences is on the horizon, but even here some counties lie outside existing wireless corridors in the region and may not be suitable locations for wireless access under current plans. Regardless of the projections for wireless coverage throughout the region, extensive deployment of the technology is still years away. Meanwhile, the digital gap expands.

Although national Internet service providers (ISPs) such as America Online (AOL) are available to Appalachian residents, for community development to benefit from the Internet, local ISPs are required. The issue is not simply the presence of ISPs, but the amount of bandwidth, calculated in bits per second, that best measures the capacity and quality of the connectivity available to a community. Without local ISPs, residents cannot access service without incurring long-distance fees. Local ISPs also become advocates for Internet use and encourage the formation of support and training organizations within communities. The number of local Internet service providers has increased since 1997 (Bohland and Puckett 2000). However, even when we assume extended coverage to adjacent counties, substantial gaps in coverage exist, particularly in eastern Kentucky and Tennessee.

Local ISPs provide access to the Internet through their points-of-presence (POPs). POPs are facilities, often space rented from a larger, incumbent telecommunication carrier such as Sprint or Verizon, in which equipment required to establish network connectivity (routers, servers, switches, and so on) is housed. The number of POPs a service provider has is sometimes used as a measure of size or growth of the ISP. To maximize potential, local ISPs must connect to facilities and services that reach major access nodes of national and international communication networks (Virginia Tech eCorridors Program 2003). Typically, local ISPs buy connections to larger service providers in order to provide their customers with access to the global Internet.

To develop the physical and organizational infrastructure needed for Internet sustainability in rural or disadvantaged communities, federal and state governments and nonprofit organizations have instituted programs to assist in infrastructure development. At the federal level, the Community Technology Center (CTC) sponsored by the Department of Education, the Neighborhood Network project (HUD), the Department of Education's Twenty-First Century Community Learning Centers, and the Telecommunication and Information Infrastructure Assistance Program (Department of Commerce) represent initiatives designed to create community networks. Managing Information with Rural America, a Kellogg Foundation initiative, is targeted to help rural communities create the capacity for electronic information sharing and conversations. A relatively small number of these initiatives operate in the Appalachian region. For example, while three hundred community technology centers have been formed since the program began (see http://www.ed.gov/fund/grant/apply/AdultEd/CTC/index.html), fewer than ten are in Appalachia and most of these are in larger cities or in university communities within the region.

In assessing future roles for using information technology for community building (in this case universal access to e-mail), Anderson and his colleagues concluded that "there are no fundamental technical barriers to the provision of universal access to e-mail within the United States" (1995, 76). The cost and time required to upgrade the present information infrastructure in many Appalachian communities makes that assessment very problematic in the region.

Place and the Internet in Appalachia

"Place" infuses every aspect of Appalachian life and not just in a geographical or analytic sense of proximal spatial arrangements in relation to cultural patterns (Allen 1990; Martin 1990; Stewart 1996). "Place" is a term used frequently and meaningfully in Appalachian conversational and sacred language. In Appalachian speech, "place" entails not only geographical locale (specific hollows, valleys, ridges, or coves) but also specific interpersonal relationships that are based in cultural roles and positions. To say one is "out of place" or to address someone by saying "that's not your place" is to accuse them of being outside the social order, apart from a negotiated and accepted network of human-land relationships (Puckett 2000). When new and encompassing technologies of the power and scope of Internet technologies are introduced into these existing matrices of relationships, they do not enter undefined—they quickly become immersed into local systems of meaning that are predicated on how individuals place themselves in relation to each other, their landscape, and to the new technologies. For much of rural Appalachia, place relations affect informal and formal political economic patterns, gender relations, and speech practices. These patterns structure how the technologies are used and who benefits from them. They direct the shape and direction of the digital divide.

Place and communicative patterns that establish place assign rights to control and use of valued resources in most rural Appalachian counties. Those well placed in terms of family name, land ownership and location, and access to political economic resources frequently have near total control over how any nonlocal resource enters the county or community and who can gain access to it (Batteau 1985; Beaver 1986; Fisher 1993; Hicks 1976). Computers, Internet software, and supporting building infrastructures (T1 lines, fiber-optic lines, or modems, for example) tend to enter these networks from outside sources—charitable donations, government funding, or corporate contributions. Local political power brokers are in positions to filter who receives the benefits of these contributions according to local priorities and political privilege (Puckett 1997). These cultural patterns lead to the following "digital divide" issues.

Local need is minimally met by local computer businesses. With high poverty rates in many counties, few can afford a new or good used computer and the necessary software. Donated ones are circulated among those well placed politically, regardless of financial need. Consequently, those have-nots who could benefit significantly from information technology (IT) often do not have access to the networks in which IT resources are being exchanged and circulated. Significant exceptions to this pattern exist in some counties. Hancock County, Tennessee, for example, had a local organization distributing upgraded used computers to interested local residents who might or might not have been members of politically privileged networks.

Public placement of computers becomes problematic in terms of both geographic and political access. Public sites in towns, such as public libraries, require residents "out in the county" to travel significant distances (twenty-five to thirty-five miles) to use IT equipment. They may not have the time or reliable transportation to make such trips. If they do attempt to log on, they may find that no one at the site can or wants to train them to use the computer or the software. They may interpret lack of assistance in political terms, noting the family connections of the staff. Furthermore, town sites may invoke place violations for county residents: town sites may be too secular, too politically charged, or too "proper," leaving them feeling "out of place." Finally, public placement may be interpreted as too public. Residents may feel that their lack of expertise or their specific task (such as searching for a job, researching genealogical histories, or exploring legal issues) is too public, leaving their personal reputation and place in the community open to examination.

Placement of ITs in educational settings means placement of electronic networking technologies into highly political entities. County school systems are one of only a few stable employment opportunities in many Appalachian counties and are noted for their political structuring (Batteau 1982; Whisnant 1994). Distribution of resources tends to be on the basis of privilege as well as or rather than competency. At the same time, schools have been targeted by government and corporations as appropriate receptors of Internet equipment, often with insufficient or no training support staff. The results have been uneven use of ITs in local school systems. One West Virginia ISP reports that the equipment his company donated was simply thrown in the corner of a classroom, totally unused, due to lack of knowledge about how to use it and disputes over who was to have access. Pike County, Kentucky, schools, however, established integrated systems for providing help to students that supported skills relevant to employment at a local call-in center. A few other counties replicated the Pike County model or have initiated their own systems of IT training. Nevertheless, placement is uneven and in many ways channeled according to preexisting networks for distributing political-economic resources.

Senses of place in much of the Appalachian South apply to gendered roles and a gender-based distribution of resources. Women in their place tend to control resources pertinent to home life, education of children, child care, health, and moral and religious activities. Men in their place tend to control resources related to the public and private exercise of authority, making and use of money, political power and office holding, and ownership of capital resources including automobiles and land. Variation occurs and women's roles as professionals and breadwinners are increasing, but expectations regarding the division of labor lead to interpretations of behavior that strongly affect how Internet technologies are diffused into community life. Men are expected to engage in physical labor involving the use of heavy machinery or in a business that caters to these activities (hardware sales, heavy equipment or automobile manufacturing or distribution, mining or logging company operations, or truck driving). Even those holding political office or involved in education are expected to demonstrate proficiency in male-gendered physical activities in their spare time or on the job. In general, behavior requiring inside desk work, including the use of computer keyboards, run counter to the cultural constructions of male identities. These patterns appear to be changing among primary and secondary students, but older residents still exhibit these gendered patterns of usage.

Women are expected to engage in indoor domestic activities that enhance the domestic sphere and influence the moral character of family members, including children. Many of these domestic activities are extended into workplace activities such as office work, teaching, and nursing. These activities overlap with dominant Internet technological uses for information, computation, and long-distance communication, but contrast with male-controlled spheres of money management and decision making. Personal and home uses of Internet technologies can conflict with expected and gendered control of resources.

Most women publicly affirm a strong Christian faith and regularly attend church, while many men at least espouse a belief in a Christian God. Within their role as moral paragons, women tend to impress meaning onto Internet technologies according to their religious orientations. Men who affirm a strong Christian orientation may also interpret the existence and use of ITs from a religious framework. Sometimes positive, these orientations can also lead to highly negative evaluations including demonic ones. These meanings are often constructed within church communities and strongly affect who will consider using ITs at a group rather than individual level and in terms of what usages are appropriate or not.

Women tend to control reading and writing activities while men are commonly assumed to be better thinkers and decision makers, at least in areas related to political or economic resource domains. Men are not expected to be skilled at literate tasks and may reject Internet technologies simply because their literacy skills are low. Except for verification of scriptural quotations, this division of literate labor devalues reading and writing as only social and entertainment tasks that are controlled by women. Since IT information is generally reading-based, e-commerce, online banking, and other political economic functions of the Internet are rejected. In some cases, a woman or adolescent may interpret these functions for her husband or adult male relatives, who then decide what to do.

Much colloquial speech in the Appalachian South conforms to characteristics of Appalachian English, a highly stigmatized English vernacular. Individuals who are deeply "placed" in community life must rely on this vernacular to maintain and enhance local networks that will provide them with services, goods, and capital. The widespread use of this variety as the preferred speech results in the following issues affecting incorporation of electronic networking technologies.

Lexicon for and ways of talking about illness, health, and medical care are significantly different. Not only is there a distinct vocabulary for disease and ill health (for example, "smothering," "high blood," and "sugar"), ways of talking about illness and disease constitute an orientation toward one's body, the role of formalized medicine, and the functions of faith healing that is different from those found at reputable Internet sites such as WebMD or databases such as Medline. Much Internet material on disease diagnosis and cure becomes meaningless when contrasted with these linguistic patterns. Other central cultural domains such as law, formal education, wage labor behavior, and religion also have distinctive vocabularies and speaking practices. Vernacular web sites have been reported as being potentially useful in addressing this aspect of Internet technology rejection.

Most rural communities in the Appalachian South are small and rely extensively on oral communications. Residents usually know each other well, often from birth, and can have roots in the community extending back six or seven generations. "Getting along" is expected. Consequently, public politeness is well developed in the local vernacular. Verbal instructions, directions, and ways of requesting also reinforce the need to respect personal identities and independence without jeopardizing future social interactions (Puckett 2005). These social interactional patterns construct very different ways of learning new tasks than is reported for corporate settings and highly urban contexts (Drew and Heritage 1992; Ervin-Tripp 1976). Nonlocal instructors in Internet uses frequently violate local norms of how to teach ("learn" in local vernacular), while knowledgeable locals who are familiar with the vernacular are in short supply. In order to overcome the linguistic barrier to sustainable implementation of ITs, it is mandatory to develop culturally sensitive models for training local residents that are also sensitive to gender. Speaking practices related to the exercise of political power are distinct and highly significant to those wanting or needing to gain access to resources (Puckett 2000). Recognition of how these linguistic forms are structured, who can use them and under what interactional and contextual conditions, and why they are significant to the diffusion and sustainable use of Internet technologies is crucial to breaking down the digital divide.

A Persistent Future

The futures promised by integration of Internet technology into Appalachian communities are compelling. Certainly, within the region some notable successes are evident. The Blacksburg Electronic Village, for example, is a groundbreaking innovation in televillages. As successful a model as the Village has become, one must recall its unique (some would say anomalous) context within Appalachia—a university community on the edge of the region.

At present, successful televillages in Appalachia are sparse. As we have demonstrated, for the future some important constraints on expansion of sustained Internet networks exist. These constraints are the result of an underdeveloped physical telecommunication infrastructure that requires significant capital investment to attain the requirements necessary for full integration of Internet technology into the region's economic and social structure. Yet, as we have argued, even with those investments in building infrastructure, some fundamental cultural and social barriers will persist. These are deeply rooted and will require more than capital investments to overcome. Thoughtful and sensitive approaches to implementation of the technology at the community scale will be required. Place counts in Appalachia.

References

Allen, Barbara. 1990. The Genealogical Landscape of the Southern Sense of Place. In *Sense of Place: American Regional Cultures*, ed. Barbara Allen and Thomas Schlereth, 152–63. Lexington: University Press of Kentucky.

Anderson, R., T. Bikson, S. A. Law, and B. Mitchell. 1995. *Universal Access to E-Mail. Feasibility and Societal Implications*. Santa Monica, CA: RAND.

Andrew, T. N., and D. Petkov. 2003. *The Need for a Systems Thinking Approach to the Planning of Rural Telecommunications Infrastructure. Telecommunications Policy* 27:75–93.

Batteau, Allen. 1982. Mosbys and Boomsedge: The Semantics of Class in an Appalachian Kinship System. *American Ethnologist* 9 (3): 445–66.

———. 1985. A Contribution to the Critique of Political Economy. *In The Many Faces of Appalachia*, ed. Sam Gray, 41–46. Proceedings of the Seventh Annual Appalachian Studies Conference. Boone, NC: Appalachian Consortium Press.

Beaver, Patricia, 1986. *Rural Communities in the Appalachian South*. Lexington, KY: University Press of Kentucky.

Bohland, J., M. Papadakis, R. Worral, and D. Zellmer. 2001. The Digital Divide in Virginia. *Virginia Issues and Answers* 9:17–23.

Bohland, J., and A. Puckett. 2000. Decline of Space, The Ascent of Place: Internet Technology in Appalachia. In *A Geographic Perspective of Pittsburgh and the Alleghenies:*

From Precambrian to Post-Industrial, ed. K. Patrick and J. Scarpaci, 182–88. Washington, DC: Association of American Geographers.

Castells, M. 2000. *End of Millennium. Oxford:* Blackwell Publishers.

Drew, P., and J. Heritage, eds. 1992. *Talk at Work: Interaction in Institutional Settings.* New York: Cambridge University Press.

Ervin-Tripp, S. 1976. Is Sybil There? The Structure of Some American English Directives. *Language in Society* 5:25–66.

Fisher, Stephen, ed. 1993. *Fighting Back in Appalachia: Traditions of Resistance and Change.* Philadelphia: Temple University Press.

Hicks, George. 1976. *Appalachian Valley.* New York: Holt, Rinehart and Winston.

Kitchin, Rob. 1998. *Cyberspace: The World in the Wires.* New York: John Wiley and Sons.

Martin, Charles. 1990. Creative Constraints in the Folk Arts of Appalachia. In *Sense of Place: American Regional Cultures*, ed. Barbara Allen and Thomas Schlereth, 138–51. Lexington: University Press of Kentucky.

Martin, Cortney V. 1997. Managing Information in a Community Network. In *Community Networks: Lessons from Blacksburg, Virginia*, ed. Andrew Cohill and Andrea Kavanaugh, 235–76. Boston: Artech House.

Mitchell, William, J. 2000. *E-topia: "Urban life, Jim— but not as we know it."* Cambridge: MIT Press.

Moss, Mitchell L., and Anthony Townsend. 1998. Spatial Analysis of the Internet in U.S. Cities and States. Presented at the Technological Futures-Urban Futures conference, Durham, England, April 23–25, 1998.

National Telecommunications and Information Agency. 1995. *Falling Through the Net: A Survey of "have nots" in Rural and Urban America.* Washington, DC: U.S. Department of Commerce.

———. 1998. *Falling Through the Net: New Paths on the Digital Divide.* Washington, DC: U.S. Department of Commerce.

———. 1999. *Falling Through the Net: Defining the Digital Divide.* Washington, DC: U.S. Department of Commerce.

———. 2000. *Advanced Telecommunications in Rural America: The Challenge of Bringing Broadband Services to all Americans.* Washington, DC: U.S. Department of Commerce, http://www.ntia.doc.gov/reports/ruralbb42600.pdf.

Oden, Michael, and Sharon Strover. 2002. *Links to the Future: The Role of Information and Telecommunications Technology in Appalachian Economic Development.* University of Texas, April 2002.

Patterson, Scott. 1997. Evaluating the Blacksburg Electronic Village. In *Community Networks: Lessons from Blacksburg, Virginia*, ed. Andrew Cohill and Andrea Kavanaugh, 55–71. Boston: Artech House.

Puckett, Anita. 1997. *Cultural Issues Affecting Electronic Networking Technology Implementation in Rural Appalachia: Suggestions for Research.* Appalachian Regional Commission, Dept. of the Interior. Emerging Issues research report.

———. 2000. *Seldom Ask, Never Tell: Labor and Discourse in Appalachia.* New York: Oxford University Press.

———. 2005. Negotiating Rural Southern Mountain Speech. In *Appalachian Cultural Competency: A Guide for Medical, Mental Health, and Social Service Professionals*, ed. S. E. Keefe, 31–55. Knoxville: University of Tennessee Press.

Rural Task Force. 2000. The Rural Difference. White Paper 2, http://www.fcc.gov/wcb/universal_service/whitepaper2.pdf.

Stewart, Kathleen. 1996. *A Space on the Side of the Road: Cultural Poetics in an "Other"America.* Princeton: Princeton University Press.

Ward, Luke. 1997. Community Network Technology. In *Community Networks: Lessons from Blacksburg, Virginia,* ed. Andrew Cohill and Andrea Kavanaugh, 159–234. Boston: Artech House.

Whisnant, David. 1994. *Modernizing the Mountaineer: People, Power and Planning in Appalachia.* Rev. ed. Knoxville: University of Tennessee Press.

Wresch, William. 1996. *Disconnected: Haves and Have-Nots in the Information Age.* New Brunswick, NJ: Rutgers University Press.

Zook, Matthew. 2000. *"Connected" Is a Matter of Geography. netWorker* 5 (3): 13–16, http://www.zooknic.com/info//Zook-netWorker-2001.pdf.

TWELVE

Appalachia

RICH IN NATURAL RESOURCES, POOR IN HUMAN OPPORTUNITY

Risa Whitson, Lawrence E. Wood, Kurt Fuellhart, and Amy K. Glasmeier

Appalachia, a sprawling region that straddles the major mountain belt of the eastern United States, has been one of the nation's poorest areas for the last one hundred years. Today, while the urban reaches of the region look increasingly like the nation as a whole in terms of levels of income, employment, and other measures of economic well-being, the rural portions of Appalachia appear surprisingly untouched by postwar economic development. The peculiar fate of the region, tied as it has been to massive natural resource exploitation, today reflects a landscape of uneven development in which many communities live in isolation, locked out of the nation's growing prosperity.

Pittsburgh is the northern urban industrial anchor of Appalachia. The once enormous steel center was an important market for metallurgical coal disgorged from the mountains of West Virginia, Kentucky, Pennsylvania, Tennessee, Ohio, and Virginia. Today, a tour of the region would find steel mills largely silent and former steel communities still largely in disarray. Among these ruins, the demand for Appalachian coal is declining both as a feedstock for industry and as an energy source for power generation.

The poverty so evident in Appalachia today arises from a complex history. Despite billions of dollars of federal and state development funds expended since the late 1960s, the heart of the region remains stagnant and distinct from economic trends experienced both nationally and within the urban areas of the region.

In this brief chapter, we present three stories that are interconnected by time, politics, and economy. We begin by tracing the history of the region and role of resource exploitation in its socioeconomic evolution. We then turn to the policy debates of the 1960s, which led to the formulation of a federal regional development program that was designed to combat regional poverty. From a broad view of the policy context, we briefly examine the fate of the most troubled parts of the region, which have been immune to the effects of conventional policy of the last thirty years. We conclude by way of summary to link the long-term regional dependence on natural resource exploitation with the enduring hardship of the region's most vulnerable citizens.

Looking Forward from the Nineteenth Century

Initially inhabited by large numbers of Native Americans, including Cherokees, Tuscaroras, Shawnees, and Senedos (Dunaway 1995; Finger 1995), the Appalachian Mountains were first settled on a large scale by Europeans during the eighteenth century. Successive waves of immigrants settled central and southern Appalachia by pushing down the Shenandoah Valley into Virginia, the Carolinas, and the Appalachia plateau to the west (Dunaway 1995; Salstrom 1994, 1995).

From the earliest stages of European settlement in Appalachia, high levels of concentrated absentee land ownership have characterized the region. In preindustrial Appalachian landholding of the early 1800s, central and absentee individuals and corporations held 75 percent of southern Appalachia (Dunaway 1995). The estimate is higher in the mountainous coal counties, with four-fifths of the land claims in eastern Kentucky made by absentee speculators and up to nine-tenths of the land owned by absentee landholders in West Virginia counties.

Farming was an important part of the early Appalachian economy. Appalachian historian Ronald Eller (1982) writes that family farming in the Appalachian Mountains prior to 1890 was the backbone of the Appalachian economy. Unlike farms in the Midwest, Appalachian farms tended to be self-sufficient and diverse, with surplus used for trade in the local barter economy. This was especially the case in the central region of Appalachia, where farmland was scarce due to steep, rugged terrain. After the timber boom in 1890, farming remained an important part of the economy throughout Appalachia, but in a different context. Ronald Lewis (1995) writes that with the rise in the timber industry, there came a move toward both the commercialization of farming and shrinking farm size in the hollows of central Appalachia.

The timber boom between 1890 and 1920 signaled the onset of industrialization in Appalachia characterized by an economic system that was extractive, resource based, and controlled by absentee interests. As logging and mining companies moved into Appalachia, local farmers sold much of the land at what appeared to the previous owners to be high prices. This had the double effect of decreasing local landholding as well as increasing consolidation of absentee land ownership.

Thus, while most Appalachian landholders sold their property voluntarily, they often did so without an understanding of the value of the land or minerals to outside economies. This type of transaction was common until the turn of the century, when Appalachian residents realized the consequences of land sales. Not all of the land was purchased by land agents, however, as many local elites in the area consolidated landholdings for themselves and outside interests.

While logging was the first industry to have a large-scale effect on Appalachian land ownership and working patterns, it was not long before coal mining rose to ascendancy. Coal was first mined in Appalachia on a small scale in the late 1870s, but it was not until the late 1890s that coal production in Appalachia began to thrive. At this time, the coal industry in the United States had already experienced a high level of consolidation in northern and Great Lakes states. By the turn of the century, the workers in these areas also had organized to form a powerful national union: the United Mine Workers of America (Dix 1977; Long 1989). This organization of labor had not extended south into the central Appalachian region, however, giving coal operators in the area a prime advantage over operators in the north, who were forced to set mining wages through a collective bargaining process. As a result of the already high level of consolidation in the industry, as well as consolidation of landholding in Appalachia, in its earliest stages, large, absentee corporations working with nonunion employees (Eller 1982) characterized the early coal industry in Appalachia.

Although it was the logging industry in Appalachia that heralded a dependency on wage employment and the introduction of company towns, the coal industry cemented these changes. Between 1900 and 1920, hundreds of thousands of people flowed into remote areas of West Virginia, Kentucky, Virginia, and Tennessee to work in the booming coal mines. Many more people who already lived in the central Appalachian Mountains also chose to work in the mines, frequently prompted by the "subsistence crisis" that had resulted from small farming plots and increased environmental degradation resulting from clear-cut logging (Salstrom 1995).

The initial coal boom that began at the turn of the century lasted through the First World War until 1923, after which the declining importance of American-produced coal in world markets and the recession of 1921–1922 began to be felt in Appalachia. By 1927, increased competition among operators

FIG. 12.1. The Totz coal tipple in Harlan County, Kentucky, a region still living the legacy of coal.

to sell coal at low prices resulted in lower wages, shortened working hours, and the closing of many small mines. Factors such as wartime overproduction, increased shipping costs, increased use of oil and gas, and mechanization of the mining process aggravated the decline in the coming decades (Eller 1982). Thus, while levels of coal production increased during World War II, the general trend until the oil crises in the 1970s was one of decline in the industry. The 1973 OPEC oil embargo began to be felt in the Appalachian coal industry around 1975, beginning the most recent upsurge in coal production in Appalachia. This boom lasted through 1982, supported by high levels of export demand due to Polish and Australian strikes (Harvey 1986). From that time until the present, decreased demand and increased mechanization have resulted in yet another major decline in employment in the industry (figure 12.1). This decline led to the loss of over 100,000 mining-related jobs in the region in just over a ten-year period, between 1980 and 1992.

Kennedy's Legacy and the Search for Appalachian Economic Development

In 1960, on the eve of his presidential campaign, Senator John Kennedy journeyed on a tour bus into the inner reaches of Appalachia. He found families living in shacks with no running water or indoor toilets, minimal dirt roads, and a landscape left wasted, filthy, and poisoned by years of opportunistic coal mining and timber cutting. Jobs were scarce and the powerful meted out jobs in return for obedience. One hundred years of exploitation and external control created a society economically dependent.

In the early 1960s, President Kennedy set up the President's Appalachian Regional Commission to study the fate of the region. Governors of the then eleven affected states proposed creating a federal agency to help resolve the enduring economic problems of the region. Kennedy died before he could secure funding for the agency; but in 1965, to fulfill his legacy, Johnson pushed legislation through a divided Congress and brought to life the Appalachian Regional Commission (ARC), a state-federal agency with the responsibility to bring economic development to the region. By the end of the 1960s, the ARC region included 397 counties; 2 more counties were added in the 1980s; and in 2002 the ARC added 7 counties to the region, bringing the total number of ARC counties to 406.

The commission's broad mandate was to provide support for health, education, child development, community development, and water, sewer, and road construction. The broad focus of the program was abruptly changed in the early 1970s, when the governors overturned the code and abolished categorical spending. For the next ten years the commission turned away from human development needs and emphasized infrastructure. As the decade wore on, there was less and less congressional resolve to support a federal role to overcome "poverty and development problems," which eventually led to a hostile attempt by Congress to eliminate all federal funding for development initiatives, including the commission.

On December 31, 1981, the eve of the new year, the thirteen governors of the ARC filed with Congress "A Report to Congress from the Appalachian Governors," which gave birth to the concept of a Distressed County Initiative (Decker 1994). At the time of the issuance of the Finish-up Program, the administration, Congress, and the public had come to focus on the need for a less costly national government and thus sought to reduce the size and number of domestic development agencies, including the ARC. Like many federal development agencies during the 1980s the ARC began to feel pressure to articulate a "finish-up" strategy designed to identify within limits a plan to bring the agency's mission to completion.

Yet the defining moment for the creation of the distressed county designation cannot be understood outside the pressures the agency felt as it stared down its possible imminent demise. Creation of the designation can be understood as a final effort to secure some level of support for those counties in the thirteen-state region that had not benefited from the early days of the program due to their small, rural, and remote conditions (Appalachian Regional Commission 1982).

At the time of its creation, the Distressed Counties Program explicitly cited as an area of greatest need the provision of clean water and adequate sewers. Hence, the program's emphasis has been and continues to be primarily on support for water and sewer systems. The initiative set aside a share of existing funds, but did not step outside of the broad institutional mandates that had come to characterize the program after 1975.

With the acceptance of the 1981 report, the Finish-up Program, planned around a five-year cycle, gave the commission time, but more importantly it established the cycle of program development for a series of new initiatives, one of which was to provide special assistance to areas deemed of greatest need. The set-aside's mandate coincided with a drastic decline in overall program funds. Any hope of coupling substantial development funding with water and sewer funding was never realized. Unfortunately, implementation of the program did not emphasize the complex and multifaceted needs of residents in counties with the most severe problems, nor were the program targets able to counter or reduce the deeper underlying problems facing these areas. Distressed program funds have largely emphasized the provision of basic infrastructure. Relatively little of the set-aside resources have been targeted to the social needs of these communities. Additionally, these funds were not of a type or magnitude to confront the deeper underlying problems that precipitated distressed counties' social needs.

Twenty Years Later: The Legacy of Domination and the Persistence of Distress

Since the early 1980s, the ARC has mandated that states allocate a certain level of ARC funds to what the commission defines as "distressed counties." The ARC annually determines distressed status. To be considered distressed, a county must meet the following three criteria. First, it must have a poverty rate of at least 150 percent of the US average. Second, its unemployment rate must be at least 150 percent of the US average (three-year average). Third, its per capita market income (income less transfer payments) cannot exceed two-thirds of the US average. However, if a county has poverty rates that are at least 200 percent of the national average, then it only needs to match one of the two remaining criteria to be considered distressed. The ARC believes that its distress measure is a sufficiently objective and reasonable basis for policy and appropriations (ARC 1989).

There was a notable decline in the number of distressed counties in

TABLE 12.1. Distressed Counties by State

State	*Total ARC Counties*	*1960*	*1970*	*1980*	*1990*	*2000*	*Dist. 1960 and 2000*	*Dist. 1960, not 2000*
AL	35	24	13	3	7	3	3	21
GA	35	14	3	1	0	0	0	14
KY	49	44	41	33	38	34	34	10
MD	3	1	1	0	0	0	0	1
MS	21	20	19	6	9	7	7	13
NC	29	15	13	2	2	1	1	14
NY	14	0	0	0	0	0	0	0
OH	29	7	6	1	10	5	3	4
PA	52	2	0	0	2	0	0	2
SC	6	0	0	0	0	0	0	0
TN	50	37	27	15	11	8	8	29
VA	21	14	8	1	5	4	4	10
WV	55	36	30	7	30	23	21	15
Total	399	214	161	69	114	85	81	133

Appalachia between 1960 and 1980, as the number of distressed counties fell from 214 in 1960, to 161 in 1970, to 69 in 1980 (table 12.1). This trend, however, had reversed itself by the 1980s, as the number of distressed counties rose to 114 by 1990. Between 1990 and 2000, however, the number of distressed counties had declined again to 85. The pattern of declining and rising distress in Appalachia mirrors national trends during the period 1960 to 2000, though by the distress measure Appalachia has performed slightly better than the rest of the nation over time.

A few patterns emerge from the analysis of distressed counties in the region. One is a pattern of persistent distress for many counties in Appalachia. Eighty-one of the 214 distressed counties in 1960 also were distressed in 2000. Many of these counties are in the central Appalachian states of Kentucky and West Virginia. Thus, a more general pattern that emerges from the study involves subregional trends in distressed status. There was notable improvement over time in Southern Appalachia, while there was persistent distress in Central Appalachia and relatively good economic conditions marked by little change in Northern Appalachia. Approximately half of the Appalachian counties that moved out of distress between 1960 and 2000 were in Southern Appalachia. The decline in the number of distressed counties in Southern Appalachia between 1960 and 2000 was partially the result of broader regional and macroeconomic trends (figure 12.2). These forces included increased industrialization and urbanization in much of the southern United States during the second half of the century. Together, they

12.2. Tourism and urbanization have led to explosive growth in Sevier County, Tennessee.

12.3. Remote, mountainous sections of West Virginia remain economically distressed.

contributed to economic improvement not only in Southern Appalachia, but also throughout the rest of the South as well.

The success throughout much of the South contrasts with economic trends for a number of Central Appalachian counties, especially in Kentucky, West Virginia, and Mississippi, which have remained persistently distressed over time. About 70 percent of the ARC counties in Kentucky and approximately one-third of the ARC counties in both West Virginia and Mississippi were distressed in both 1960 and 2000. The region's relative isolation from major urban areas and its continued dependence on extractive industries, particularly coal, explain the poor economic conditions in Central Appalachia (figure 12.3).

A third regional trend is the consistent lack of distressed counties in Northern Appalachia, especially in New York and Pennsylvania. Again, as was the case with Southern Appalachia, this success can be understood in a broader regional context, as economic conditions in Northern Appalachia were at least somewhat reflective of historically strong economic conditions in the northeast United States. However, a number of counties that had never been distressed or had not been distressed since 1960 became distressed in 1990. For example, there was a striking increase in the number of distressed counties in Ohio between 1980 and 1990, from one to ten, though this number had fallen to five by 2000. Much of this incipient distress is the result of manufacturing jobs leaving the North, as a number of counties in Ohio, and indeed in other northern Appalachian states such as Pennsylvania as well, lost a significant number of manufacturing jobs during the period studied. In general, however, the Northern Appalachian subregion had relatively few distressed counties between 1960 and 2000.

Approximately 20 percent of the Appalachian counties that were distressed almost four decades ago remained distressed in 2000, indicating that poverty, low wages, and limited employment opportunities have been a way of life for many people in such counties. In general, changing distress status during the period studied was related to subregional trends within Appalachia as well as broader trends especially affecting the northern and southern United States.

In addition, there were key differences between counties that either remained distressed or had moved out of distress by 2000. The counties that moved out of distress demonstrated significantly improved rates of educational attainment, had become more urbanized, and had a fairly even demographic distribution. Counties that remained distressed showed much less improvement in rates of educational attainment, were highly rural, and had a large percentage of young and elderly residents.

The Fate of Troubled Areas

Clearly, the description of distressed counties presented here represents a far more complex set of issues than can be dealt with by a program that largely emphasizes basic water and sewer services. And while the ARC attempts to address other issues of development in the region as well, the agency is hindered by having limited funds with which to work. In addition to the statistical analysis, we also can look back on the case study research to find important attributes of the region.

Distressed counties have many needs, such as jobs, skills training programs, social programs to care for children (allowing parents to work), health programs to provide elderly and children with access to needed services, and geographic access to more developed portions of the region. While the Distressed Counties Program was never intended to eradicate the underlying problems facing these challenged areas, the original and far broader ARC program was. Evidence from the case studies of successful counties highlights the importance of the early years of the ARC program, when expenditures for education and community welfare enjoyed equal footing with infrastructure.

Looking Back, Looking Forward

Appalachia remains one of the nation's wealthiest regions on the basis of natural resources such as coal and timber, yet the territory is home to some of the country's poorest communities. The legacy of exploitation and domination by coal and timber companies is a despoiled environment that in many places is no longer receptive to development. In the 1960s, Appalachia's problem was perceived to be isolation. Thus roads, sewers, and water systems were seen as essential for development. However, while access remains a major problem for the most remote parts of the region, new roads and water pipes alone will not remedy the deeply entrenched and highly complex problems of Appalachia's impoverished communities. A consideration of the role of institutions, the unique history of external ownership and concentrated power, and the role of the wider economy are necessary to understanding and addressing Appalachia's most persistent problems. It remains to be seen whether federal and state political actors recognize that standard economic development practice has not and will not change Appalachia's fate.

References

Appalachian Regional Commission. 1982. Transcript from the May 4th Commission meeting. ACE Federal Reports, Inc.

———. 1989. Appalachian Regional Commission Distressed Counties Program (internal memo). Washington, DC: Appalachian Regional Commission.

Decker, R. 1994. Internal Memorandum. Distressed Counties. Washington, DC: Appalachian Regional Commission.

Dix, Keith. 1977. Work Relations in the Coal Industry: The Hand-Loading Era, 1880–1930. West Virginia University, Institute for Labor Studies.

Dunaway, Wilma A. 1995. Speculators and Settler Capitalists: Unthinking the Mythology about Appalachian Landholding, 1790–1860. In *Appalachia in the Making: The Mountain South in the Nineteenth Century*, ed. Mary Beth Pudup, Dwight B. Billings, and Altina L. Waller, 50–75. Chapel Hill: University of North Carolina Press.

Eller, Ronald D. 1982. *Miners, Millhands, and Mountaineers: Industrialization of the Appalachian South, 1880–1930.* Knoxville: University of Tennessee Press.

Finger, John R. 1995. Cherokee Accommodation and Persistence in the Southern Appalachians. In *Appalachia in the Making: The Mountain South in the Nineteenth Century*, ed. Mary Beth Pudup, Dwight B. Billings, and Altina L. Waller. Chapel Hill: University of North Carolina Press.

Harvey, Curtis E. 1986. *Coal in Appalachia: An Economic Analysis.* Lexington: University of Kentucky Press.

Lewis, Ronald L. 1995. Railroads, Deforestation, and the Transformation of Agriculture in the West Virginia Back Counties, 1880–1920. In *Appalachia in the Making: The Mountain South in the Nineteenth Century*, ed. Mary Beth Pudup, Dwight B. Billings, and Altina L. Waller, 297–320. Chapel Hill: University of North Carolina Press.

Long, Priscilla. 1989. *Where the Sun Never Shines: A History of America's Bloody Coal Industry.* New York: Paragon House.

Salstrom, Paul. 1994. *Appalachia's Path to Dependency: Rethinking a Region's Economic History, 1730–1940.* Lexington: University Press of Kentucky.

———. 1995. Newer Appalachia as One of America's Last Frontiers. In *Appalachia in the Making: The Mountain South in the Nineteenth Century*, ed. Mary Beth Pudup, Dwight B. Billings, and Altina L. Waller, 76–102. Chapel Hill: University of North Carolina Press.

THIRTEEN

Living on the Fringe

A GEOGRAPHIC PROFILE OF APPALACHIAN OHIO

Geoffrey L. Buckley, Timothy G. Anderson, and Nancy R. Bain

The federal government established the Appalachian Regional Commission (ARC) in 1965 "to serve the needs of 21,000,000 people residing in one of the most economically distressed regions of the country" (ARC 1993, 7) (figure 13.1). As currently defined by the ARC, Appalachia encompasses approximately 400 counties in thirteen eastern states, including 29 counties in southeastern Ohio. In some ways, southeastern Ohio occupies a fringe within this vast area. This is especially true given its Midwestern orientation and hinterland relationships. In other, arguably more significant, ways, this portion of Ohio shares much in common with Appalachia's core, generally recognized as centered on West Virginia and eastern Kentucky. Economic development based on extractive industries, environmental alteration associated with the extraction of bituminous coal and logging activities, and postindustrial economic decline—not to mention perceptions of the area as a social and economic backwater—all seem to place southeastern Ohio firmly within the context of the "Appalachian experience." In still other ways, the territory north and west of the Ohio River remains distinct, not easily defined solely in Appalachian terms yet clearly not Midwestern in character.

Philliber (1994, xv–xvi) has noted that defining a region is "often a matter of consensus—a consensus that is strong about the center but weak around the edges." Numerous authors have shown over the years that there is little consensus in defining the boundaries of an Appalachian region (Ford 1962;

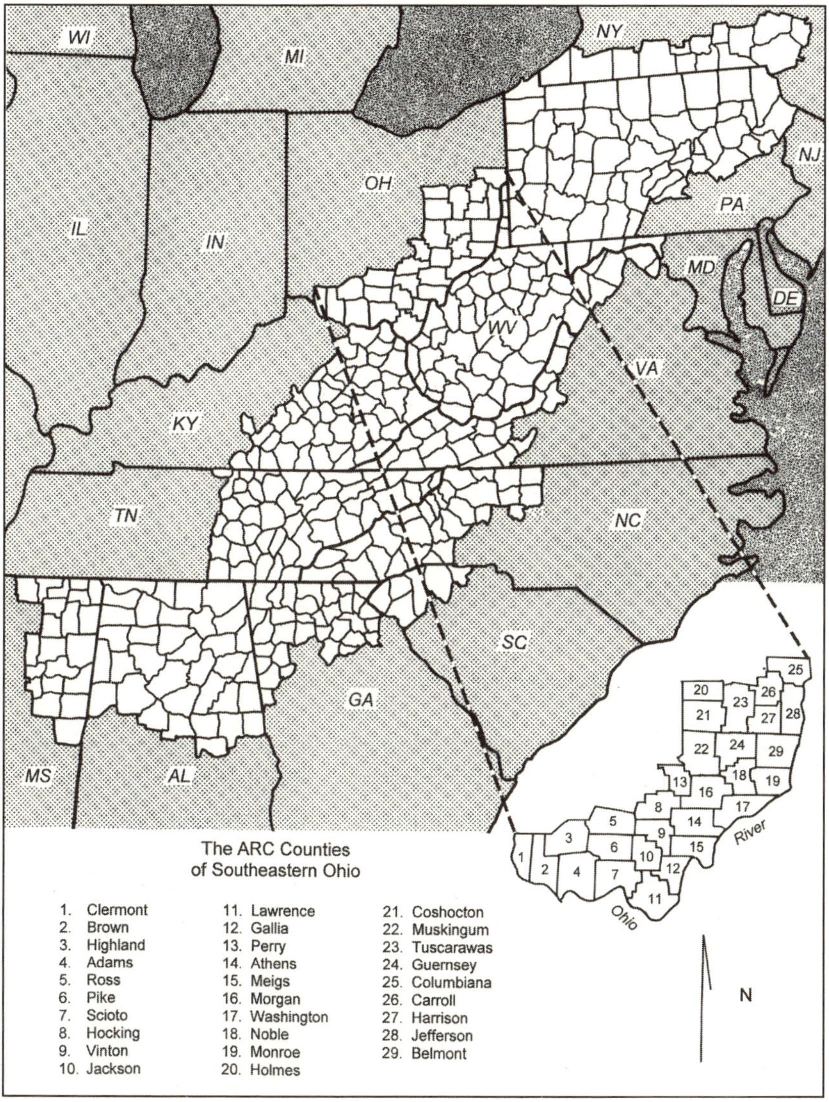

FIG. 13.1. The ARC counties of southeastern Ohio. Appalachian Regional Commission 1993.

Raitz and Ulack 1984; Appalachian Regional Commission 1985; Salstrom 1994; Williams 2002). Although one could argue that southeastern Ohio occupies an "edge" or "fringe" position within Appalachia, some authors do not include it in their delimitation of the region. Appalachia has been described as a "region of contradictions: rich yet poor; exploited yet underdeveloped;

scarred yet beautiful" (Appalachian Regional Commission 1985, 7). Whether part of Appalachia or not, perhaps no other single statement can be applied so readily to southeastern Ohio.

We argue that the southeastern counties of Ohio constitute a fringe region with respect to metropolitan Pittsburgh, Appalachia, and Ohio. In short, it is a place that does not fit neatly into any North American region delineated by geographers over the years. We base our fringe supposition on three primary factors. First, the area possesses a distinctive historical settlement geography, one that distinguishes it clearly from much of the rest of Appalachia. Second, while its history of resource extraction and subsistence agriculture is comparable to that of Appalachia, its economic orientation and hinterland relationships set it apart. Third, the area can be viewed as being a fringe in relation to the rest of the state of Ohio. Indeed, lower income levels, a decaying physical infrastructure, and persistent sociocultural stereotyping reinforce perceptions of the area as an economic backwater.

Historical Settlement Geography

With the possible exception of Texas, no other section of the United States exhibits such a wide variety of land subdivisions and survey systems as does Ohio, including the southeastern counties under scrutiny here. This distinctive settlement geography stems from processes cast during the period in which Anglo settlers from the East Coast populated the area. A special set of circumstances derived from a federal form of government shaped the settlement and land alienation within the so-called Northwest Territory (or Old Northwest).

In order to facilitate and encourage Anglo settlement in the newly acquired territory, between 1785 and 1820 the federal government enacted several policies to address these special circumstances. First, Congress brokered the cession of most of the territory west of the Appalachians that had been claimed by eastern states by virtue of royal charter and prior appropriation. Second, the human barrier represented by Native Americans was largely removed through military intervention and the signing of territory-ceding treaties with dozens of tribal groups. Third, congressional approval of the Land Ordinance of 1785 established an orderly system of land survey and alienation in the newly acquired lands. The so-called Seven Ranges in southeastern Ohio became the first area to be surveyed under the township and range system (Meinig 1993, 241–43).

By 1786, all of the eastern states that had claimed territory in what would become Ohio agreed to relinquish their claims to the federal government. Connecticut and Virginia, however, negotiated with Congress to retain large

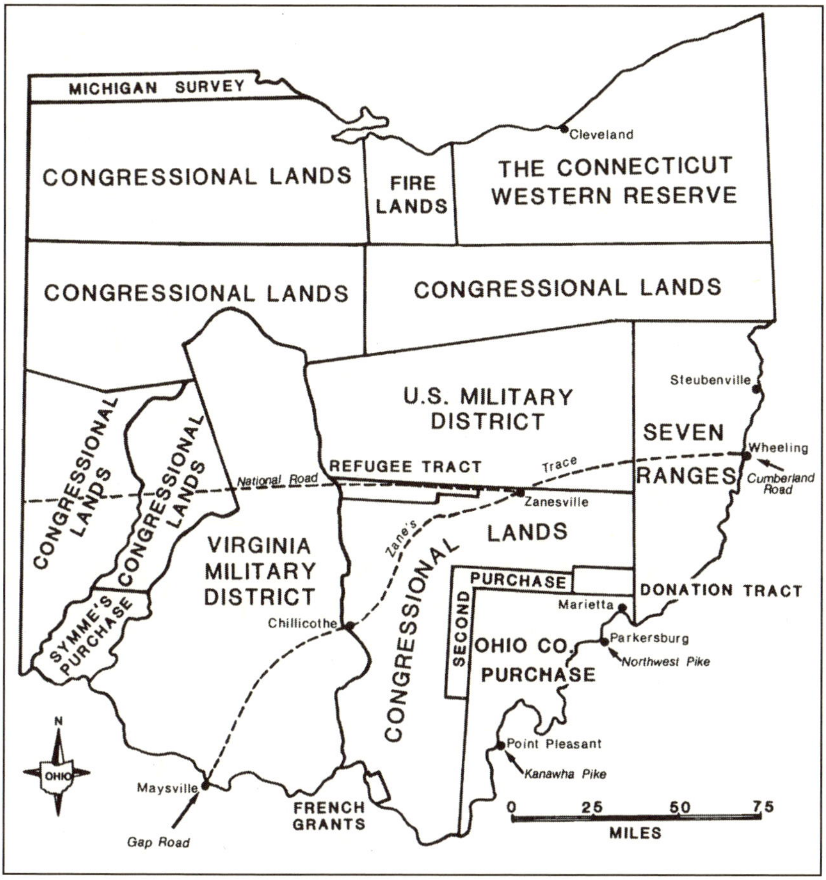

FIG. 13.2. Original Ohio land subdivisions (after Sherman 1925; Burke 1996; Wilhelm 1982).

tracts to satisfy debts owed to state militia members who had served during the Revolutionary War. Likewise, Congress reserved some two million acres in 1796 within which to locate military warrants from the Revolution that had not yet been satisfied (the United States Military District).

Congress also authorized the sale of two substantial tracts within the territory to private companies. Both the Ohio Company (1787) and the Symmes Company (1794) surveyed and subdivided their respective tracts before reselling parcels to private individuals. They surveyed these tracts according to different systems. On the one hand, the Virginia Military District employed an irregular metes and bounds system reminiscent of the territory east of the Appalachians. The rectilinear system prevailed in the Western Reserve, the Ohio Company purchase, the United States Military District, and the so-called Congress Lands. In effect, Ohio became a testing ground for federal land policies during the early national period. The result was that by 1820 the Ohio Territory resembled a patchwork quilt of subdivisions and districts reflecting various land division policies and survey systems (Sherman 1925, 89–90; Burke 1996, 23) (figure 13.2).

What did this mean for the Anglo settlement of Ohio? Moreover, from where did the first settlers hail? To begin with, the differential subdivision of the state played a critical role in directing streams of migrants from the major East Coast culture hearths. The early routes of ingress into the territory, such as Zane's Trace and the National Road, influenced settlement in the region. Detailing the exact origins of early settlement groups in Ohio (and the Midwest in general) is problematic. However, geographers Gregory Rose (1985) and John Hudson (1988) provide insight here. They demonstrated that the 1850 federal census, the first to record the nativity of each person counted, remains the most accessible and accurate source of such population data, at least at the level of large groups of migrants.

When one analyzes these data for Ohio, it is clear that settlers from each of the three major East Coast culture hearths (New England, the Mid-Atlantic States, and the Tidewater South) populated Appalachian Ohio during its formative stages. More significant is the fact that streams of migrants from each of these areas clearly settled among each other, forming subregions within the broader region. Figure 13.3 maps the nativity of the population not born in Ohio in 1850, at the township level and by the East Coast region of origin.

In these counties, of the nearly 157,000 people not born in Ohio in 1850, six in ten hailed from the Mid-Atlantic states, those states comprising the Midland culture hearth. A vast majority of these Midland migrants came from southeastern Pennsylvania and settled primarily in public domain lands ("Congress lands") and tracts in the Virginia Military District left over after federal warrants had been satisfied (Wilhelm 1982). Migrants from the South made up about one-third of this frontier population. The majority of these settlers were born in Virginia and Kentucky and settled within the boundaries of the Virginia Military District or along the Ohio River (Wilhelm 1982). New Englanders constituted the smallest early population group settling in Appalachian Ohio, accounting for just 4.5 percent of the migrant population. As might be expected, the majority of these settlers came from the core states of New England: Massachusetts, Rhode Island, and Connecticut. They settled for the most part in Athens and Meigs counties in the Ohio Company purchase, a private land venture established by New England aristocrats and Revolutionary War heroes.

This distinctive settlement geography produced a mixed frontier popula-

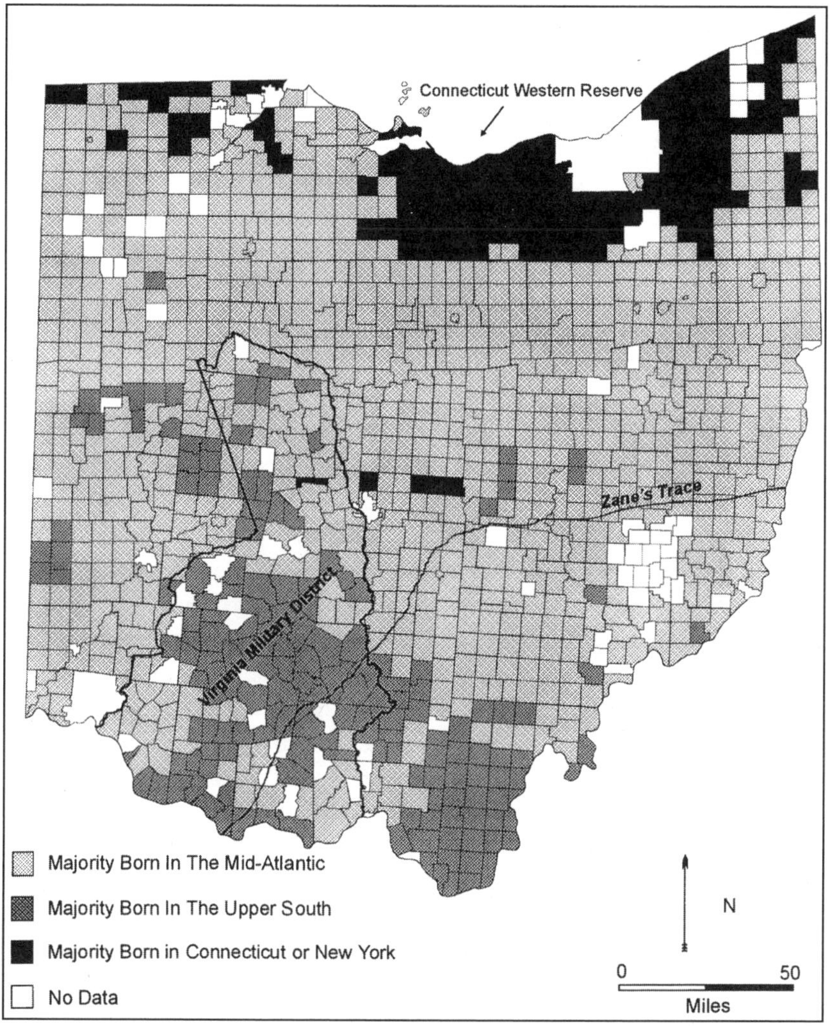

FIG. 13. 3. Origins of the non-Ohio-born population, 1850 (after Wilhelm 1982).

tion in Appalachian Ohio and resulted in the construction of a hybrid cultural landscape. In contrast to other parts of Appalachia, Ohio's southeastern counties attracted settlers from each of the East Coast culture hearths, the majority coming from the Midland hearth. Predictably, the cultural landscape of Appalachian Ohio represents a mix of elements and signatures from each of the hearths, but the Midlanders dominate. In Adams County, the traveler is likely to encounter Upland South landscapes dominated by tobacco farms and barns, transverse bay barns, and Upland South toponyms. Farther east, in Athens County, a bit of New England can be seen in several elongated villages centered on large, open public spaces—called the village green or common in New England. Only a few miles farther north, in Fairfield County, the Pennsylvania-German influence is conspicuous—forebay bank barns, Midland toponyms, federal style I-houses, and Reformed churches dominate the landscape. In this manner, the landscapes, values, and traditions typically associated with Appalachia have been tempered in southeastern Ohio by other cultural influences.

Land and Economy in Early Appalachian Ohio

What attracted settlers to southeastern Ohio? Endowed with a wealth of natural resources, including fertile valley bottoms, extensive forests, and plentiful water, Appalachian Ohio offered much to the prospective agriculturist. Early diaries suggest a positive assessment of this potential, but soon the realities of woodland agriculture in a river-dissected environment became apparent. Ohio Company investors failed to make the profit they expected and found the area bypassed in favor of the flatter, open areas to the west (Cutler 1820–1829, 20). Beginning in the late eighteenth century, woodland agriculture transported and modified from the East Coast gained a foothold in southeastern Ohio and then spread to the north and west. For the most part, the wide, flat valleys supported a mostly family-based rural economy in the unglaciated country of southeastern Ohio. Early settlers arriving via the Ohio River and its tributaries or by overland routes (for example, Zane's Trace from Kentucky and the National Road from Pennsylvania) used abandoned Indian clearings to plant their crops. They also cleared trees from the lower slopes. As both figures 13.4 and 13.5 suggest, this pattern of wooded upper slopes and cultivated lower slopes and valleys has been a common one for two centuries. In both scenes, the impact of woodland agricultural practices on the soils and vegetation is stark.

By 1840 Ohio ranked first in national output of corn and wheat. According to Bidwell and Falconer (1941), the parts of Appalachian Ohio closest to Cincinnati figured prominently in the corn boom. In turn, the region was a major food supplier of the South via New Orleans, while the wheat economy prevailed on the northern edge of the region. Until canals were constructed, however (mostly outside this region), the cost of transport limited marketing of corn to a twenty-mile radius and the marketing of wheat to a fifty- to seventy-five-mile distance (Bidwell and Falconer 1941). Thus, except for these fringe areas of major commercial activity, agriculture in the region retained a subsistence character.

Residents in this somewhat isolated fringe area sold farm produce, bought manufactured goods, and generally maintained contact with distant

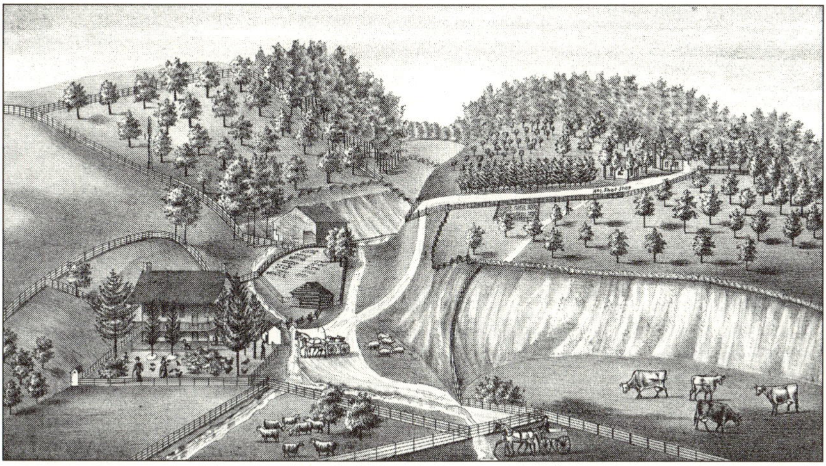

FIG. 13.4. Residence of John W. Bowman, Perry County, Ohio. *Atlas of Perry County, Ohio*, 1875, p. 30.

FIG. 13.5. Farm in southeastern Ohio, ca. 1940. W. E. Peters Papers, Ohio University Archives.

communities. This contact resulted through the agency of merchant capitalists who moved across the area selling their wares and collecting materials for sale in eastern markets. For instance, early settler Julia Cutler (1820–1829) reported that agents of John Jacob Astor passed through the region, buying furs and skins, especially bear. A local state legislator also collected steers and hogs and drove the animals to markets in the Great Valley and Baltimore. The numbers were modest at first but herds of several hundred animals were

FIG. 13.6. Coal mining in the Sunday Creek Valley, Athens County, Ohio. Buhla Collection, Ohio University Archives.

not unusual by the 1820s. The limited records of the day show that materials moved either on the hoof or were value-added products transported by wagon. Besides drovers moving cattle, canal and river records show bacon, flour, lard, and dairy products being exported, along with other important commodities such as staves, lumber products, and hemp (Bidwell and Falconer 1941). The construction of canals during the early nineteenth century succeeded in linking much of Ohio to the Great Lakes market, but records show that much of southeastern Ohio remained unconnected (Bidwell and Falconer 1941). Not until the arrival of railroads and the emergence of coal as a valuable energy source did parts of the region integrate further with the rest of the state.

Indeed, it was the development of the coal industry that would dominate the region's economy for the next 150 years (figure 13.6). Beginning about the second half of the nineteenth century, Ohio's economy shifted from one based primarily on agriculture to one increasingly dependent on mineral extraction. Vast deposits of bituminous coal located in eastern and southeastern sections of the state fueled this transformation (Collins 1976). Although small amounts of coal were mined prior to the Civil War, it was not until the postwar era that coal mining in Ohio took off. Critical to the expansion of the industry at this time was the introduction of the railroad, which connected the coal mining areas with key markets such as Columbus and cities such as Toledo, Gary, and Chicago on the Great Lakes (Grant 2000; Williams 2002). According to Crowell (1995, 6), "Between 1850 and 1880, Ohio's railroad system grew at a tremendous rate, facilitating the movement of coal to market as well as becoming a major consumer of coal for steam-generated locomotion."

Ohio registered its first year of coal production in 1800, when settlers mined approximately one hundred tons in Jefferson County. While production increased steadily over the next few decades, it did not surpass one million tons until 1853. Spurred on by Ohio's growing industrialism and increased mechanization in the mines, production soared, reaching nearly forty-eight million tons during the last year of World War I. Ohio's coal workforce also reached new heights at this time, topping out at more than 50,000 miners in 1918. As was the case in other parts of Appalachia, production figures sagged during the 1920s and 1930s before World War II sparked an increase in the demand for coal (Collins 1976, 5; Crowell 1995, 5–6, 10). Coal production peaked in Ohio until 1970 when the sector extracted a record 55,136,699 tons of coal (Collins 1976, 1). Since then, production has slipped to pre–World War II levels due to a combination of factors including increased transportation costs, enforcement of environmental regulations, and conflicts between management and labor (Ray 1993; Crowell 1995, 10).

Coal mining in southeastern Ohio currently relies on underground and surface techniques. After World War II, however, surface mining emerged as the preferred method of removal (Crowell 1995, 17). The reasons for surface mining's ascendancy are several. First, the use of electric-powered steam shovels—many of which reached mammoth proportions—allowed operators to mine more coal at a faster rate. Second, surface mining presented fewer risks to worker health and safety. Third, coal companies could cut costs by employing fewer workers. To illustrate, between 1950 and 1970 coal production in Ohio rose steadily despite a 90 percent decrease in the number of underground mines and an 83 percent drop in the size of the labor force (Crowell 1995, 6, 10). Regardless of the methods used or the size of the workforce, one thing is certain: coal mining has left its mark on southeastern Ohio's physical environment. In addition to the company towns, gob piles, and derelict equipment one often associates with historic mining districts, the coal industry in southeastern Ohio has left behind a legacy of environmental alteration with which present and future generations must contend. Among the more pressing problems are land subsidence, widespread acid mine drainage, and extensive deforestation.

Appalachian Ohio Today

Decades of declining coal production, high rates of unemployment, and a deteriorating physical infrastructure (most notably, the condition of its public schools) have prevented Appalachian Ohio from sharing in the economic prosperity that other parts of the state have enjoyed in recent years. Worse, hard economic times have permitted old stereotypes of the region as an economic and social backwater to persist. For instance, editorial cartoons in a Cleveland newspaper in 1997 and 1999 made light of the state's contentious school-funding debate while lampooning residents of rural southern Ohio (figure 13.7; Darcy 1997, 1999). The cartoons prompted an angry response from Sixth District US congressman Ted Strickland: "This is an insult, not only to people in my rural southern Ohio district, but to all those in other Ohio communities that have not shared in our state's economic good fortune. I am very disappointed that the *Plain Dealer* continues to use cultural stereotypes to poke fun at rural Ohioans who are simply fighting to make sure their kids get what they deserve—an adequate education" (Strickland 1999).

Appalachian Ohio trails much of the rest of the state and nation accord-

FIG. 13.7. Editorial cartoon, *Plain Dealer*, March 26, 1997. Courtesy of the *Plain Dealer*, Cleveland, Ohio.

ing to several key economic indicators. With regard to personal per capita income, for example, Ohio's Appalachian counties lag far behind the rest of the state and the nation. In 2000, per capita income for Appalachian Ohio was $21,607, compared to $27,977 for the state of Ohio and $29,469 for the United States. In Athens County, one of six "distressed" counties in the region in fiscal year 2004, the figure stood at $18,660 (Appalachian Regional Commission 2004). Similarly, while poverty rates at the county and regional levels declined between 1990 and 2000, they remained relatively high compared to state and national figures. While great strides have been made since the establishment of the Appalachian Regional Commission in 1965, a great many challenges lie ahead.

Betwixt and Between

We have argued that southeastern Ohio occupies a fringe or edge position within the Appalachian region. In some ways the area has much in common with the Midwest; while in other, perhaps more important ways, it is strongly connected to Appalachia.

In terms of historical settlement geography, southeastern Ohio is more closely linked with the rest of Ohio and the greater Midwest. Located along one of the primary migration routes to the West, the area attracted settlers from all three eastern culture hearths. The clear majority of settlers came from Pennsylvania, followed by upland southerners mainly from Kentucky and Virginia. It is this diversity which sets southeastern Ohio apart from much of the rest of Appalachia, dominated as it is by cultural landscapes and traditions imparted by a dominant Scots-Irish frontier settlement majority.

Southeastern Ohio shares much in common with the rest of Appalachia in terms of economies and land use. Small-scale woodland agriculture, economies based on extractive industries, large-scale environmental alteration and degradation, comparatively low rates of economic development, and sociocultural stereotypes of the region's inhabitants by outsiders—all are indicative of a link with the rest of Appalachia.

References

Appalachian Regional Commission. 1985. *Appalachia: A Special Issue on the 20th Anniversary of the Appalachian Regional Commission.* Washington, DC: Appalachian Regional Commission.

———. 1993. Directory of Local Development Districts in the Appalachian Region. Washington, DC: Appalachian Regional Commission.

———. 2004. http://www.arc.gov/

Bidwell, P. W., and J. I. Falconer, 1941. *History of Agriculture in the Northern United States, 1620–1860.* New York: Peter Smith.

Burke, T. A. 1996. *Ohio Lands: A Short History.* Columbus: Ohio Auditor of State.

Collins, H. R. 1976. *Coal Production in Ohio, 1800–1974.* Columbus: Ohio Department of Natural Resources, Division of Geological Survey.

Crowell, D. 1995. *History of the Coal Mining Industry in Ohio.* Columbus: Ohio Department of Natural Resources, Division of Geological Survey.

Cutler, Julia. 1820–1829. *Annals.* MS Collection, Cutler Papers, Marietta College, Marietta, Ohio.

Darcy, J. 1997. The Hon. Judge Roy Bean Linton Lewis Jr., Edyoukation Zar of Ohio. Cartoon. *Plain Dealer,* March 26.

———. 1999. I will ensure every Ohio student. . . . Cartoon. *Plain Dealer,* March 2.

Ford, T. R., ed. 1962. *The Southern Appalachian Region: A Survey.* Lexington: University Press of Kentucky.

Grant, H. R. 2000. *Ohio on the Move: Transportation in the Buckeye State.* Athens, OH: Ohio University Press.

Hudson, J. C. 1988. North American Origins of Middlewestern Frontier Populations. *Annals of the Association of American Geographers* 78:395–413.

Jones, Robert L. 1983. *History of Agriculture in Ohio to 1880.* Kent, OH: Kent State University Press.

Meinig, D. W. 1993. *The Shaping of America: A Geographical Perspective on 500 Years of History.* Vol. 2. New Haven: Yale University Press.

Philliber, W. W. 1994. Appalachia and the Study of Regionalism. In *Appalachia in an International Context: Cross-National Comparisons of Developing Regions,* ed. P. J. Obermiller and W. W. Philliber, xv–xvi. Westport, CT: Praeger.

Raitz, K. B., and R. Ulack. 1984. *Appalachia, a Regional Geography: Land, People and Development.* Boulder: Westview Press.

Ray, R. G. 1993. Portal to Portal: My Experience Mining Coal in Ohio. *Appalachian Journal* 21:24–29.

Rose, G. 1985. Information Sources for Nineteenth Century Midwestern Migration. *Professional Geographer* 37:66–72.

Salstrom, P. 1994. *Appalachia's Path to Dependency: Rethinking a Region's Economic History, 1730–1940.* Lexington: University Press of Kentucky.

Sherman, C. E. 1925. *Original Ohio Land Subdivisions,* Vol. 3, *Final Report.* Columbus: Ohio Department of Natural Resources, Division of Geological Survey.

Strickland, T. 1999. Strickland Says "Enough is Enough," to the *Plain Dealer.* News Release, Congressman Ted Strickland, March 29.

Wilhelm, H. G. H. 1982. *The Distribution of Settlement Groups: Ohio, 1850.* Athens, OH: H. G. H. Wilhelm.

Williams, J. A. 2002. *Appalachia: A History.* Chapel Hill: University of North Carolina Press.

FOURTEEN

Central Appalachia's Whitewater Recreation Industry

Lizbeth A. Pyle

The pursuit of whitewater adventure lures more than 250,000 rafting enthusiasts to Central Appalachian rivers each year (figure 14.1). Companies with names like Appalachian Wildwaters or Mountain River Tours eagerly provide equipment and experienced guides to customers looking for whitewater thrills. These commercial outfitters hold licenses issued by state natural resource regulatory agencies and have offered whitewater rafting trips since the late 1960s. The necessary combination of steep stream gradients, ample rainfall, upstream impoundments, and access to large population centers including Pittsburgh and Philadelphia, Washington DC and Baltimore, or Columbus and Cleveland allowed the industry to prosper in this section of Appalachia.

Three rivers account for the majority of this whitewater recreation: the New and Gauley rivers in southern West Virginia, and the Youghiogheny River as it follows a northwesterly course through western Maryland into southwestern Pennsylvania (figure 14.2). Smaller amounts of commercial use also exist on the Cheat and Shenandoah rivers, while commercial rafting on the Tygart River virtually disappeared in recent years. Commercial rafting accounts for a major portion of all river running on these streams, but many individuals with their own canoes and kayaks also enjoy paddling on them and their numerous tributaries. This chapter describes patterns of whitewater use on each of these Central Appalachian rivers and then profiles whitewater rafters' characteristics and their economic impact around the New, Gauley, and Cheat rivers in West Virginia. It concludes with a discussion of other economic activities developing within the tristate area's whitewater recreation industry as it matures.

FIG. 14.1. Whitewater rafters on the Gauley River.

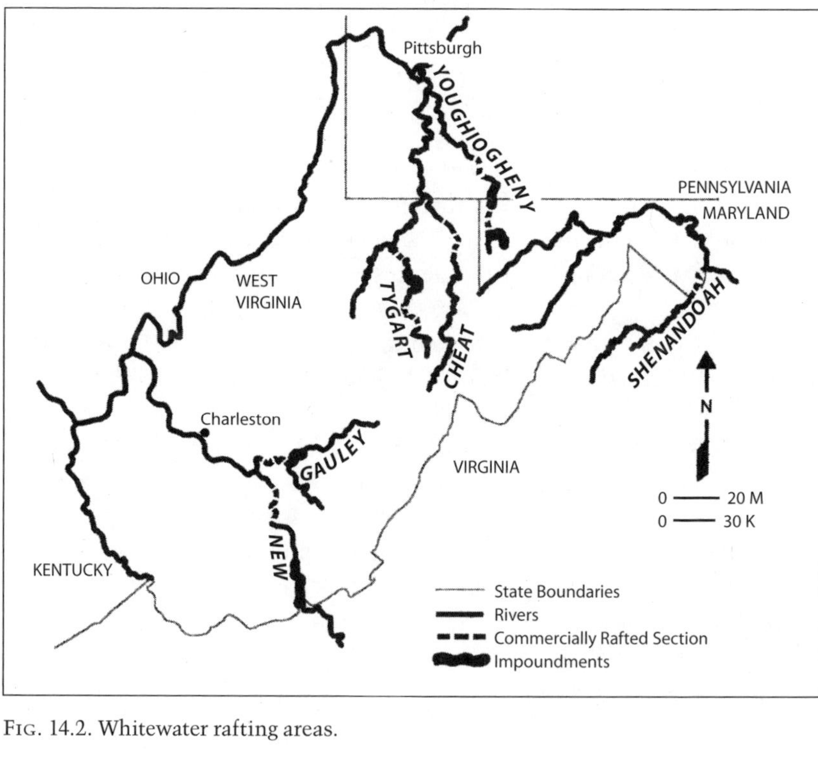

FIG. 14.2. Whitewater rafting areas.

Patterns of Commercial Whitewater Use

Commercial rafting in the East gained a foothold in the late 1960s and then began to expand rapidly in the 1970s and 1980s. Some have related the rapid expansion to the 1972 release of *Deliverance,* a film that featured Burt Reynolds on an ill-fated whitewater canoe trip, because it drew national attention to the thrill of running whitewater (Imre Szilaygi, personal communication, 1999; Mayfield and DeHart 1996). A classic example of this rapid expansion occurred on the Chattooga River, part of the South Carolina–Georgia border, where *Deliverance* was filmed. Commercial rafting on the Chattooga expanded in 1972 to 21,000 people and approached 95,000 by 1994 (Mayfield and DeHart 1996). Rafting on other rivers also increased, including popularly run sections of the New and Youghiogheny rivers (Palmer 1984). In recent years, commercial rafting on the Central Appalachian rivers considered here has leveled off or declined, suggesting a mature industry. The rapid gains made during the 1970s and 1980s have disappeared, yet most of the rivers continue to draw from a fairly stable marketing base. This section describes the settings and patterns of use on rivers in West Virginia, southwestern Pennsylvania, and western Maryland.

New River

With more than 150,000 customers in a typical year, the New River receives the majority of commercial whitewater use in the Central Appalachians (table 14.1). Geologically, it is a very old river, though not necessarily the second oldest river in the world as claimed by some local boosters (Morgan and Mayfield 1994). The New River rises in North Carolina and is impounded before reaching the stretches that are commercially rafted in West Virginia. It has the longest season of any of these rivers, lasting from the spring through summer and into the fall, because of the large size of its drainage basin. The most popular rafting section is known as New River Gorge, and twenty licensed commercial outfitters offer trips on this segment of the river. Here the river drops at a rate of twelve feet per mile through boulder-strewn rapids that have tumbled from cliffs towering above the river. Commercial outfitters also offer easier trips that are geared to novice rafters and families upstream of the more popular gorge section. The New River Gorge is part of a 53,000-acre unit managed by the National Park Service as a National River. About fifty river miles and surrounding land are included in the unit. Early in the 1900s, the gorge supported a number of coal towns that thrived during the heyday of mining in this region of West Virginia. Today, it is best known for the popular fourteen-mile whitewater run that ends below a long steel

FIG. 14.3. The New River Gorge, West Virginia.

TABLE 14.1. Recent Changes in the Number of Commercial Rafting Customers

River Segment	*1998*	*1999*	*2000*	*2001*	*2002*
New (WV)	158,771	155,543	157,070	147,497	154,063
Gauley (WV)	65,089	59,132	62,393	59,940	58,501
Cheat (WV)	8,487	4,264	7,394	6,903	4,011
Shenandoah (WV)	19,367	7,936	22,853	22,853	5,852
Tygart (WV)	207	174	49	14	0
Lower Youghiogheny (PA)	61,419	54,922	58,551	54,650	51,274
Upper Youghiogheny (MD)*	3,078	2,172	2,877	3,153	2,484

*Use figures for the Upper Youghiogheny are estimates based on total number of rafts running the river with three customers and one professional guide per raft.

Sources: West Virginia Department of Natural Resources in Charleston, WV, Ohiopyle State Park in Ohiopyle, PA, and Deep Creek Lake Recreation Area in Oakland, MD.

arch bridge, spanning the gorge about 870 feet above the river (figure 14.3). Each fall, half of the bridge is closed to vehicular traffic on Bridge Day to provide the opportunity for people to walk across or parachute off the well-known structure. In recent years, rock climbing on the cliffs above the river has become an increasingly popular recreational pursuit in the New River Gorge.

FIG. 14.4. Gauley River rafters.

GAULEY RIVER

Nearby, the Gauley River offers world-class whitewater runs almost exclusively in the fall. During a limited number of scheduled water releases from the Summersville Dam, the lake pool behind it is drawn down to accommodate winter and spring snowmelt. The launch site for the more difficult upper section is alongside the earthen dam. During the brief period each fall when the lake level is drawn down, more than half the rafters that run the New River over a six-month period descend the Gauley River in just six weeks of scheduled water releases (figure 14.4). Twenty licensed outfitters offer trips on the Gauley. The Gauley's popularity is due to its equally spectacular scenic gorge and the increased level of difficulty of its steeper rapids. The sixteen-mile Upper Gauley section drops at a rate of about twenty-eight feet per mile, while the eight-mile Lower Gauley stretch falls at about twenty-six feet per mile (Burrell and Davidson 1972). This river is considered to be among the best whitewater runs in the East by rafters and expert kayakers who routinely make the trip to southern West Virginia from locations scattered between the Carolinas, Michigan, and New York. In 1988, the National Park Service took over management of a twenty-five-mile stretch of the river with the creation of the Gauley River National Recreation Area (United States Department of the Interior 1996). Just downstream of the lower section, the Gauley joins the New River to form the Kanawha, an industrial river that serves West Virginia's capital city of Charleston before flowing into the Ohio River.

Cheat River

The Cheat River in northern West Virginia is less than two hours from Pittsburgh and about four hours from Washington DC, so it also draws heavily from those two metropolitan areas and some others in Ohio. Nine outfitters operate commercial rafting trips on the Cheat, which drops at about twenty-five feet per mile during the eleven-mile stretch of river known as the Cheat Canyon (Burrell and Davidson 1972). Unlike the New and Gauley, where use has fluctuated only slightly in recent years, the Cheat has experienced precipitous declines in commercial use. Five streams converge along their northerly flowing course to form the Cheat River, and it remains the largest unchecked watershed (that is, there are no upstream dams) above Pittsburgh.

The Cheat's free-flowing status is both an attraction and a liability. While some rafters and kayakers are drawn to "wild" rivers that are free of dams, commercial use is usually restricted to the spring when snowmelt and rainfall provide sufficient in-stream flows to support the rafting industry. During this time, six- to eight-person rafts usually can be used, but when flows are too low, commercial outfitters switch to inflatable kayaks that can tolerate lower water levels. Problems with water variability and the lack of other organized recreational activities to draw visitors to the area have been exacerbated by complaints about unsightly and unpleasant acid mine drainage from coal mines in the vicinity (David Bassage, personal communication, 1999; Imre Szilagyi, personal communication, 1999). As a result, commercial use has plummeted from levels of more than 20,000 customers annually in the 1980s to less than 5,000 since the year 2002.

Other West Virginia Rivers

West Virginia state government also monitors commercial whitewater use on the Shenandoah River, which forms its northeastern border with Virginia. Thanks to its proximity to the Washington DC metropolitan area, its moderate use levels have been sustained. Only four outfitters are licensed by the state of West Virginia to offer commercial trips on the popularly run seven-mile stretch of the Shenandoah. The whitewater run ends near the historic town of Harpers Ferry, West Virginia, where the Shenandoah joins the Potomac River in the Ridge and Valley section of the Appalachian Mountains. The final stream whose commercial use is monitored by the state of West Virginia is the Tygart River. It flows northward into the Monongahela River about twenty-five miles south of the Mason-Dixon Line. With scarcely more than two hundred customers in 1998 and none in 2002, its two licensed commercial outfitters clearly have focused their marketing efforts on other rivers instead. The Tygart River, like the Cheat, also has suffered from coal mining activities in its watershed.

Youghiogheny River

A dramatic waterfall on the Youghiogheny River that drops about eighteen feet forms the centerpiece of Ohiopyle State Park, a 19,000-acre unit in southwestern Pennsylvania. The river and land around the Youghiogheny received state park protection after the Kaufmanns and Mellons, two wealthy families engaged in Pittsburgh merchandising and banking interests, acquired the land and then transferred it to the state's conservation agency (Palmer 1984). In addition to providing a public benefit, the action also served to further protect the private estates that both families owned in the area. Fallingwater, a home designed for the Kaufmann family by Frank Lloyd Wright and reputed to be the world's most famous private residence, is just a few miles away on Bear Run, a tributary of the Youghiogheny. The state park regulates the commercial raft trips that launch near the base of the waterfall. The seven-mile stretch of river below the falls, known as the Lower Yough, is heavily used, especially on weekends. Individuals taking part in guided commercial trips, as well as those who rent rafts without the benefit of a guide, enjoy the river's challenging rapids from spring through the fall. Throughout most of the Lower Yough run, the river drops at a rate of thirteen feet per mile. The first mile has a much greater stream gradient, though, resulting in nearly continuous rapids during the initial stretch of this trip (Burrell and Davidson 1972). Many private boaters, who paddle the river in their own canoes and kayaks, also flock to Ohiopyle year-round. An annual race inaugurated in 1999 allows the most highly skilled among these private boaters an opportunity to paddle their boats over the state park's waterfall legally during a September weekend (figure 14.5).

In the 1940s, the US Army Corps of Engineers built Youghiogheny Dam upstream of what eventually became the state park to provide flood control for the city of Pittsburgh. The existence of the reservoir benefits the whitewater industry because it also guarantees minimal flows to ensure commercial rafting as well as private recreational boating and fishing all summer long. Downstream of its whitewater sections, the Youghiogheny continues to flow north to meet the Monongahela River just south of Pittsburgh.

There is another commercially run section of the river in western Maryland, known as the Upper Yough, located upstream of the reservoir. Today this stretch of river is managed as a wild and scenic river within the Maryland State Wild and Scenic Rivers System. Commercial use on the Upper Yough is made possible by limited releases from a hydropower-generating plant on

FIG. 14.5. Running Ohiopyle Falls on the Youghiogheny River.

Deep Creek Lake, Maryland. Ten outfitters based in Pennsylvania, Maryland, and West Virginia offer commercially guided trips on this difficult 10-mile stretch of river. In addition to its commercial use, this part of the river is also popular with expert kayakers and canoeists. Its stream gradient averages 48 feet per mile, though one 3.5-mile segment of the river drops at the very steep rate of 116 feet per mile (Burrell and Davidson 1972). Maryland's commercially rafted section of the Upper Youghiogheny is much narrower and boulder-choked, so only four-person rafts can be used. The lower guide-to-customer ratio in smaller rafts coupled with greater skill requirements for guides results in higher trip fees for rafting customers.

Profile of Rafting Customers in West Virginia and Their Expenditures

The West Virginia Department of Natural Resources commissioned a survey of rafters on the New, Cheat, and Gauley rivers as part of their ongoing river management. Conducted during the summer of 1995, the survey provided information about the characteristics of rafting customers and their expenditures (Whisman et al. 1998). The study found that about 52 percent of the rafters on the New and Cheat rivers were males, but the more challenging rapids of the Gauley River lured many more males than females (73 percent male on the Gauley). A majority of all the rafters on these West Virginia rivers fell within an age range of twenty to forty, and more than half of them

(53 percent) had earned a bachelor's degree or higher. While median family incomes ranged between $50,000 and $75,000, incomes at the upper end of the scale corresponded with raft trip prices on the three rivers. Trips are least expensive on the Cheat, and only 9 percent of the rafters on this river reported incomes of $100,000 or more. Due to the greater difficulty of the Gauley, trips on it are most expensive. Among those rafting the Gauley, 16 percent had incomes of $100,000 or more. On the New River, 13 percent had incomes of $100,000 or more. Travel patterns also corresponded with river difficulty. The average one-way travel distance for a trip on the Cheat was 269 miles, 304 to the New, and 436 to the Gauley. West Virginians account for only about 3 percent of the commercial rafting participants. Most of rafting customers drove from New York, Ohio, Michigan, Virginia, Pennsylvania, Maryland, and Indiana to run the Cheat, New, and Gauley rivers.

In addition to paying the rafting company for their guided trip, customers frequently purchase souvenir T-shirts, videos, or photographs of their river trip from the whitewater outfitter. The 1995 survey of rafters in West Virginia on the Cheat, New, and Gauley rivers suggested that rafters spent an average of $87, $96, and $174, respectively, for their raft trip and related expenditures like photographs. (Note that each year the prices of commercial trips and related souvenirs increase. In 2003, the weekend cost for just the guided trip alone on these rivers averaged about $82 on the Cheat, $101 on the New, and $139 for the Gauley.) The economic benefit of commercial whitewater rafting extends beyond revenues generated by the raft companies themselves. For example, most of the rafting customers purchase overnight lodging in the area, meals in local restaurants, and gasoline for their trip home. The 1995 study reported that expenditures in the local area for these items averaged $104, $151, and $148 for the Cheat, New, and Gauley rivers, respectively, providing a further boost to the economies of communities around these rivers (Whisman 1998).

Diversification within the Whitewater Industry

The whitewater industry also benefits local and state economies indirectly through the creation of other businesses with direct linkages to existing whitewater recreation. Examples from communities located in the Central Appalachian whitewater area discussed in this chapter illustrate different types of diversification occurring within the industry. The largest of the spin-off businesses is Ohiopyle Prints, named for the Pennsylvania town on the Youghiogheny River where the company got its start. More than twenty years ago, two young men started this imprinted sportswear company to meet the needs of local whitewater outfitters wanting to sell souvenir T-shirts to their

Fig. 14.6. Whitewater-related manufacturing.

customers. Today the company employs over one hundred people. Ohiopyle Prints supplies not only local outfitters, but also far-flung ones running rivers like the Colorado in the Grand Canyon. They also market their products to ski resorts across the country. A few other businesses with strong roots in the local whitewater industry, though considerably smaller, also got their start not too far from Ohiopyle. One company focuses its production on a small maneuverable raft called a Shredder. Another one that designs and manufactures specialized clothing and related equipment for whitewater boating got its start just a few miles upstream in the small town of Confluence.

A second community where whitewater manufacturing businesses have congregated is Friendsville, Maryland. This small town on the Upper Youghiogheny River boasts one company that has manufactured rafts since 1982 and another that got its start making spray skirts for kayak cockpits before expanding into special clothing for water sports as well (figure 14.6). A company that manufactures helmets worn by whitewater boaters also incubated in Friendsville, but moved elsewhere in Garrett County when operations expanded. Across the Maryland border into Preston County, West Virginia, another small inflatable craft manufacturing company is located not far from the Cheat River. A second imprinted sportswear company operates in West Virginia's small town of Davis, located on a headwater stream that combines with others to form the Cheat River. Two self-employed individuals that make custom canoe and kayak paddles also live in communities near the Cheat and Youghiogheny rivers.

Some final examples of diversification within the whitewater industry can be found in the small southern West Virginia town of Fayetteville. Diversification in southern West Virginia developed a service-oriented focus rather than the manufacturing one that emerged around the Youghiogheny and Cheat rivers. For example, a catering service and a transportation company in this vicinity gave outfitters on the New and Gauley rivers the option of outsourcing both the preparation of lunches provided on the river for customers and the shuttling of customers to and from the river. A photography company also set up shop on the main street in Fayetteville to provide rapid duplication of souvenir photographs and videos so customers can purchase them at outfitters' base camps after their trips. Guest services like restaurants or lodging establishments also have expanded more in this area, given the large combined volume of commercial rafting on the New and Gauley rivers in southern West Virginia.

Future of the Whitewater Industry

Commercial outfitters on the New, Gauley, Cheat, Shenandoah, and Youghiogheny rivers package recreational experiences for people drawn to the thrill of running whitewater. During the past three decades, the whitewater industry experienced periods of rapid growth, stabilization, and decline in customer numbers. Such growth has been welcome in a region where out-migration is high and the economic base, mining, has become increasingly mechanized. However, further expansion of commercial rafting is constrained by a number of factors, including regulatory controls set by state agencies on the number of commercial permits and daily use capacities for river segments, and seasonal limits in water availability or comfortable temperatures to support the activity (Mayfield and DeHart 1989; Imre Szilagyi, personal communication, 1999). In an effort to expand their commercial ventures, rafting companies vie for an increased market share through improved service, or, more importantly, try to diversify their operations. Many have added retail stores and restaurants to their operations. In recent years, some companies have worked hard to extend the time customers stay in the area by offering packaged vacations that combine rafting with lodging and mountain biking, horseback riding, rock climbing, or other activities in the area.

The longer customers remain in the area, the more money they will spend, benefiting outfitters and communities. The local economies of small towns near these rivers diversified as the whitewater industry developed and matured. Further economic growth in the Central Appalachian tristate area may occur as outfitters, communities, and states more aggressively market whitewater rafting and related recreation and tourism activities. Additional product development and manufacturing also may occur if highly skilled boaters with innovative ideas and entrepreneurial skills continue to congregate within this whitewater region.

References

Burrell, Bob, and Paul Davidson. 1972. *Wild Water West Virginia*. Hillsborough, NC: Menasha Ridge Press.

Mayfield, Michael W., and Jennifer DeHart. 1989. Whitewater Rafting in the Southeastern United States: Current Status and Constraints on Future Growth. *Sport Place* 3 (3): 15–19.

———. 1996. Carolina Whitewater. In *Snapshots of the Carolinas: Landscapes and Cultures*, ed. G. Gordon Bennett, 91–94. Washington, DC: Association of American Geographers.

Morgan, John, and Michael W. Mayfield. 1994. The Second Oldest River in the World? *Southeastern Geographer* 34 (2): 138–44.

Palmer, Tim. 1984. *Youghiogheny: Appalachian River*. Pittsburgh, PA: University of Pittsburgh Press.

United States Department of the Interior, National Park Service. 1996. General Management Plan, Gauley River National Recreation Area, Nicholas and Fayette Counties, West Virginia. Glen Jean, WV: National Park Service.

Whisman, Steven A., et al. 1998. A Summary of Economic Impacts of Commercial Whitewater Rafting in West Virginia. Final Report Submitted to the West Virginia Department of Natural Resources by the West Virginia University, Morgantown, WV.

FIFTEEN

Going to the Mountains

DEER HUNTERS IN THE ALLEGHENY NATIONAL FOREST REGION

Deborah Che

"I'm thinking about the deer. I like the trees, you know. I like the way the trees are in the mountains, all different."
—*Michael Cimino,* The Deer Hunter

Pennsylvania's northern tier has long been renowned as big game (deer, bear) country. Northwestern Pennsylvania's Allegheny National Forest (ANF), with over half a million acres of publicly owned forest lands open to hunting, has attracted hunters from urban western Pennsylvania and eastern Ohio. This paper will examine the tradition of these urbanites from cities like Pittsburgh, New Castle, Sharon, and Erie, Pennsylvania; and Cleveland, Akron, and Youngstown, Ohio; who have been termed "flatlanders," "up-here's," and "Ohio-sians" by permanent residents of the ANF region, coming up to the mountains to hunt. First, I will discuss how human landscape modifications produced the area's bountiful deer populations and deer hunting reputation. Then I will review changes in the area's hunting tourism with the development of farm tourism and hunting camps. Finally, I will examine how the orange-clothed army of flatlander, up-here, and Ohio-sian hunters has changed due to shifts in the regional economy and in statewide deer populations.

The Deer Hunting Tradition in the Mountains

Deer hunting is big business in Pennsylvania. In 2001, in-state trip and equipment hunting expenditures equaled $901 million (USDI Fish and Wildlife

FIG.15.1. The mountains along the Allegheny River, Tidioute, Pennsylvania.

Service and USDC Bureau of the Census 2003). The first day of buck season (the Monday after Thanksgiving) is a de facto holiday, with over a million hunters estimated to be in the woods (Sajna 1990, 3). During the 2002 deer season, hunters in Pennsylvania harvested 517,529 deer (Pennsylvania Game Commission 2003e). Pennsylvania's northern tier, its traditional big game and hunting camp country, which includes northwestern Pennsylvania's ANF counties (Warren, McKean, Forest, Elk) and north-central counties where state forest and game lands preponderate (Potter, Tioga, Bradford, Cameron, Clinton, and Lycoming) accounted for 19 percent of the 2002 harvest (Pennsylvania Game Commission 2003e). This region earned its legendary hunting reputation during the 1930s and 1940s when it was one of the few areas in the state with deer. The northern tier yielded from 33 percent up to 67 percent of Pennsylvania's total deer harvest then (Pennsylvania Game Commission 1998a) (figure 15.2).

Past human modifications of the landscape, especially timber harvesting and hunting, produced the northern tier's reputation for good deer hunting. Before permanent European settlement, northern Pennsylvania had ten to fifteen deer per forested square mile (McGuinness 1997). Predators, Native American hunters, and the food availability in the mature and old growth hemlock-beech forest kept the deer population in check. The subsequent European settlement, with its bounty and meat market–oriented hunting and

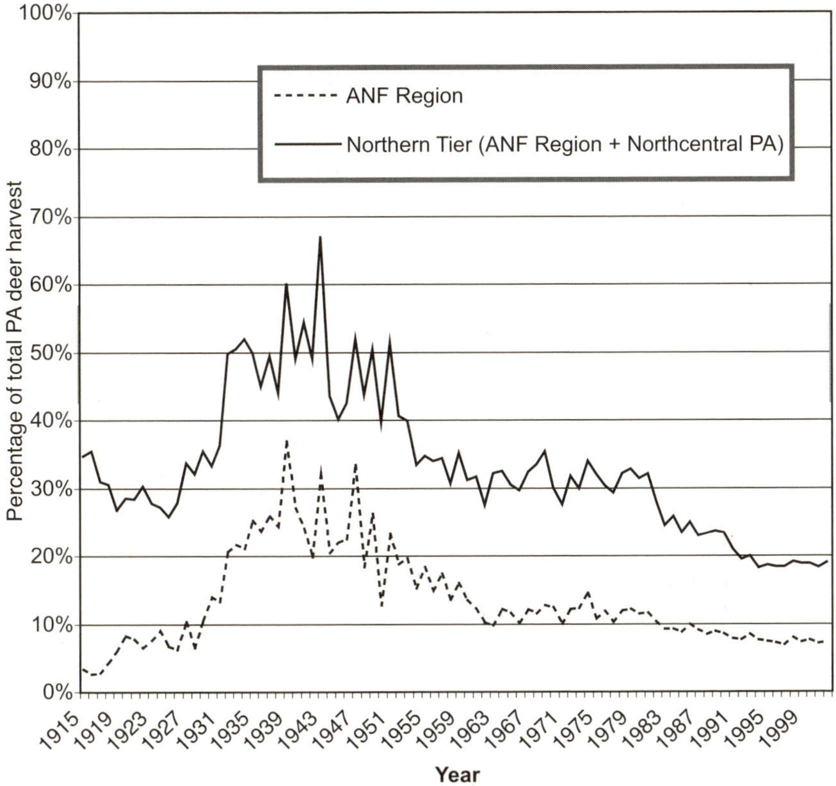

FIG.15.2. Northern tier deer harvest (Pennsylvania Game Commission 1998a; 2003a; 2003b; 2003c; 2003d; 2003e).

industrial timber harvesting, greatly altered the native forest and impacted the deer population. Hunting eliminated major predators such as the gray wolf and mountain lion and nearly eliminated the white-tailed deer by the turn of the twentieth century, as venison was desired in urban meat markets and logging camps. The pattern of timber harvesting greatly altered the deer carrying capacity of the Allegheny plateau forests. Old-growth white pine and then hemlock were removed for use in construction and in leather tanning, respectively. During the capital-intensive, steam-powered, logging railroad era (1890–1920), the remaining virgin and partially cut pine, hemlock, and hardwoods were clear-cut to produce wood distillation chemicals (Marquis 1975). The clear-cutting of entire hillsides allowed shade-intolerant Allegheny hardwood (black cherry, maple, and ash) saplings and seedlings, which were adapted to the open conditions, to replace much of the formerly dominant hemlock and beech (Marquis 1975; Whitney 1990).

This new Allegheny hardwood seedling-sapling forest provided the re-

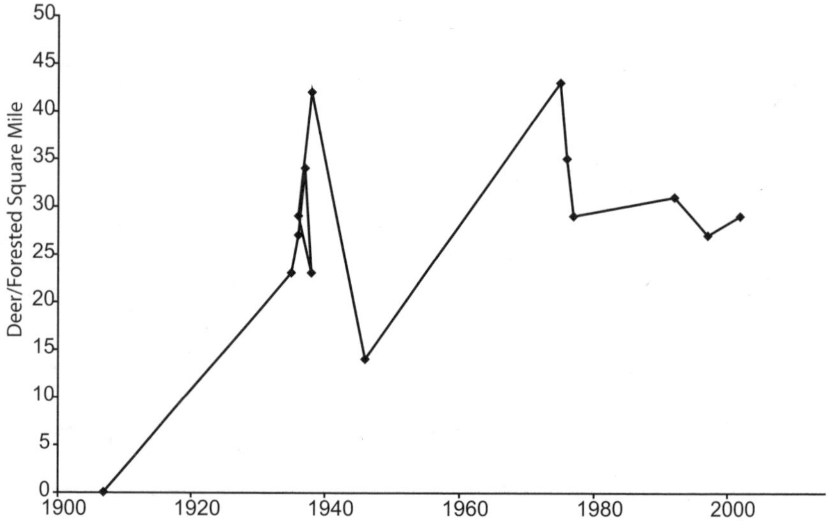

FIG.15.3. Deer densities in the Allegheny National Forest (Pennsylvania Game Commission 1998; Pennsylvania Game Commission 2002; Redding 1995).

maining deer population, protected and augmented with stocking by the Pennsylvania Game Commission, with a man-made, predator-free habitat with plenty of browse. The ANF region's deer population density exploded from near zero to an average overwinter density of more than forty deer per forested square mile in the 1930s (Redding 1995) (figure 15.3). An abundant food supply produced the high deer populations and legendary trophy bucks with large weights and racks. Hunters who came of age then reminisced about seeing one hundred deer in a day and a "buck behind every tree." The abundance of deer in northern Pennsylvania contrasted with the lack of deer in the heavily populated, industrialized, and agricultural southern tier counties (Sajna 1990). The first of many deer population busts occurred in the 1940s when the Allegheny plateau forest reached the pole-timber stage, which provided limited browse and could only support five deer per forested square mile. The ANF region's deer population alternately boomed and busted from the 1940s through the 1970s. These population fluctuations followed variances in forage availability that increased with timber harvests and decreased with severe winter weather (Redding 1995).

The northern tier's land ownership patterns also fostered its legendary deer hunting reputation. Importantly for future public hunting access, much of the lands deforested in the northern tier fell through purchase or tax default into state or federal ownership, since timber companies that were shifting operations west largely deemed them worthless. In north central Pennsylvania, much of these cutover lands became state forests. In north-

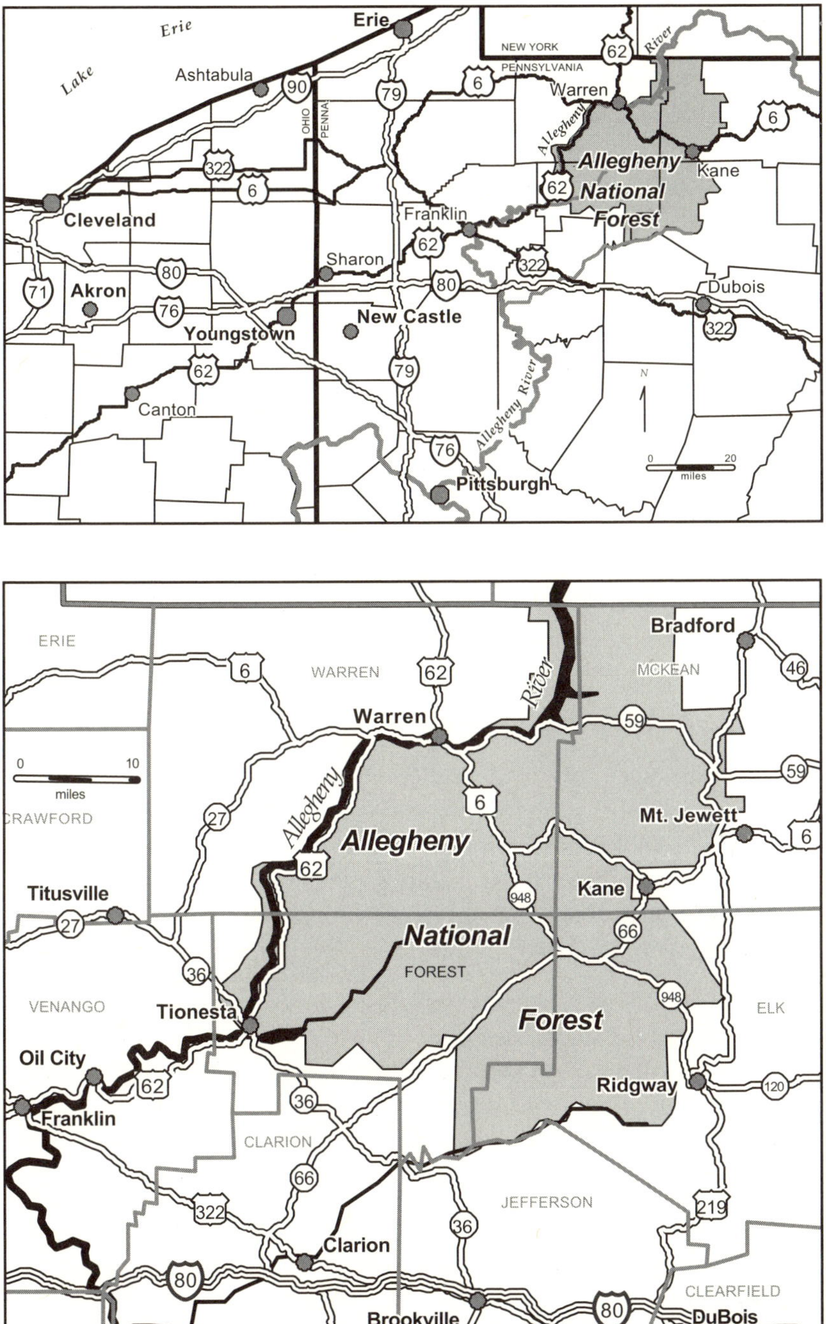

Fig. 15.4. Regional map of the origin area for Allegheny National Forest hunters and seasonal residents (above), with map of the Allegheny National Forest region (below).

western Pennsylvania, the USDA Forest Service, which was authorized by the Weeks Act of 1911 to purchase, reforest, and manage watersheds of navigable waters, became the primary landholder. The agency acquired cutover land in the Allegheny watershed in Forest, Warren, McKean, and Elk counties for a few dollars an acre. This land would become part of the Allegheny National Forest (ANF), which was created in 1923 (Frank 1998). The ANF grew to encompass 500,000 acres of quality deer hunting land, which drew residents of deer-poor urban and industrial western Pennsylvania and eastern Ohio. The ANF region's permanent residents referred to these outside visitors according to their resident origins: "up-here's" are visitors from the Pittsburgh SMSA (standard metropolitan statistical area) who would say, "We're up here in the mountains for the weekend"; "Ohio-sians" are visitors from Ohio; and "flatlanders" are visitors from both Ohio and southwestern Pennsylvania. All these terms signify outsider status and have, to some degree, a negative connotation. The use of these terms throughout the northern deer country should be viewed in the context of local, rural anxiety over the more affluent urban visitors' competition for land, hunting spots, and women/spouses (Glimm 1983). The flatlanders, Ohio-sians, and up-here's became the foundation of the ANF region's evolving hunting tourism.

Coming up to the Mountains: Agritourism?

Through the first decades of the ANF era (1920s–1950s), hunting tourism in the region involved elements of what today is called agritourism. Urban hunters from western Pennsylvania and eastern Ohio boarded in private homes and farms in the northern deer counties. One resident of a farm bordering thousands of acres of deer habitat in the national forest reminisced about annually housing hunters from Cleveland from the late 1920s to the 1950s:

> Back in the good old days, many of the farm folk in deer country took in hunters. They would board as few as one or two on up to a dozen or more, depending on their accommodations. Usually the hunters were kept for a minimum of three days, which was about as long as many of them thought the hunting was good for. But some did stay for as long as a week, which was about as long as their hosts were good for. (Ogrin 1975, 21)

Over the decades, the type of Cleveland hunters hosted by this resident's family changed. Initially first-generation Eastern European immigrants who owned taverns, grocery stores, or hardware stores stayed at the farm. As these hunters, who rarely ventured out into the surrounding woods or bagged deer, had come from countries where hunting was a sport restricted to the nobility, their primary reward was in just being able to hunt deer. Gradually younger hunters, who worked in Cleveland's factories and mills, replaced the first-generation immigrants. To this latter group, it was important both to trade their everyday industrial labor for days in the woods *and* to get their deer (Ogrin 1975).

One Forest County woman who grew up on a farm similarly recalled the tradition of housing Pittsburgh area hunters every hunting season: "From 1954–56, up until 1960, we'd put up a sign 'room and board' and open up our homes for hunters and put up extra beds. Had twenty at a time, the McDonald (Pennsylvania) fire department. Sometimes we would have a group or one hunter by himself needing a place to stay. The same ones came back every year saying, 'I need a place to stay when I return'" (Che 2000).

Boarding a group of hunters required extra work on the farm, as everyone would be up early to prepare breakfast and a bag lunch so that hunters could be out in the woods at the break of dawn. In the evenings, hunters consumed a big dinner consisting of the farm's own pork and beef. The extra work during hunting season provided all members of the farm family with financial benefits, as the former Forest County farm girl recalled, "After the hunters paid mom and dad, $10 (per week per person), they would tip me and my sister $1 because we served the tables. We thought we had a lot—the $20–$25 would be our Christmas money" (Che 2000). Boarding hunters, like agritourism today, helped maintain working farms while providing visitors with accommodations and full country meals.

Hunting Camp Development in the Allegheny National Forest Region

Permanent hunting camp development, some of which occurred concurrently with the farm tourism, became the dominant element of hunting tourism in the ANF region from the 1950s onward. Improved transportation and the booming, manufacturing-based economy in western Pennsylvania and eastern Ohio increased demand for camps that could be used during both hunting season and the summer. The Eisenhower-era development of the interstate highway system, with Interstate 80 to the south, Interstate 79 to the west, and New York's Southern Tier Expressway to the north of the ANF, facilitated weekend getaways in the mountains. Interstates 90 and 80, coming out of Cleveland and Youngstown, respectively, made the ANF region more accessible to Ohio hunters than to those from parts of southern Pennsylvania (Sajna 1990).

The post–World War II economic boom in the region's cities also fueled camp development. It drove camp demand by highly paid, blue-collar, urban workers from Pittsburgh, Cleveland, Youngstown, Akron, and Erie who worked in steel and other manufacturing plants and had six to thirteen

TABLE 15.1. Forest County Camp Ownership, by Owner Origin Area

Camp Owner Origin Area	*Total Camps (#)*	*Total Camps (%)*
Pennsylvania		
Pittsburgh SMSA	1301	41
Lawrence (New Castle) & Mercer (Sharon) counties	404	13
Erie SMA	148	5
Other Western PA	747	23
Other PA	9	1
Ohio		
Cleveland SMA	165	5
Akron SMA	55	2
Youngstown-Warren SMSA	159	5
Canton-Massillon SMA	29	1
Other Eastern OH	89	3
Other OH	38	1
New York	18	1
Other States	42	1
Total	3204	101[a]

[a]Due to rounding.

Source: Forest County Assessment Office 1978

weeks of annual leave. Additionally the manufacturing boom increased the supply of private land for camps, which mainly consisted of former farms. In the ANF region, as in other parts of Pennsylvania, returning GIs left farms and small towns for regional cities with higher-paying manufacturing jobs. Once their parents who farmed passed away, sons who had "seen the world and suddenly saw Forest County as too small" sold or abandoned farmland (D. Carlson, interview by author, July 23, 1999). The already limited number of farms in this mountainous county declined as many of these farms were subdivided into lots as small as 50 by 150 feet for hunting camps (Che 2000). Pennsylvania residents from Pittsburgh, New Castle, Sharon, and Erie and Ohio residents from Cleveland, Akron, and Youngstown purchased this land for camps. These cities were prominently represented as origin areas for hunting camp owners (table 15.1).

Camp development changed the landscape of the ANF region. In Forest County, like much of the ANF region and rural Pennsylvania, weak land use planning and controls have resulted in haphazard recreation settlement patterns on private lands. In Forest County, most camps in both large developments on former farms and on roadside lots were established prior to any sewage or minimum lot size regulations. Some large camp developments can be more accurately described as "camp cities." They have high housing densities but lack urban levels of garbage and sewage service (Forest County Conservation District and Planning Department 1998). The individual camps vary widely in quality from converted school buses and tar paper shacks to cottages and rustic log cabins having open fireplaces, running water, and equipped kitchens. This haphazard development on rural private land sharply contrasts with the limited, planned recreational development on northern tier public lands that hold most of the natural and scenic attributes (Zelinsky 1995).

In addition to the effect on the landscape, the influx of hunters associated with the camp development also culturally impacted the sparsely populated ANF counties. During the peak hunting camp decades of the 1950s–1970s, the population of Forest County, which then had fewer than 5,000 permanent residents, swelled to as many as 40,000 during buck season (*Forest Press* 1984). The origin areas of incoming hunters mirrored those of camp owners in the ANF region. A 1977 study of the spatial distribution of Pennsylvania deer hunting found that out of the 11.7 percent of hunters who reported successfully bagging a buck in the ANF region, 70 percent came from outside the immediate region (Hess 1977, 116). Of those from outside the region, 93 percent were from other parts of western Pennsylvania. More than 50 percent were from the Pittsburgh SMSA. Large numbers of successful hunters in the ANF region came from Erie, Mercer (Sharon), and Lawrence (New Castle) counties (Hess 1977, 117). Ohio hunters, especially those from the Cleveland and Youngstown areas, too were attracted to the ANF which offered nearby, quality deer hunting areas then lacking at home (Hess 1977, 144).

Deer hunting season, with its influx of hunters, was a notable annual event in the northern big game counties. In areas of Forest County outside the main towns, the hunters' arrival resulted in the loss of electricity for several hours as they turned on electric heaters in the camps and overwhelmed the then-limited distribution capacity. In the towns, the "sea of orange" would run so thick that crossing the streets or walking down sidewalks became difficult. Special, temporary phones would also be installed for hunters to use. While locals noted inconveniences with the influx of hunters who often stayed a week at camp, hunting season represented the last chance for local businesses to make money needed to survive winters until seasonal recreation users returned to camp in the spring. The summer and sporting seasonal trade often made up at least half of local stores' and restaurants' business (Che 2000).

The Relative Decline in Hunting Tourism

Hunting tourism in the ANF region has declined since the era of major camp development. According to the ANF, deer hunting use of the forest has declined. The national forest has tracked the number of on-forest hunters by counting the number of cars along a standard survey route on the opening and second mornings of antlered (buck) and antlerless (doe) seasons (table 15.2). According to the ANF, its car counts, which were the only quantitative data that specifically measured hunting in the region, may overestimate the decline in hunting. During the years the ANF counted cars, it also constructed new forest roads that gave hunters alternative access to the forest off the survey route. But by using the car-count data in conjunction with Pennsylvania Game Commission statistics that show a decline in hunting licenses, ANF managers conclude hunting has declined on the forest, although numbers have stabilized somewhat in recent years (USDA Forest Service 1989; USDA Forest Service 1993; USDA Forest Service 2002).

Changes in the regional economy, in leisure demographics, and in the deer population statewide have negatively affected hunting tourism in the ANF region. The deindustrialization and economic restructuring of cities like Pittsburgh, Cleveland, Youngstown, and Akron (Bluestone and Harrison 1982; Buss and Gemmel 1990; Fitzgerald 1990; Hill 1990; Shanahan and Goe

Table 15.2 Hunter Use of Allegheny National Forest (Car Count Data)

		Buck/Antlered Season			Doe/Antlerless Season		
Year	*Day of Season*	*Total Miles*	*Total Cars*	*Cars/ mile*	*Total Miles*	*Total Cars*	*Cars/ mile*
1975[1]	1	186.2	3944	21.0	186.9	1404	7.5
1981[1]	1	240.1	4063	16.5	240.8	1491	6.1
1984[1]	1	233.3	3090	13.6	237.2	1034	4.4
1988[1]	1	230.0	2498	11.0	234.0	1071	4.5
1989[2]	1	115.1	1171	10.2	114.0	596	5.2
1990[2]	1	252.4	2045	8.1	240.3	1133	4.7
1991[2]	1	186.0	2565	13.7	152.0	1016	6.7
1992[2]	1	110.8	1577	14.2	107.3	566	5.3
1994[3]	1	227.2	2494	11.0	215.7	1261	5.8
1975[1]	2	219.2	2977	13.6	183.4	677	3.7
1981[1]	2	60.6	490	8.15	244.0	744	3.0
1984[1]	2	245.1	1883	7.87	243.1	491	2.0
1988[1]	2	147.0	1024	6.9	115.0	281	2.45
1994[3]	2	225.1	1693	7.5	221.4	616	2.8

Sources: [1]USDA Forest Service 1989, 22
[2]USDA Forest Service 1993, 21
[3]Nelson 1994, Allegheny National Forest Deer Season Car Counts

1990) that the campers called home have affected camper visitation patterns. By the early 1980s, several years after steel plant closings in Pittsburgh and Youngstown, former steelworkers' year-round and hunting season use of their camps in Forest County dramatically shifted as their unemployment benefits ran out. According to the editor of the county's weekly newspaper, this "high-spending group," which used to come up every weekend through the 1970s, may only come one weekend a month (*Forest Press* 1984). Locally, the decline in steel translated into campers' shorter stays, from one week down to a few days. During hunting season, receipts are lower at stores, restaurants, and at church and community organization fundraisers, such as hunters' breakfasts on the first day of buck season (Che 1997). For local tourism service providers whose sales had increased with the good hunting seasons of the 1970s, business decreased by 5 to 8 percent following the manufacturing decline (*Forest Press* 1984).

Changes in the leisure time and preferences of seasonal camp owners too have altered the hunting camp tradition. These changes are due in part to regional economic changes and camp turnover. Some original camper families who lost high-paying manufacturing jobs in Rust Belt cities and could no longer afford to pay property taxes on these second residences have sold them. In other camps, ownership has passed to a second generation of campers. Compared to the original generation of camping families, who came primarily for hunting and fishing and had a single wage earner, the newer owners are frequently younger, two-income families with less leisure time. Their children are also interested in a variety of activities at camp such as hiking, canoeing, biking, all-terrain vehicle riding, and horseback riding. Hunting and fishing are less dominant than in the past. The children also are involved in multiple activities at home (for example, soccer, Scouts) that leave less time for getaways in the mountains. Given both changing interests and time constraints, ANF area businesses reliant on the seasonal trade note that newer campers tend to stay shorter periods of time and come less frequently than steelworkers' families (Che 1997) whose "weekly arrival at camp with the car packed by the wife could be timed according to when the husband's shift ended."

The decline in both overall leisure time and time allocated to hunting among ANF campers mirrors nationwide trends. Americans now work an additional 140 hours, or three more weeks, a year than in 1969 (Rieger 1997, 36). The time allocated for hunting, too, has similarly decreased. Due to decreasing leisure time and competing family activities, American sportsmen today are lucky to go hunting for a weekend. In comparison, their 1950s counterparts often hunted for ten days to two weeks a year. Hunting interest groups view decreased hunting time with concern, as it may hamper development of the next generation of hunters who learn the sport from older relatives (Rieger 1997).

In addition to the regional economy and interest in hunting, changes in Pennsylvania's deer population have also affected the hunting camp tradition. As noted earlier, in the 1930s and 1940s, hunters from southern Pennsylvania had to travel to the northern tier counties to find deer. But since World War II, deer populations have increased statewide. Hunting has gradually improved in southern Pennsylvania's suburban and agricultural counties. A 1953–1957 Pennsylvania Game Commission study found that deer with spiked antlers, which were uncommon in the better food (agricultural) areas, made up over 30 percent of the legal antlered kill in Forest County. The study also found that the antler points on bucks killed in the "big game" ANF and north-central counties, where earlier deer overpopulation had degraded the habitat, were fewer than four to four and a half, compared to six or more points in suburban Philadelphia and southwest Pennsylvania (Bowers 1958).

While the northern tier counties hold legendary reputations for deer hunting, deer population densities now are greater in southern Pennsylvania, which has limited cover but abundant food. Post–World War II farm abandonment and later suburban and exurban development and clearing

TABLE 15.3 Selected Characteristics Affecting Suitability of Land for Deer Hunting

Counties	*% Public Land*[1]	*% Forest Land*[2]	*Square Miles of Forested Land*[2]				*2001-2 Winter Deer Density (deer/ forested sq. mile)*[2]
			Seedling/ Sapling	*Pole Timber*	*Saw Timber*	*Total*	
ANF Region							
Elk	49.6	91	64	137	552	753	24
Forest	48.2	93	50	43	304	397	34
McKean	25.6	81	90	237	485	812	26
Warren	31.6	79	62	109	527	698	32
Pittsburgh, PA, MSA							
Allegheny	0.3	36	34	35	191	260	N/A
Armstrong	1.6	54	98	43	214	355	58
Beaver	4	48	33	60	117	210	38
Butler	5.1	50	75	110	212	397	54
Fayette	11	61	74	114	292	480	27
Washington	2.3	50	132	113	182	427	68
Westmoreland	5.7	51	137	98	283	518	48

Sources: [1]Center for Rural Pennsylvania 2000
[2]Pennsylvania Game Commission 2002

of mature stands have turned southern Pennsylvania's forests back to the seedling-sapling stage, which can support sixty deer per forested square mile over the winter. Southern Pennsylvania's forests and deer population densities are at the same stage as the ANF's in the 1930s (Pennsylvania Game Commission 2002) (table 15.3). Since the 1970s, the deer population in previously deer-poor northeastern Ohio has similarly expanded (Shafer-Noland 1997). In contrast, the ANF's maturing second-growth forests (saw timber stage), which provide good cover for deer and moderate amounts of browse and mast, have an overwinter carrying capacity of twenty deer per forested square mile. Currently the ANF counties average around thirty deer per forested square mile, which is too high for foresters, farmers, and wildflower enthusiasts, if not for hunters who would like to sight more potential targets (McGuinness 1997).

The Continuing Draw of Deer Camp

Despite the relative difficulty of getting a trophy buck in the mountains compared to hunting near home, thousands of flatlanders, Ohio-sians and up-here's still take deer up north and leave money that supports otherwise marginal businesses (*Potter Leader-Enterprise* 1998). As deer harvests in individual ANF counties may exceed the number of resident hunters in those counties, harvest volumes can indicate the influx of hunters from outside. Nonresident hunters in 4,888-person Forest County likely accounted for a significant share of the county's harvest, which totaled 7,007 deer in 2002 (Pennsylvania Game Commission 2003e). Because the four ANF counties offer greater acreages of public land open to hunting, these counties with lower deer densities than those in metropolitan Pittsburgh (table 15.3) can still attract out-of-the-region hunters and have high deer harvests. The ANF region's total deer harvest equaled 37,204 deer in 2002 (Pennsylvania Game Commission 2003e).

The continuing trek of hunters to the big woods where one may have a lower chance of getting a buck or doe than in suburbia indicates that deer hunting involves more than getting a buck or doe. In a study conducted for the US Fish and Wildlife Service, Steven Kellert found the actual harvesting of a deer far down on the list of reasons to go hunting, behind (in descending order of importance) nature, escapism, companionship, shooting, skill, vicarious satisfaction, and trophy display (Kellert in Sajna 1990, 195–96). Going to the deer camp, rather than hunting in one's suburban backyard, involves the most important reasons for hunting. Deer hunting in the "big woods" provides a special nature experience for urban and suburban hunters.

FIG. 15.5. Deer hunters at camp, Allegheny National Forest region. Photo courtesy of USDA Forest Service, Allegheny National Forest.

One hunter described the north country: "It's just a different world. It's so peaceful out in the woods. The quiet is deafening" (Sajna 1990, 31). Going to camp also allows hunters to get away from their daily routine and gather with friends and relatives that they often haven't seen since last season. The deer camp experience plays an integral part in the lives of its participants. In one study, 60 percent of the deer hunters interviewed could think of nothing in their lives that compared to the pleasures of deer camp. *Pittsburgh Post-Gazette* outdoors writer Mike Sajna, who participated in the trek from Pittsburgh to the ANF for buck season, perhaps best summed up the allure of deer camp as a "firm, replenishing oasis in a world that yearly becomes more disjointed, baffling and artificial" (Sajna 1990). Because deer camp provides what hunters rank as the most important reasons for participation in the sport and because it is so intertwined with the identities of its participants, the yearly tradition of coming up to the mountains will likely continue, even if in an abbreviated form.

The Evolving Getaway in the Mountains

Since the 1930s, northwestern Pennsylvania's Allegheny National Forest (ANF) region has drawn hunters from industrial and urban centers of western Pennsylvania and eastern Ohio. Human landscape modifications, including timber harvesting and the elimination of major predators, produced the mountains' bountiful deer populations and deer hunting reputation. The tradition of deer hunters from the regional cities of Pittsburgh, New Castle, Sharon, and Erie, Pennsylvania; and Cleveland, Akron, and Youngstown, Ohio, coming up to the ANF region to pursue their game changed in the last fifty years. Hunter accommodations shifted from farm stays to permanent camp developments that enabled highly paid blue-collar workers from the surrounding regional cities to purchase their "little piece of paradise." Largely unplanned camp development altered the landscape and supported large seasonal influxes of urban hunters. Since 1980, however, regional economic restructuring, declining overall leisure time and more diversified leisure preferences, and the expansion of the deer herd in previously deer-poor urban western Pennsylvania and eastern Ohio have contributed to a decline in the ANF region's hunting-based tourism. While deer hunting is still an economically and culturally important part of the region's tourism industry, getaways in the mountains increasingly include a diversified group of outdoor recreation activities such as canoeing, riding ATVs, hiking, mountain biking, and horseback riding. The region's tourism geography has responded to regional deindustrialization in ways unanticipated just a few decades ago.

References

Bluestone, B., and B. Harrison. 1982. *The Deindustrialization of America: Plant Closings, Community Abandonment, and the Dismantling of Basic Industry.* New York: Basic Books.

Bowers, G. L. 1958. The Pennsylvania Deer Story 1958. *Pennsylvania Game News* 29 (10): 33–48.

Buss, T. F., and D. Gemmel. 1990. Youngstown/Warren, Ohio: A Reflection of the Boom and Bust of the Steel Industry. In *Economic Restructuring of the American Midwest: Proceedings of the Midwest Economic Restructuring Conference of the Federal Reserve Bank of Cleveland,* ed. R. D. Bingham and R. W. Eberts. Boston: Kluwer Academic Publishers.

Center for Rural Pennsylvania. 2000. *Ranking of Public Land as Percent of Total Land Area by County, 2000.* Chart. Harrisburg, PA: Center for Rural Pennsylvania.

Che, D. 1997. *Forest County Ecotourism Feasibility Study.* Forest County Action Team/ Penn Soil RC&D, Tionesta, PA.

———. 2000. *Tourism, Timber, and Manufacturing: Rural Restructuring, Commodification, and Institutional Relationships in Forest County, Pennsylvania.* PhD diss., Clark University.

Fitzgerald, J. 1990. Pittsburgh, Pennsylvania: From steel town to advanced technology center. In *Economic Restructuring of the American Midwest: Proceedings of the Midwest Economic Restructuring Conference of the Federal Reserve Bank of Cleveland,* ed. R. D. Bingham and R. W. Eberts. Boston: Kluwer Academic Publishers.

Forest County Assessment Office. 1978. *Alphabetic Listing of Camp Names in Forest County 1978.* Tionesta, PA: Forest County Assessment Office.

Forest County Conservation District and Planning Department. 1998. *Comprehensive Plan.* Tionesta, PA: Forest County Conservation and Planning Department.

Frank, K. 1998. History of the Allegheny National Forest—Before 1923. *Allegheny Brambles,* April 17, 1998.

Glimm, J. Y. 1983. *Flatlanders and Ridgerunners: Folktales from the Mountains of Northern Pennsylvania.* Pittsburgh: University of Pittsburgh Press.

Hess, T. L. 1977. *A Spatial Study of Pennsylvania Deer Hunting.* MS thesis, Pennsylvania State University.

Hill, E. W. 1990. Cleveland, Ohio: Manufacturing Matters, Services Are Strengthened, but Earnings Erode. In *Economic Restructuring of the American Midwest: Proceedings of the Midwest Economic Restructuring Conference of the Federal Reserve Bank of Cleveland,* ed. R. D. Bingham and R. W. Eberts. Boston: Kluwer Academic Publishers.

Marquis, D. A. 1975. *The Allegheny Hardwood Forests of Pennsylvania.* Upper Darby, PA: USDA Forest Service, Northeastern Forest Experiment Station.

McGuinness, B. 1997. Deer Carrying Capacity: Too Few, Too Many, and for Whom? *Allegheny Brambles,* January 29, 1997.

Nelson, B. 1994. 1994 Allegheny National Forest Deer Season Car Counts.

Ogrin, F. T. 1975. The Deerslayers. *Pennsylvania Game News* 46 (7): 21–24.

Forest Press. 1984. "Tionesta: Dry, Dead, and Lost?" October 31.

Pennsylvania Game Commission. 1998a. *Pennsylvania Deer Harvests and Road Kills.* Harrisburg, PA: Pennsylvania Game Commission.

———. 1998b. *Pennsylvania Deer Statistics 1982–1997.* Harrisburg, PA: Pennsylvania Game Commission.

———. 2002. *Pennsylvania Deer Statistics 1982–2001.* Harrisburg, PA: Pennsylvania Game Commission.

———. 2003a. Deer Total: 1998 Harvest Map, www.pgc.state.pa.us/pgc/cwp/view.asp?a=493&q=159204 (accessed February 17, 2004).

———. 2003b. Deer Total: 1999 Harvest Map, www.pgc.state.pa.us/pgc/cwp/view.asp?a=493&q=159148 (accessed February 17, 2004).

———. 2003c. Deer Total: 2000 Harvest Map, www.pgc.state.pa.us/pgc/cwp/view.asp?a=493&q=159113 (accessed February 17, 2004).

———. 2003d. Deer Total: 2001 Harvest Map, www.pgc.state.pa.us/pgc/cwp/view.asp?a=493&q=159071 (accessed 17 February 17, 2004).

———. 2003e. Deer Total: 2002 Harvest Map, www.pgc.state.pa.us/pgc/cwp/view.asp?a=493&q=159029 (accessed February 17, 2004).

Potter Leader-Enterprise. 1998. Whitetail Vital to Northern Tier. *Potter Leader-Enterprise/Reporter Argus,* September 30.

Redding, J. 1995. History of Deer Population Trends and Forest Cutting on the Allegheny National Forest. In *Proceedings, 10th Central Hardwood Forest Conference,* ed. K. W. Gottschalk and S. L. C. Fosbroke. Radnor, PA: US Department of Agriculture, Forest Service, Northeastern Forest Experiment Station.

Rieger, G. 1997. Prince William's Deer. *Field and Stream* 101 (12): 34, 36.

Sajna, M. 1990. *Buck Fever: The Deer Hunting Tradition in Pennsylvania.* Pittsburgh: University of Pittsburgh Press.

Shafer-Noland, A. L. 1997. The Science and Politics of Deer Overabundance at Cuyahoga Valley National Recreation Area. *Wildlife Society Bulletin* 25 (2): 457–62.

Shanahan, J. L., and W. R. Goe. 1990. Akron, Ohio: Regional Economy at the Turning Point. In *Economic Restructuring of the American Midwest: Proceedings of the Midwest Economic Restructuring Conference of the Federal Reserve Bank of Cleveland,* ed. R. D. Bingham and R. W. Eberts. Boston: Kluwer Academic Publishers.

USDA Forest Service, Allegheny National Forest. 1989. *Allegheny National Forest FY 88 Forest Plan Monitoring and Evaluation Report.* Warren, PA: USDA Forest Service, Allegheny National Forest.

———. 1993. *Allegheny National Forest Fish and Wildlife Monitoring and Evaluation Report.* Warren, PA: USDA Forest Service, Allegheny National Forest.

———. 2002. *Allegheny National Forest Monitoring and Evaluation Report for FY 2000.* Warren, PA: USDA Forest Service, Allegheny National Forest.

US Department of the Interior, Fish and Wildlife Service, and US Department of Commerce, Bureau of the Census. 2003. *2001 National survey of fishing, hunting, and wildlife-associated recreation: Pennsylvania.* FHW/01-PA-Rev.

Whitney, G. G. 1990. The History and Status of the Hemlock-Hardwood Forests of the Allegheny Plateau. *Journal of Ecology* 78:443–58.

Zelinsky, W. 1995. Recreation and Tourism. In *A Geography of Pennsylvania,* ed. E. W. Miller. University Park, PA: Pennsylvania State University.

SIXTEEN

American Heritage Rivers

A NEW MODEL FOR WATERSHED PLANNING IN APPALACHIA

Richard A. Roth

Practitioners and academicians perennially affirm the idea that the watershed is the most appropriate geographic unit for regional planning and natural resource management. Planning over the extent of a large watershed, however, is difficult to reconcile with the existing political geography of state and local governments. Large watershed or river basin planning has been attempted in different forms and for different purposes for nearly a century, usually either by the federal government or, as in the case of interstate compacts, with the permission of the federal government (Black 1987).

The federal government chose Southern Appalachia for the first and only federally mandated experiment in comprehensive regional planning on a watershed basis: the Tennessee Valley Authority (TVA), whose jurisdiction encompassed the entire Tennessee River Basin. This large watershed includes much of Tennessee as well as parts of Alabama, Georgia, Kentucky, Mississippi, North Carolina, and Virginia. The TVA serves as a model of watershed-based planning imitated throughout the world (Newson 1992), exemplifying the idea of "regional socioeconomic development through publicly owned hydropower" (Goldfarb 1994, 487). However, some critics bitterly criticized it for top-down, technocratic planning that disproportionately favored industrial elites (e.g., Chandler 1984).

Another watershed-based planning process is underway in Southern Appalachia: the American Heritage Rivers project on the New River. Like the TVA, it was initiated by the federal government, but unlike the TVA, proponents describe it as a bottom-up, locally driven process. For example,

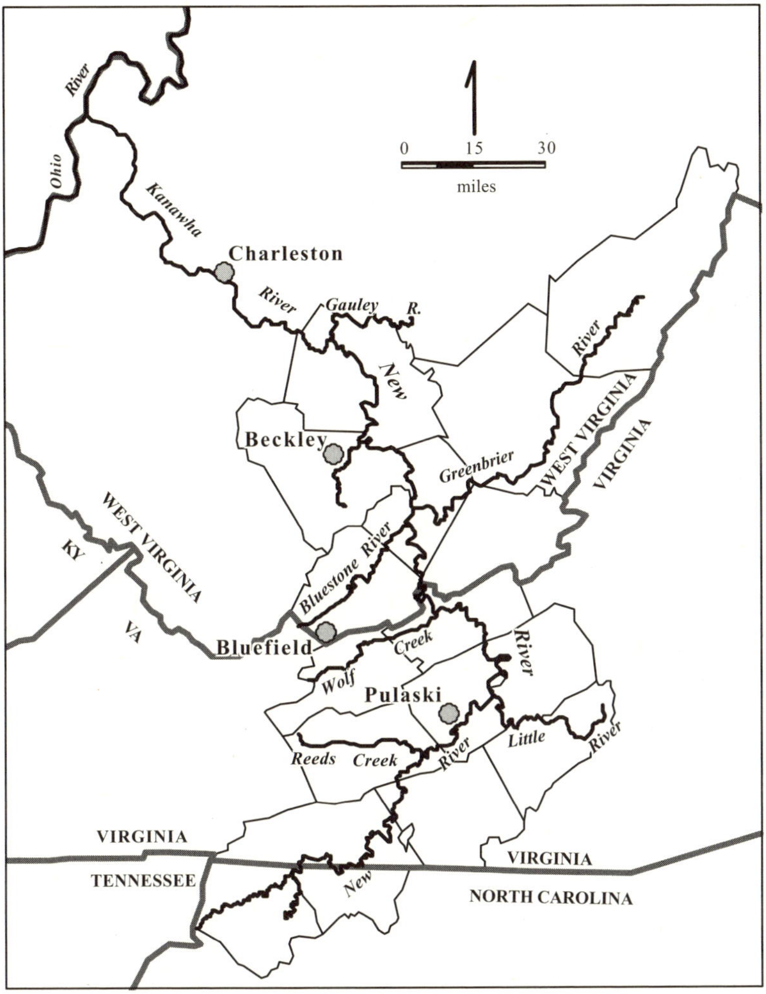

FIG. 16.1. The New River and its major tributaries (North Carolina, Virginia, West Virginia).

one brochure published by New River Community Partners (NRCP), the nonprofit organization managing the planning process, states that "based on goals *determined by the communities*, environmental, economic, and social concerns will be addressed through an action plan *designed and driven by local residents*" (NRCP 1998, my emphasis).

The New River has its headwaters in North Carolina, flows northward through western Virginia, and continues northwest through West Virginia before joining the Gauley River to form the Kanawha near Charleston (figure 16.1). Its waters eventually spill into the Gulf of Mexico via the Ohio and the Mississippi rivers. Its watershed includes all or a major part of fifteen counties in three states.

Thirty years ago a unique coalition of local citizens, national environmental and recreational organizations, and politicians successfully defeated a proposed hydroelectric dam in the headwaters region of the New River. Now the inaptly named New (it is one of the oldest rivers in the world) is the focus of an unusual multi-jurisdictional exercise in regional planning organized on a watershed basis. The stimulus for the planning activity was the 1998 naming of the New as one of fourteen American Heritage Rivers by President Clinton.

In this chapter, I describe how people in localities in all three states—North Carolina, Virginia, and West Virginia—developed plans for their communities, which were combined into a single "work plan" for the New as an American Heritage River. As one who participated in the development of the work plan, I also offer some reflections on the planning process. Did it live up to the rhetoric of its federal government instigators, to make it a bottom-up process rather than a federally directed top-down one? Did it facilitate local conversations about appropriate or sustainable development, or was it simply a bandwagon on which anyone's pet project could be piled?

The American Heritage Rivers Initiative

In his 1997 State of the Union address to Congress, President Clinton announced his intention to designate ten American Heritage Rivers. In an executive order of September 11, 1997, the White House outlined the process by which rivers would be selected, the roles of federal agencies in implementing the initiative, and the purpose of the initiative, which was to promote "natural resource and environmental protection, economic revitalization, and historic and cultural preservation" in the river communities (Executive Office of the President 1997a).

The executive order described the initiative as one that would create no new regulatory authority and would not interfere with state, tribal, and local prerogatives. Federal agencies would assist designated communities to reach their own expressed goals: "communities shall nominate rivers as American Heritage Rivers and the federal role will be solely to support community-based efforts to preserve, protect, and restore these rivers and their communities" (ibid.). The mandate directs federal agencies to facilitate access to federal assistance in communities along designated rivers. Five elements constitute the initiative: participation by communities would be voluntary; communities would nominate themselves (that is, rivers would not be nominated by federal agencies or representatives); nominations would have to have broad community support; federal agencies would be required to make information widely available; and members of Congress would be able to veto nominations within their district (Clark 1998). Opposition by congressional representatives led to the elimination of nine rivers and fourteen stretches of rivers from consideration during the selection process (ibid.).

Deliberations allowed communities across the nation to nominate their "river, river stretch, or river confluence" for designation as an American Heritage River. The chair of the federal Council on Environmental Quality (CEQ) coordinated the selection process and was directed to create a diverse selection committee representing a variety of perspectives: " natural, cultural, and historic resources; scenic, environmental, and recreation interests; tourism, transportation, and economic development interests; and industries such as agriculture, hydropower, manufacturing, mining, and forest management" (Executive Office of the President 1997a). The chair of the CEQ ensured that the chosen rivers were themselves diverse, representing a variety of sizes, conditions (both "pristine" and "degraded rivers in need of restoration"), and geographic settings.

An interagency task force, through a process of public meetings across the country as well as soliciting comments and suggestions, designed the initiative to meet the needs and concerns of local communities. A Federal Register notice elicited more than 1,700 comments, and the CEQ summary of those comments reveals the deep ambivalence about the federal government so evident in American politics in the 1990s:

> Many respondents wrote in favor of the initiative, citing increased coordination of federal services, the attention to environmental, economic and cultural/historic values in the design of the initiative, the integrated method to river restoration and revitalization, and the community-driven approach. Many appreciated the fact that no new regulations would be imposed as a result of the initiative.
>
> Many of the respondents wrote in opposition to the initiative. Many were opposed to federal involvement of any kind in restoring and revitalizing rivers and often expressed concern about property rights and the role of the United Nations along designated rivers. (Executive Office of the President1997b)

A set of criteria defined the quality of the applications: the "natural, economic, agricultural, scenic, historic, cultural, or recreational" characteristics of the river that render it distinctive or unique; the "effectiveness" of the applicant community's plan and the extent to which the plan addressed the three American Heritage River objectives of economic revitalization, natural resource protection, and cultural and historic preservation; the "strength and diversity of community support"; and the willingness and capability of the community to forge partnerships and agreements to implement their plan to meet their goals and objectives (ibid.).

One hundred twenty-six applications reached the review office. On July 30, 1998, the president and vice president flew to the Boggs Community Farm on a floodplain along the New River in Ashe County, North Carolina, and announced the designation of fourteen rivers as American Heritage Rivers, including the New River in North Carolina, Virginia, and West Virginia. Designated American Heritage Rivers, according to federal directives, receive national publicity and expedited and refocused federal assistance. The one definite and substantial federal contribution to each of the designated rivers is the assignment of a federal bureaucrat to work full time on behalf of the communities in the river's watershed, interceding and negotiating the tortuous paths of the federal bureaucracy.

The New River's American Heritage River Plan

In 1997, in the four-county headwaters region of the New River, which includes Alleghany, Ashe, and Watauga counties in North Carolina and Grayson County in Virginia, civic groups, community leaders, and local area "boosters" teamed with the Conservation Foundation, a nonprofit environmental organization, to develop an "action plan" to enter in the American Heritage Rivers competition. They created a nonprofit organization, New River Community Partners (NRCP), to organize the effort and implement the plan if it was chosen. Even though the NRCP invited other communities in Virginia and West Virginia to join the four-county area in its application, none chose to participate. This lack of interest may reflect an abiding distrust of federal programs and projects in the Appalachian region. For example, in the Blue Ridge Mountains of Virginia, some local residents, recalling how their parents' land was taken by the federal government for the Shenandoah National Park in the 1930s, have lobbied Congress to limit the ability of the US National Park Service to acquire more land for park expansion, even through voluntary agreements (*Roanoke Times* 1995). Hard feelings remain, too, in the Tennessee Valley Authority region over the agency's exercise of eminent domain (Chandler 1984; Walker 1998).

New River Community Partners also received several grants that allowed it to hire a full-time coordinator, who then organized the watershed-wide planning effort. The action plan at the heart of NRCP's successful application had four primary objectives: historic and cultural preservation, economic revitalization, natural resource and water quality protection, and education. The action consisted of phases, with the first one focusing on the headwaters region, while the second and third included the rest of the New River watershed in Virginia and West Virginia (NRCP 1998).

After the New River's designation, the NRCP accelerated the inclusion of downstream communities, sending its coordinator, Mr. Craig White, to facilitate meetings and organize planning processes in interested communities. In Virginia, which is organized into multicounty planning district commissions, the New River Valley Planning District Commission took the lead in organizing citizen planning activities in Floyd, Giles, Montgomery, and Pulaski counties and the city of Radford (known collectively as the New River Valley of Virginia). In West Virginia, planning was done on a county-by-county basis.

The publicity created by President Clinton and Vice President Gore's visit to Ashe County attracted interest in communities outside the headwaters area. Undoubtedly, the promise of "streamlined access" to federal resources for homegrown projects was a primary motivator in community interest.

In the New River Valley, the staff of the local planning district commission, working with NRCP, invited local citizens, elected officials, organizations, and businesses to a planning meeting. Four committees emerged from those meetings: a Natural Resource Protection Committee, an Economic Revitalization Committee, an Education and Training Committee, and a Cultural and Historic Preservation Committee. Participation in the committees was open and voluntary. The initial participants brainstormed who else should be invited and invitations to subsequent meetings were sent.

The committees each met several times over a period of two months. The process, facilitated by NRCP coordinator Craig White and assisted by planning district commission staff, consisted of brainstorming, then refining a list of projects to be included in a watershed-wide "work plan." Although Mr. White and NRCP board members described the process as one that would create a space for a discourse and perhaps consensus on a sustainable future for the New River Valley, in practice there was little time for dialog among groups. The reality is that it is difficult to involve volunteers in a sustained effort, and so meeting time is at a premium. No one has patience for lengthy and possibly conflict-ridden negotiations. The lure of streamlined access to federal money meant that everyone who had a pet project needing funding put their project forward for inclusion in the work plan, and that few were motivated to do anything more than push for their projects.

There was little discussion of the merits of projects within groups, no criticism, and no ranking. Even less discussion took place among groups. Clearly, the possibility, even likelihood, of conflict existed: projects aimed at expanding the regional or local economies are unlikely to also benefit

TABLE 16.1. New River Community Partners Work Plan Projects

Historic/cultural preservation: Many of the historic/cultural preservation projects are tied to promotion of tourism.
Establish Historic Districts in Pocohontas County (WV) Communities
Restore a Working-Class [Coal] Miner's Home
Historic Study of New River Crossing
Civil War Tours in the New River Valley
Education and training: Projects in this category addressed curriculum development, training for workers, development of information and outreach resources, library enhancement, and literacy.
Watershed-based Environmental Education in the New River Headwaters
Community Training in Sustainable Development
Strengthen Public School Agricultural Programs
Appalachian Studies Program for Grayson County (VA) Schools
New River Watershed Atlas
Technology Magnet School
Job Training and Skill Development in Alleghany County
Economic revitalization: This category included a wide variety of projects promoting tourism, community development, infrastructure, small businesses and entrepreneurship, health and human resources facilities, industry, and community leadership development.
Low Interest Loan Program for Community Development
Housing Construction and Rehabilitation in the Mt. Rogers District
Peterstown (WV) Sidewalk Replacement
Establish a Resource Center to Promote Downtown Revitalization
Ansted (WV) Visitors and Interpretive Center
National Whitewater Hall of Fame
Develop Senior Assisted-Living Centers in Pocohontas County (WV)

continued

natural resource protection, and projects aimed at natural resource protection or historic preservation are unlikely to benefit the economy, except perhaps for tourism.

I am aware of only one instance in which members of one committee (in the New River Valley planning process) expressed any reaction to a project put forward by another committee. This was a proposal for a new road linking Blacksburg in Montgomery County and Dublin in Pulaski County, which would necessitate another river crossing. Several members of the Natural Resource Protection Committee reacted negatively and even threatened to pull out of the planning process if the road were included. Ultimately, the road was not included, not because of opposition but because in subsequent meetings of the economic development committee no one championed it.

Lists of proposed projects ("action items") from the committees working in the headwaters, the New River Valley of Virginia, and West Virginia

TABLE 16.1. *continued*

Natural resource protection: Natural resource protection projects focused on clean-ups, stream restoration projects, open space and land preservation, natural resource inventories and studies, and development of parks and improved recreational facilities.

Promote Sustainable Forestry
Watershed-based Hazard Mitigation
Floodplain Management and Riverfront Development in Boone (NC)
Adopt-a-Stream Clean-up Program
Stream Bank Restoration and Buffer Projects
Eliminate Direct Piping of Sewage
"Environmentally Friendly" Model Development
Cleanup of Old Howes Tannery Site
New River Comprehensive Water Quality Study

Agriculture: Agricultural projects focused on maintaining agriculture as a viable economic activity and land use, particularly in the face of anticipated declining importance of tobacco.

Investigate Alternative Agricultural Opportunities
Agricultural Laborer Education
Produce Craft Raw Materials
Demonstration Aquaponics Project in Headwaters
Controlling Multiflora Rose and Other Shrubs with Goats
Develop Creamery to Support Local Dairies

Transportation and trails: Transportation projects focused primarily on trail networks and hiking-biking facilities attractive to tourists.

US 219 Study and Improvements in Monroe County (WV)
Develop Bike Lanes and Paths along Pocohontas County (WV) Roads
Complete and Extend New River Trail to Galax (VA)
Rails to Trails Project in Oak Hill (WV)

were eventually combined into a single document, the American Heritage Rivers New River Work Plan. Projects categories are as follows: historic and cultural preservation (73 projects); education and training (66 projects); economic revitalization (76 projects); natural resource protection (73 projects); agriculture (22 projects); and transportation and trails (17 projects). North Carolina's communities contributed 19 percent, Virginia's 39 percent, and West Virginia's 42 percent of the projects (NRCP 1999). Table 16.1 lists representative projects of each of categories. In its 2001 report, NRCP stated that over 13 million dollars was "leveraged" from governmental and private sources to support the projects in the work plan. In addition, NRCP cites the following accomplishments (2001, 2):

Projects include sustainable agriculture, aquatic ecosystem restoration, all-hazard mitigation planning, sewer and water infrastructure, river access (blueways), riparian corridor planning and preservation (greenways), conservation easements, trails development, historic preservation, tourism, economic development and education. Considerable efforts have been made toward capacity building in the watershed. Several workshops have been conducted or co-hosted by NRCP to address a wide variety of needs. Some of the more popular topics include: grantsmanship, niche industry development, wastewater management, stream bank stabilization, communication, and agricultural interests. Numerous meetings have been held throughout the watershed with stakeholders and community partners to facilitate and build consensus, provide technical consultation, advise on sources for program and project information, provide funding source information, and offer support for new teaming efforts and partnerships.

The successes of the NRCP are consistent with those reported by other American Heritage River organizations (US EPA 2001, 2002), although it must be pointed out that there has been no independent evaluation of either the program or of its individual river projects. The US Environmental Protection Agency recommended that the program be continued by the administration of President George W. Bush.

Reflections on the American Heritage Rivers Planning Process

Many years have passed since the United States government initiated regional planning on a watershed basis in Appalachia. The Tennessee Valley Authority remains a powerful presence in the Tennessee River Basin. Besides TVA, vestiges of a preeminent federal presence in large-scale river basin planning exist. The US Army Corps of Engineers exerts widespread authority over navigation, flood control, and other aspects of water resources and is organized on a watershed basis. Although it operates a number of projects in the region (for example the Bluestone Dam on the New River), the scope of its authority does not extend to regional socioeconomic development. The Reagan administration terminated federal support for the river basin commissions created by the Water Resources Planning Act of 1965; the Ohio River Basin Commission survives as an advisory group but its influence is very limited. The TVA remains the only large-scale watershed authority in Appalachia created by the federal government with a broader mission than water resources development and management. Its focus, however, has largely shifted from comprehensive economic development planning and natural resource conservation to electric power generation. From the start, TVA epitomized the top-down watershed planning of a paternalistic federal government (Chandler 1984).

Goldfarb (1994) recounts a history of regional development-oriented watershed-based programs pursued by federal government during the first six decades of the twentieth century. The program established under the Reclamation Act epitomizes the principle that regional economic development can and should be encouraged by large-scale federal water projects. The American Heritage Rivers Initiative can hardly be compared with any of the development-oriented federal interventions described by Goldfarb. It is not technocratic, and it is not an experiment in social engineering. The planning has not been top-down and the role of the federal government has been carefully circumscribed. The language of the public pronouncements regarding the program (apart from President Clinton's 1997 State of the Union address) is cautious, careful not to arouse fears of heavy-handed governmental action. Executive Order 13061, which spelled out details of the initiative, states that federal agencies involved in the American Heritage Rivers Initiative "shall act with due regard for the protection of private property provided for by the Fifth Amendment to the United States Constitution. No new regulatory authority is created as a result of the American Heritage Rivers Initiative. This initiative will not interfere with matters of State, local, and tribal government jurisdiction" (Executive Office of the President 1997a, section 1d).

Federal involvement in the American Heritage Rivers Initiative is completely unlike the federal role in the Tennessee Valley during the New Deal era. It represents the gentlest encouragement of local and regional efforts in the three specified areas (economic revitalization, cultural and historic preservation, and natural resource protection), and that is all. On its face, this initiative reflects a far less paternalistic role for the federal government. Although some concerned with property rights and states' rights fear heavy-handed intrusion on local communities and property owners (for example, see Marzulla 1998; Sutton 1999; or Sterling 2000), American Heritage River planning in the watershed of the New River does not support this view.

At least in the New River Valley, the American Heritage River planning process lived up to the promise of being a grassroots effort. Although the planning district commission directed the process and one of its staff facilitated committee meetings, volunteer participants were the source of all project ideas. There was no federal presence except at the later meetings, when Mr. Ben Borda, a career Army Corps of Engineers employee based in Huntington, West Virginia, was in attendance. His presence was low-key and nondirective, and had no influence on the types of projects being promoted. The planning process was in part supported by federal funds from the US Forest Service and the Environmental Protection Agency, yet they had virtually no influence on the substance of the work plan.

The diversity of projects included in the work plan reveals the grassroots nature of the process. The projects do not reflect a shared vision for the region, but rather the contradictory impulses shared, no doubt, by many Americans: the desire for more development and prosperity, together with a reluctance to change livelihoods, lifestyles, and the cultural landscape. While the planning process had the potential to nurture a discourse about how to bring about continued economic development while at the same time preserving traditions, nature, and the cultural landscape, that discourse did not happen, at least in the New River Valley.

The lack of implementing institutions reflects the grassroots nature of the planning process. Those who proposed the work plan's projects also implemented them. It is noteworthy that although state or federal agencies may have had personnel who participated in the meetings, they did not implement them. A project's inclusion in the work plan is no guarantee that funds will be made available for it, or that it will actually happen. That depends on the tenacity and skill of its proponents.

The grassroots planning approach exemplified by the New River American Heritage River Initiative is consistent with what Goldfarb (1994) describes as "an emerging body of institutional theory" supporting a consensus-driven decision-making process for watershed planning and management. Such a consensus-driven process would be "participatory," "flexible," "responsive," and "bottom-up" rather than "universal," "standardized," and "top-down," and "existing institutions should be used wherever possible" (Goldfarb 1994, 498). Still, it is difficult to see how only existing institutions (state agencies, regional planning districts, and local governments) can do more than try to protect and advance their own parochial interests. Of the 327 projects listed in the NRCP work plan, only a handful address problems or needs common to the watershed as a whole (NRCP 1999). Given that no new authority has been created and no new federal money has been authorized or appropriated for the American Heritage Rivers program, its impact on the communities in the watersheds of designated rivers is likely to be modest at best. The process so far has done little to foster a unified vision for the future of the region defined by the watershed.

References

Black, Peter E. 1987. *Conservation of Water and Related Land Resources.* Totowa, NJ: Rowman and Littlefield.

Chandler, William U. 1984. *The Myth of TVA: Conservation and Development in the Tennessee Valley, 1933–1983.* Cambridge, MA: Ballinger Publishing Company.

Clark, Ray. 1998. American Heritage Rivers: A Community-Based Approach to Economic Development and Environmental Protection. In *The American Heritage Rivers Initia-*

tive: A Magnificent Idea or the Great Land/Power Grab? ed. G. C Landrith III, 13–24. Washington, DC: National Legal Center for the Public Interest.

Executive Office of the President. 1997a. *Federal Support of Community Efforts along American Heritage Rivers*. Office of the Press Secretary, the White House. Executive Order 13061, September 11, 1997.

———. 1997b. *Notice. American Heritage Rivers Initiative*. Description of American Heritage Rivers Initiative and Information on How Communities Nominate Their Rivers. Council on Environmental Quality (CEQ). 62 Federal Register 48860, September 17, 1997.

Goldfarb, William. 1994. Watershed Management: Slogan or Solution? *Environmental Affairs Quarterly* 21:483–509.

Marzulla, Roger J. 1998. AHRI: This Baby Bureaucractic Monster is Bad for Business, Undemocratic and Un-American. In *The American Heritage Rivers Initiative: A Magnificent Idea or the Great Land/Power Grab?* ed. G. C. Landrith III, 25–49. Washington, DC: National Legal Center for the Public Interest.

New River Community Partners. 1998. The New River: America's Heritage (brochure). Sparta, NC: New River Community Partners.

———. 1999. The American Heritage Rivers New River Work Plan. Sparta, NC: New River Community Partners.

———. 2001. State of the River 2001. Sparta, NC: New River Community Partners.

Newson, Malcolm. 1992. *Land, Water and Development: River Basin Systems and Their Sustainable Management*. London: Routledge.

Roanoke Times. 1995. Goodlatte Immersed in Controversial Legislation. *Roanoke Times*, March 12, 1995.

Sterling, John A. 2000. Above the Law: Evolution of Executive Orders (part two). *University of West Los Angeles Law Review* 31:123.

Sutton, Victoria V. 1999. Have We Sold the Environment Down the River? *South Carolina Environmental Law Journal* 8 (Summer): 39.

U.S. Environmental Protection Agency. 2001. State of the River Report, http://www.epa.gov/rivers/publications.html.

U.S. Environmental Protection Agency. 2002. Annual Report, Rivers Uniting Communities, Successes of Community Partners of the American Heritage Rivers Initiative, http://www.epa.gov/rivers/publications.html.

Walker, Melissa. 1998. African Americans and TVA Reservoir Property Removal: Race in a New Deal Program. *Agricultural History* 72 (2): 417–29.

V

QUO VADIS?

SEVENTEEN

Pittsburgh and the Creative Age

Richard Florida

Pittsburgh's economic transition from a smokestack to a service economy is nothing less than remarkable. Characterizations of the city underscore its gritty industrial past, from unearthly descriptions of its nineteenth-century furnaces lighting up the night sky to stories about schoolchildren having to change their clothes twice a day to rid themselves of soot. In the new millennium, however, Pittsburgh's leading employer is the University of Pittsburgh, specifically, its chain of medical and teaching hospitals and research and development complexes related to the health sciences. Carnegie Mellon University also provides a significant edge in high-tech and related fields.

This chapter highlights what I call the "creative economy," which took root in the United States in the 1980s and 1990s. I identify the attributes of place that fuel this transition (see Florida 2002, 2004) and examine Pittsburgh's relative position among several indicators of regional performance. I argue that Pittsburgh's rich history in providing safe haven, work, and housing for European immigrants and African Americans needs to be reinvigorated so that a new wave of new residents find the city a worthwhile place to live and work. Changes in the city's university district (Oakland) and recreational facilities are necessary if Pittsburgh wishes to be a national leader in the new economy.

The Rise of the Creative Economy and the Creative Class

The changes the US economy is going through are much larger and more enduring than the set of technology shifts that we call the Internet, or even the so-called new economy. What is really new about our economy and our society is much bigger than technology, high-tech industries, or technology-based clusters; it's bigger than the ups and downs of the NASDAQ or the latest gyrations of the stock market, or the latest technology fads, whatever they may be—optic electronics or a wireless world.

Scholars and the public are bogged down in a debate that fails to get at the fundamental cornerstone of this issue. On one side of the debate are the techno-utopians. They claim that technology and the new economy will change everything. Workers, they contend, will be free from the constraints of long commutes and from the demands of overbearing government. In fact, America's workforce will be free from the constraints of a workplace. They could not be more wrong.

On the other side, we have witnessed the rise of a whole set of techno-pessimists, who discuss the age of access or the white-collar sweatshop or the way in which technology is causing us all to toil longer, harder, and be more exploited and oppressed than ever before. Inherent in this idea is the notion that somehow the decline of the stock market and of technology stocks will force us all back to work in even more oppressive conditions.

I contend that this debate is largely unfounded. Rather, I argue that we are going through a long-term, enduring set of changes in the way we live, work, and build communities. These are not necessarily even associated with the new economy, although the economic shifts of the early 2000s pushed them to the fore and accelerated their visibility. Nonetheless, those changes have been going on since perhaps the 1970s. This change is not just about technology, and not even about new technological developments. It is a move from a company-centered economy to a people-driven economy.

In the old economy, companies directed the nature of work in a comprehensive fashion. One attached oneself to a company and would remain for many years with the same one, often in the same house in the same community. Today, we live in an economy that is people driven. Cities of significant economic and demographic growth thrive because they are places where people want to live (Jacobs 1961). Phoenix, for instance, began growing in the 1950s and 1960s as a retirement center and now New Yorkers choose it as a place to live and work because they enjoy the lifestyle.

The people-driven economy is not a panacea. The flip side is that in addition to having more freedom and choice, individuals also bear more risk. Many information and technical workers are essentially on their own, with little in the way of company or social supports. As the economy turns down, we are seeing the disadvantages of bearing this risk.

The key to understanding this shift lies in two factors. First is the rise of creativity as the fundamental source of economic value. In everything we do, creativity has come to be the underlying source of economic growth. Second, the rise of creativity as an economic force has brought a new social class to the fore—the creative class. It has grown from roughly 5 percent of the workforce in 1990 to more than 30 percent today. With 38 million people, it is larger in numbers than the industrial working class and has emerged as the dominant norm-setting class of our time.

The New Era of Economic Development

The rise of creativity as the fundamental source of economic value and the rise of the new creative class has deep implications for economic development and for public policy. For economic developers or those of us who care about the future of regions, the question becomes very simple. People, or their talents, are the key factor of production in this new system. They are what matter. Economic growth, thus, will be shaped much more in the future by the distribution of people or talent than by the distribution of firms.

Conventional economic development indicators touted the number of corporate headquarters in a city. Pittsburgh has more corporate headquarters than Phoenix, but the latter is growing about nine or ten times faster than Pittsburgh. Why? The answer is that Phoenix is attracting people who attract companies. So the key economic development question is this: How do you develop, attract, and retain the talent that you have and that you can bring in from the outside? The question is important because we now know that economic growth will be shaped much more in the future by the distribution of talent than by the distribution of firms.

At the 1999 annual meeting of the National Governors Association in Washington DC, Carly Fiorina, then the CEO and president of Hewlett-Packard, spoke about the very core of the new economy. In so many words, she said:

> We don't need any more tax incentives. We don't need any more big incentive packages. We don't even need highway interchanges. Of course, in some instances, we'll take them. We will go where the highly skilled people are. If you have the people, we will come to your jurisdiction. If you don't have the people, we can't come no matter how much money you want to pile up and shove in front of us. We will go where the highly skilled people are.

Those remarks underscore the nature of the shift and underscore that the new economy is much bigger than technology; it has to do with what we want and the way we live today. The shift from a company-centered to a people-driven economy manifests itself in two fundamental dimensions of life: work and place

The No-Collar Workplace

The workplace is being radically transformed. In the mid-twentieth century, the workday used to run from nine to five. Now the workday is 24/7. Americans work from home, and we play at work. Many workplaces have a gym, a café, and showers. Men do not necessarily wear ties anymore. It is remarkable how the dress code of workplaces has changed. On a recent visit to the offices of Pittsburgh's leading securities law firm I found myself in one of the conservative institutions on earth wearing blue jeans and a polo shirt. Concerned, I asked my hosts, "Will I be embarrassed?" They said "No, everybody here dresses like this." Indeed, in nearly every high-tech company the dress code is casual. As the former provost of my university said when he visited a high-tech spin-off, "This looks more like a graduate seminar than an office." Firms are responding to this new workplace. Goldman Sachs, for instance, is building a new corporate headquarters across the river from Manhattan, a large state-of-the-art facility that will be devoted to providing all of the working, playing, and learning amenities that its workforce desires so that it can attract the people it needs.

Peter Drucker said it best: "You can't bribe knowledge workers" (Drucker 1999). Knowledge workers are not only motivated by money and stock, they want to make a difference, to be challenged, to participate, to do great work, and to work around great people. In the old system you traded time for money. Our parents worked nine to five every day and overtime on Saturdays to make a great way of life for their families and their children. The current generation of knowledge workers, aged roughly twenty-one to forty, trades time for money, but they also have the freedom to choose what they want to do. In short, we trade time and money for the autonomy to do what we love.

What Do People Want?

What do people want in a job? They want the ability to design their own work, to work flexibly and to blur the boundaries between life and work, and to be themselves in the workplace. They do not want to be a different person at home than at work. In two surveys—one 1999 survey taken at the height of the new economy stock boom and one taken in February 2000, when the market headed downward—what respondents said they wanted in a workplace was the same: challenge and responsibility in the workplace, flexibility, job stability, base pay rather than stock options, and the ability to express themselves in their schedules and their dress.

One example, perhaps quite anecdotal, comes from when I taught at

Carnegie Mellon University, which produces some of the best and the brightest. Microsoft is the number one recruiter of Carnegie Mellon students and many graduates go on to work at Oracle and Intel. Most of the top technical staff at Microsoft consists of my former colleagues. My former colleagues are the top technical staff at Red Hat, and my former colleagues formed Sun Microsystems. They are in major capital venture firms. Carnegie Mellon lost many faculty members to start-up companies. So, what do high-tech firms do to go after our students?

In spring of 2000, I walked out of my office, going to the faculty club with an older colleague, and I came across a round table where everybody was dressed a bit more casually. There were three young women at the table who had T-shirts that said "Trilogy at CMU." There was a guy at the table with spiked hair, "full metal," and many visible tattoos. When I asked him what he was doing, he said he was going to work for Trilogy. When I asked why, he said, "because they're a great company with great people, and they're in Austin, Texas—where I really want to live."

I discovered later from my colleagues that he was a top student and a highly paid recruit. One of the senior recruiters from the company told me: "He's a rock star." That's how important his talent was. "He's a rock star, and we treat him like an athlete or a rock star, and we want him to work here. And you know what? When General Motors or General Electric come down and ask who's going to work on their project, we wheel him out, because we show them the really cool guy that we've got to work on their project."

The Place of Place

What do people want in terms of a community? If people are the key factors of production, if they attract companies and build wealth, and if a region's future will be decided more by its ability to attract people than to attract firms, then this is an important question. I argue that place has replaced company as the fundamental organizing unit in our economy.

New economy pundits like George Gilder (2000) or Kevin Kelly (1998) would tell us that in this great wireless world of the Internet, place is irrelevant: people can choose to live anywhere as long as they have a hookup to the Internet. They could not be more wrong. The world of the new economy makes place much more important than it ever was before, because people can choose to move, and they want to choose nice places to live with other exciting people, interesting things to do, and lots of amenities.

Companies locate near their raw materials and their markets. Pittsburgh's growth historically benefited from the resource endowments of coal and a network of rivers to float heavy materials along to steel plants. Industrial companies located around these raw materials and good transportation. These ingredients for industrial location made perfect economic sense.

But people differ from iron, ore, and coal: people can move. Companies chase talented workers, and talented workers chase companies, and the chase goes on. Companies cannot just locate and expect new economy workers to come anymore. They have to locate where workers are and where workers want to be. Therefore, companies have to attract people, and people attract companies. It works both ways.

Most econometric models that predict regional growth show that the ability to attract human capital and into a higher stock of human capital is always a significant indicator. Going back to the year 1900, one can predict regional growth by the percentage of highly educated or knowledgeable or high human capital people.

My research shows that new workers do not move just for a job anymore. Instead, they move for lots of jobs. In other words, we move not for a job with one company, we move to regions that have lots of jobs, or a "thick" labor market. This explains the attractiveness of technology meccas like the San Francisco Bay area; Seattle; Austin, Texas; or even Washington DC.

People understand that temporary attachments between people and companies are the realities of the new labor market. They will not work for a company for life, in most cases. They will move up by moving on. Moreover, they opt to be situated in a labor market that is thick with opportunities so that when the first job or second job ends, they can have another job without having to uproot their entire family. The first thing creative people want is thick labor markets.

The second feature is that place has become an important demarcation of status in people's lives. In the old days you could say, "I work for GE," "I work for AT&T," "I work for IBM," "I work for BMW," "I work for Mercedes-Benz," "I work for Toyota," and the company you worked for provided status. You could take an assignment in a not-so-great place yet feel compensated by the quality of the firm for which you worked.

Place is an important part of people's status in the new American labor force. A lot of why particularly young talented people move is because they want to live in a cool place with other interesting people looking for status as well as income level. People crave lifestyle amenities. Sunshine is great, and they want to climb rocks, ride bikes, see sporting events, go to the theater, and go out at night. Places that will grow and attract firms have to have these features. Not just three of them, all of them. Part of this preference for active outdoor recreation is directly linked to the way people work. If you're sitting behind a terminal for twelve to sixteen hours a day, you need to be able to go out and ride your bike, go careening down a mountain at noon, or climb a rock, because you can't think about what you're working on when you are up there on that rock.

This need for active outdoor recreation, interspersed with the workday, is very much related to the changing nature of work in America. People want to be around creativity and be around creative energy. David Brooks argues in his 2001 book *Bobos in Paradise* that the nature of our culture is changing. We used to have this strict distinction between the bourgeois, conservative working person or executive, and the Bohemian. Bohemians rejected the middle class and the formal corporate world. Brooks, however, essentially says this: "We're all Bobos now. We're all Bourgeois-Bohemians. You cannot tell the espresso-sipping professor from the cappuccino-gulping banker."

Our culture is fusing these two separate categories. One of our best predictors of what regions will grow and what regions will not is the Bohemian Index. The ability of a region to attract high-technology industry is directly correlated to its ability to attract and nurture a creative arts and music community.

People want diversity. Talented people come in all shapes and sizes, races, ethnicities, backgrounds, genders, and sexual orientations. Talented people want to know that the communities they live in reflect and support that diversity. Another great predictor of high-technology growth is the so-called Gay Index. Places that are open to different kinds of people and can support and nurture a gay community are the kinds of places that are open to everyone and anyone. These places prosper in ways unheard of decades earlier, when manufacturing mostly drove the American economy.

Quality of Place

People want places with unique and authentic character. What makes quality of place? I give it three dimensions: what's there—the combination of the built and natural environment; who's there—the diversity of people, the visual cues that anyone can fit in and make a life in that community; and what's going on—the vibrancy of street life, cafe culture, arts and music, and people engaging in outdoor activities.

Paul Allen's work is a good example about how the quality of place is intrinsically tied to the new economy and economic development. Allen is the second or third richest man in the world, cofounder of Microsoft, and one of the builders of the new wireless technology future. He owns the sports teams in Seattle and financed a museum dedicated to the memory of Jimi Hendrix called the Experience Music Project. It is devoted to using popular music culture and the legacy of rock music to engage young people in technology by combining music and technology. Paul Allen is investing in developments around these experience learning centers.

Another example comes from Kirk Watson, the former mayor of Austin who won his last reelection with 84 percent of the vote. He claims that Austin benefits from a convergence between technology and lifestyle (Bishop 2000). Austin made big investments in attracting the Intels and Motorolas of the world. Local and state governments invested in building up the University of Texas with federal grants for Mobile Computing Corporation and Sematech and also poured money into its computer science and electrical engineering programs. Spin-off firms, too, have been important. Witness, for instance, Dell Computer, born in Michael Dell's fraternity room when he dropped out of school, and Trilogy, the Austin-based software company.

Those factors alone would not be enough to make Austin what it is today. Austin residents were also supporting *Austin City Limits* and the Sixth Street music scene. This transformation made it the kind of place that Willie Nelson and singer-songwriters want to locate in. When you jog on the path in Austin, you see a statue not of some Austin political figure, but of Stevie Ray Vaughan, the guitar player. The South-by-Southwest Music and Film Festival has been a powerful marketing tool that says "Austin is the kind of place that's with it, that gets it, that you want to live in." Mayor Watson was fond of saying: "We benefited from a convergence between technology and lifestyle that put us on the map. It's not one; it's not the other. They both work together."

The Three Ts of Economic Development

The three Ts of economic development are technology, talent, and tolerance. Cities have to promote first-class technology. This means aggressively attracting talent. To have a creative economy, places have to be tolerant, open, and diverse. The top-ranked cities in terms of location and growth of high technology score top marks on all three: they are San Francisco, Boston, Austin, Seattle, and Washington DC. Doing any one T is not enough; each T is a necessary but an insufficient condition for success.

Pittsburgh is a premier creator of technology. The region has created technology that drives more regional growth across the United States and the world than probably any other region. Its college graduates are a top source of talent for Seattle and Austin, and even Silicon Valley. But it is not as open and diverse as it could be. It has had low rates of immigration and does not offer the creative diversity members of the creative class are looking for.

Openness to enterprising people from around the world has always been a pillar of the Pittsburgh spirit. The region was built by immigrants—the hard-working Italians, Irish, East Europeans, Jews, African Americans, and other groups that powered this region's path to greatness as a center for heavy industry. Building a thriving new economy in the region today will require a similar commitment to openness and diversity across all segments of the population.

A look at the nation's leading high-tech centers is revealing: They are places where people from virtually any background can settle. The growth and development of great cities comes from their ability to harness diversity, welcome newcomers, and turn their energy and ideas into innovations and wealth. In Silicon Valley, the world's leading high-tech center, nearly a quarter of the population is foreign born. Furthermore, almost one-third of the valley's high-tech scientists and engineers hail from foreign countries.

The Milken Institute identifies immigration as one of the two most powerful demographic trends reshaping the nation's cities and regions. Its list of "Melting Pot Metros" ranks the most diverse regions in the country (Frey and DeVol 2000). Sure enough, highly ranked regions in California and Texas, as well as Chicago, New York City, and the Washington DC area are also hot spots of economic growth. Once a haven for immigrants, Pittsburgh did not make the top twenty-one cities on the Melting Pot Metros list.

From Andrew Carnegie in steel to Andy Grove in semiconductors, immigrants have been a powerful source of innovation and entrepreneurship (Florida 2000a). Roughly one-quarter of new Silicon Valley businesses established since 1980 had a Chinese or India-born founder, according to a 1999 study by Annalee Saxenian. That figure has increased to more than 30 percent since 1995. Pittsburgh's own high-tech community also draws heavily from foreign-born entrepreneurs and technologists. My own analysis of regions with more than 700,000 people highlights the striking connection between diversity and high-tech industry (Florida 2002, 2005).

High-tech industry and talent are drawn to places where people can easily fit in regardless of race, ethnicity, gender, sexual orientation, or appearance. The ability to develop high-tech industry is closely related to openness to newcomers—specifically foreign-born scientists and engineers.

In a separate study, Florida and Gates (2001) examined the relationship between high-tech industry and a group that has traditionally been subject to considerable discrimination and ostracism—the gay population. Six of the top ten high-tech cities also number among the top ten gay cities: Seattle, Boston, Washington DC, Atlanta, San Francisco, and Los Angeles. This "gay concentration index" predicts the location of high-tech firms and workers better than any other factor.

This close relationship between tolerance and high-tech industry is not because gay people in and of themselves attract technology companies.

Rather, a place that is a comfortable home to the gay community is likely to be open to all types of people. The key to growth in the new economy is to be open and have low entry barriers for human capital.

How Does Pittsburgh Stack Up?

I now offer a quick overview of how the greater Pittsburgh region stacks up on my indicators. These are ranked on the basis of the top forty-nine largest metropolitan regions across the United States; those with populations of one million and over and for all regions for which data are available (table 17.1).

Technology

Given its background as an industrial age center, Pittsburgh does very well on the first T, technology. It is among the highest ranked of any older industrial region, ranking 22nd of the 49 largest regions and 31st of all regions on the Milken Institute's Tech-Pole Index in 2000. With 34.2 patents per 10,000 people, Pittsburgh ranked 22nd of large regions and 50th among all regions on my Innovation Index (measured as patents per 1,000 people) in 1999.

Talent

The Pittsburgh region also does reasonably well on aggregate measures of talent, the second T. With 30.2 percent of its working population in creative occupations in 1999, Pittsburgh ranked 22nd of large regions and 53rd of all regions on this basic measure of the creative class. Pittsburgh had 322,000 creative class workers as of 1999. With 21.2 percent of its population holding a bachelor's or more advanced degree in 1990, Pittsburgh ranked 36th of large regions and 87th of all regions on the basic Talent Index, defined as the percent of the population with a bachelor's degree and above.

Tolerance

The Pittsburgh region does less well on tolerance, the third T. With a foreign-born population of 3.3 percent, it ranks 39th of large regions on the Melting Pot Index and 112th overall. This compares to more than 20 percent for leading regions. On the Bohemian Index (a measure of artists, musicians, and performers) Pittsburgh ranks 44th, 102nd of all regions. Finally, Pittsburgh ranks next to last—48th of 49—of large regions and 201st of all regions on the Gay Index; and last of large regions and 193rd of all regions on the percentage of people in interracial marriages. To improve its position in the race to attract high-tech industry, the region must improve its performance on diversity.

TABLE 17.1. Creativity Index

Rank	*Region*	*Creativity Index*	*Overall Rank*	*Creative Class*	*High Tech*	*Innovation*	*Diversity*
1	San Francisco	1057	1	12	1	5	1
2	Austin	1028	2	7	13	6	23
3	Boston	1015	3	6	2	12	41
3	San Diego	1015	3	30	14	13	4
5	Seattle	1008	5	20	3	34	11
6	Raleigh/Durham	996	6	5	16	8	52
7	Houston	980	7	22	19	39	16
8	Washington DC	964	9	4	5	85	18
9	New York	962	10	25	15	54	20
10	Minneapolis	960	11	14	28	11	60
10	Dallas	960	11	55	6	40	15
12	Los Angeles	942	13	46	4	79	5
14	Atlanta	940	14	32	7	87	10
14	Denver	940	14	17	65	29	25
15	Chicago	935	16	29	10	56	46
16	Portland, OR	929	18	73	11	32	31
17	Philadelphia	927	19	27	17	36	70
18	Hartford, CT	922	21	16	41	35	61
19	Phoenix	909	22	92	8	46	21
20	Indianapolis	891	24	68	20	55	42
21	Rochester, NY	877	25	34	51	4	115
22	Sacramento	872	26	40	26	103	34
23	West Palm Beach/ Boca Raton	852	32	123	40	44	17
24	Columbus, OH	832	33	70	48	102	24
25	Kansas City	818	35	24	25	135	73
26	Tampa/ St. Petersburg	804	38	76	42	128	26
27	Salt Lake City	798	41	139	35	45	59
28	Charlotte, NC	787	42	69	46	124	51
29	Miami	775	43	99	62	138	2
30	Cleveland	774	44	71	57	42	134
31	St. Louis	770	45	57	24	76	153
32	Orlando	752	49	108	43	164	9
33	Cincinnati	742	52	119	50	23	141
34	San Antonio	737	55	84	34	126	93
35	Milwaukee	736	56	111	61	38	128
36	Pittsburgh	734	57	53	31	50	210
37	Jacksonville, FL	715	64	50	95	168	47
38	Nashville	711	66	79	70	171	45
39	Detroit	708	68	42	147	27	150
40	Providence, RI	698	70	120	80	108	71

continued

TABLE 17.1. Creativity Index, *continued*

Rank	*Region*	*Creativity Index*	*Overall Rank*	*Creative Class*	*High Tech*	*Innovation*	*Diversity*
41	Greensboro, NC	697	71	128	53	119	78
42	Oklahoma City	668	83	72	72	150	113
42	New Orleans	668	83	122	87	180	19
44	Grand Rapids, MI	639	95	197	76	52	110
45	Louisville	622	100	150	91	131	83
46	Buffalo	609	105	83	71	73	240
47	Las Vegas	561	117	257	74	178	8
48	Norfolk/ Virginia Beach, VA	555	120	97	60	200	162
49	Memphis	530	132	184	100	141	119

Source: http://www.creativeclass.org/regall.shtml. Copyright ©2003 / Richard Florida Creativity Group.

Discussion

From its industrial buildings and glorious housing stock to its ethnic neighborhoods, Pittsburgh has an authenticity that is a tremendous advantage in the new economy. Instead of uprooting its history and creating the generic features associated with malls throughout the country, public and private leaders should focus on preserving the legacy of old buildings, such as those in the Strip District, Lawrenceville, the South Side, and Downtown. The region's historic architecture and building design is perfect for conversion into tech spaces, technology incubators, and lofts, as the case of the Strip District makes clear. (See chapter 5 in this volume.)

High-tech places are built around universities that create knowledge, generate new ideas, incubate fledging companies, and act as talent magnets. If our region is serious about engaging the new high-tech economy, we need to take our university neighborhood seriously and start investing in it. Oakland is home to 35,000 students and the workplace for 100,000-plus knowledge workers. As a technology incubator and talent generator, it may well be the most strategically important area of the entire region.

Oakland, however, is a tired neighborhood that has been neglected for years. In the words of a young University of Pittsburgh student with whom I spoke: "I love the university, but Oakland is a hole." After spending four years in Oakland, it is little wonder that students want to leave when they graduate.

A central part of revitalizing Oakland is creating a more connected city. Oakland is isolated. In fact, many of the region's neighborhoods are isolated.

Part of this is inherent in Pittsburgh's topography. But there once was an extensive system of trolleys and buses to connect the city. Urban renewal has done much to disconnect neighborhoods by putting giant barriers in the form of stadiums, big box stores, circles, and parking garages between them.

In all of our focus groups and interviews, the participants expressed that the city and region needed to be more connected. Students, young professionals, and seniors expressed a preference for a subway, a light-rail system, or a more user-friendly, round-the-clock bus system, with dedicated routes connecting Oakland to other parts of the city.

With universities and a burgeoning high-tech community, authenticity, glorious rivers and topography, and a stunning built environment, Pittsburgh is poised for success in the creative age. Instead of dismissing these unique assets in a quest to be more like everywhere else, we must recognize that they are the source of real and long-lasting advantage in the new economy (Florida 2000b).

Talent, tolerance, and diversity are powerful forces in the value systems and choices of the creative class, whose members want to work for companies and live in communities that reflect their openness. The primary factor in choosing a place to live and work, these people say, is diversity. Talented people simply will not locate in places that ostracize segments of the population.

While the perception may be worse than the reality, the people in focus groups I have conducted feel that Pittsburgh is not open to minority groups, new immigrants, and gay people. Young women also say that there are substantial barriers in the way of their advancement. Talented members of racial and ethnic minorities express their desire to leave the city at a rate far greater than their white male counterparts. To compete and prosper in the creative era the region will need to become more open to diversity.

The Pittsburgh region has many resources from which to draw. World-class universities, cutting-edge research and development, and a burgeoning corps of high-tech companies position this region for a prosperous future. The region is working hard to attract young, talented people. Most important, it possesses a proud legacy of driven, hard-working immigrants building industries, neighborhoods, and the American dream. To ensure success, Pittsburgh must build on the diverse heritage of its past to engender an even more prosperous future.

References

Bishop, Bill. 2000. Havens for Artists Attract High Tech, Industry, Index Shows. *Austin American Statesman*, June 11.

Brooks, David. 2001. *Bobos in Paradise: The New Upper Class and How They Got There.* New York: Simon and Schuster.

Drucker, Peter. 1999. Beyond the Information Revolution. *Atlantic Monthly,* October 4, 47–57.

Florida, Richard. 2000a. Forum: Pittsburgh's Prosperity Depends on Diversity. *Pittsburgh Post-Gazette,* October 15.

———. 2000b. Pittsburgh, Let's Wake Up and Play. *Pittsburgh Post-Gazette,* June 11.

———. 2002. *The Rise of the Creative Class: And How It's Transforming Work, Leisure, Community and Everyday Life.* New York: Basic Books.

———. 2004. *Cities and the Creative Class.* New York: Routledge.

———. 2005. *The Flight of the Creative Class.* New York: Harper Business.

Florida, Richard, and Gary Gates. 2001. *Technology and Tolerance: The Importance of Diversity to High-Technology Growth.* Brookings Institution.

Frey, William, and Ross DeVol. 2000. America's Demography in the New Century: Aging Baby Boomers and New Immigrants as Major Players. Policy Brief no. 9. Santa Monica, CA: Milken Institute.

Gilder, George. 2000. *Telecosm: How Infinite Bandwidth Will Revolutionize Our World.* New York: Free Press.

Jacobs, Jane. 1961. *The Death and Life of Great American Cities.* New York: Random House.

Kelly, Kevin. 1998. *New Rules for the New Economy: 10 Radical Strategies for a Connected World.* New York: Viking.

Saxenian, Annalee. 1999. *Silicon Valley's New Immigrant Entrepreneurs.* Berkeley: Public Policy Institute of California.

EIGHTEEN

What Will the New Millennium Bring?

Joseph L. Scarpaci

When Louis Wirth coined the phrase "way of life" in 1938 he aimed to capture the unique features of a rapidly urbanizing America. The nation had surpassed the 50 percent urban mark only two censuses before in 1920. Essential in his conceptualization of urbanism was the idea that city living contrasted sharply with the traditional image of agrarian life. Still, there were strong ties to the countryside, in what geographers call the "hinterland." Fast-forward (a term that did not exist in Wirth's day) nearly seventy years and those city-rural linkages have blurred.

No longer do the raw materials from the countryside supply just the city center and no longer does the city exist mainly to service those small towns, suburbs, and exurban places beyond its borders (Hadden and Borgatta 1965, 3). Pittsburgh fits that characterization, as the pages in this book make plain. As far back as 1965, urbanists were arguing that "it would be difficult today to find an American metropolis in which the governmental system is in imminent danger of breakdown" (Bollens and Schmandt 1965, 330). Such optimistic assessments are rare today. Pittsburgh's near bankruptcy and quest to tap into suburban incomes and taxes mirror the problems facing many US cities. Suburbanization, deindustrialization, and a rural America that is better integrated with the rest of the nation beckon with new ways that change the relationship between town and country. Pittsburgh and the Appalachians experience that change in ways that have not always been harmonious, but the pattern is clear: An industrial heritage has left Pittsburgh with unique neighborhoods, a talented labor force, and a hinterland that has capitalized on new retailing and tourism to offset the demise of milling and mining.

The uneven economic and population growth across Pittsburgh and the Appalachians tests the limits of regional planning and public-private partnerships. If regional planning was born at the end of World War II, it is fair to say that it peaked in the 1950s and 1960s to accommodate the baby boom. Since World War II, the heart of such planning was to address suburban growth management, to ameliorate the negative aesthetic impact of industry, and to reuse deindustrialized sites located near urban cores. National trends such as these are visible in Pittsburgh's Renaissance projects, downtown revitalization, North Shore and Strip District developments, and convention centers. However, Pittsburgh's revitalization projects will require a reinvigorated tax base, even if the outlook for Appalachia will continue to witness the smaller projects that characterized the Tennessee Valley Authority and the Appalachian Regional Commission. Grand strategies may be absent, as suggested by the distinguished planner David Loeks's forecast that "regional planners may be spending much more of their time on fiscal issues than previously" (1997, 297).

The political climate in the first years of the new millennium indicates very little tolerance for public programs and planning that reallocate resources or use income-distribution schema. John Levy calls this ethos "planning from the right," and it generally assumes that the market is a more efficient resource allocator than is government. It also embraces the idea that private decisions about resource allocation (investment, development, construction) are more conducive to supporting political freedom than are public investments. To the contrary, the left sees town and country planning agencies as implementers of capitalist interests, regardless of the disparities and injustices such decisions invoke. Ultimately, the left views planning as relatively powerless and capable of implementing only palliative and insignificant reforms (Levy 1997, 334–39). Where, then, do the spread of Internet technology in Appalachia, the stadium location debacle on the North Side, the provision of affordable housing in Chatham Village, or other examples in this book lie on this right-left continuum? The answers, no doubt, are subject to the reader's ideological and political stance about the roles of markets and planning.

Pittsburgh and Appalachia's recent history exemplifies how cities and regions have been wounded. While their injuries pale compared with human disasters (civil wars, terrorist attacks) and natural ones (earthquakes, tsunamis), they are perpetually caught up in cycles of degeneration and renewal (Schneider and Susser 2003). The postindustrial era riddles the city and region with problems that undermine quality of life. Overcoming those troubles will require more than attracting corporate investment in the city or hinter-

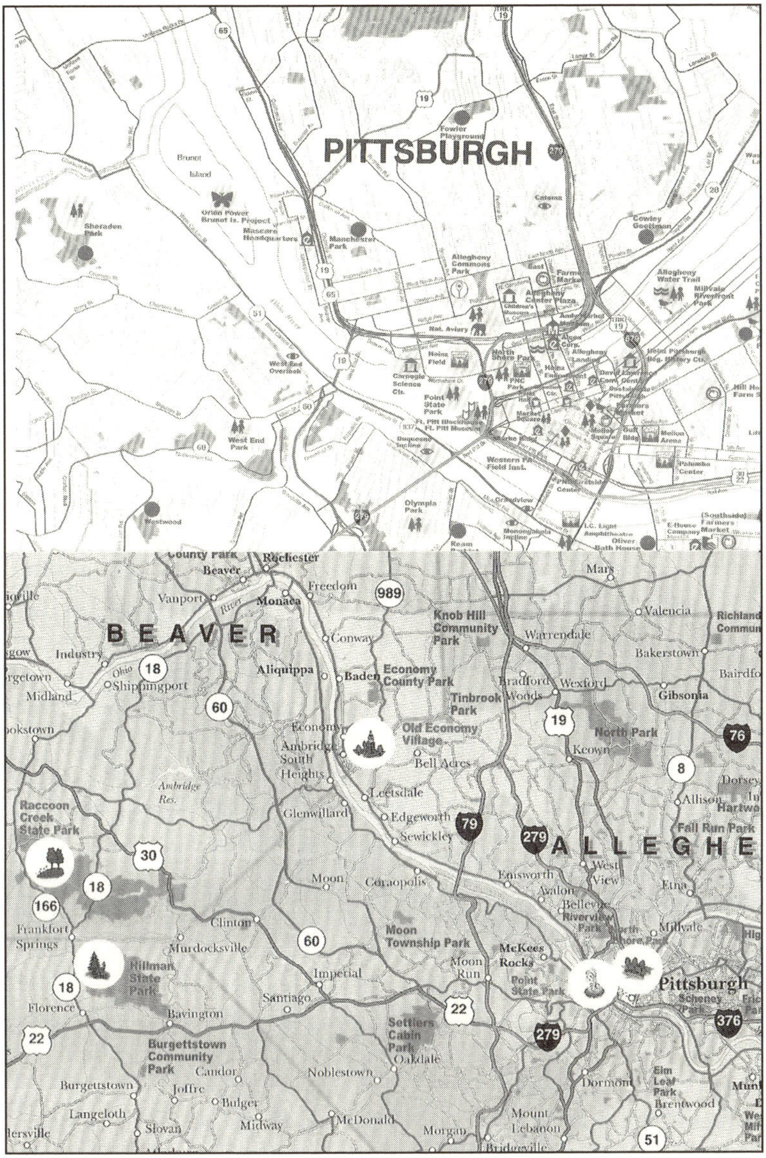

FIG. 18.1. Map from greenpittsburgh.net. **Courtesy of 3 Rivers Connect, www.3rc.org.**

land. Mom-and-pop businesses in such diverse sectors as Grove City retailing or West Virginia whitewater rafting promise some relief at the local level to problems of underinvestment. Global companies may pounce on fiscally strapped cities and regions with the promise of reviving the local economy. Privatizing public services and showcasing special places could offer isolated instances of reviving this postindustrial region. As the chapters in this book show, there are no magical formulas for harvesting the cultural and natural resources in Pittsburgh and Appalachia.

A dose of skepticism may be necessary in forecasting the future of any region. Urban historian Samuel P. Hays argues that the environmental affairs of Pittsburgh and the Appalachians have been redirected to accommodate workers in the "new technology": computers, electronics, and informatics. Recreational resources such as hiking and biking, rails-to-trails projects, and land acquisitions spearheaded by the Western Pennsylvania Conservancy have safeguarded lands along the Youghiogheny River and in the Laurel Highlands. Pittsburgh's Technology Council helped to produce a Green Map (figure 18.1) that touts the green areas of the city and region. As Richard Florida argued in the previous chapter, these are the features required to bolster the city's talent index and, in turn, forge linkages with the Appalachians. Google's recent announcement that it will open a local office in Panther Hollow (located in the Oakland district of Pittsburgh) and partner with Carnegie Mellon University underscores the city's cultural and natural resources. Google's engineering director made the decision to open a Pittsburgh outpost after he discovered that CMU graduates and researchers were reluctant to leave Pittsburgh: "'The response [always] was, "I really like living in Pittsburgh,"' he said. 'If we were gonna hire these people, we'd have to open an office here'" (Shropshire 2005). Hays, however, suggests the Technology Council's Green Map project is "another significant example of the desire of Pittsburgh leaders to 'celebrate' a grossly exaggerated environmental presence amid an exceptionally weak record of environmental performance" (Hays 2003, 214–15).

This book has provided a guided tour of the challenges, opportunities, failures, and renewals that the city and region have experienced over the past century or so. The seminal events, projects, and political decisions outlined here should not be perceived as exclusively elite-driven ones. Myriad small actors—ordinary citizens, small entrepreneurs, nonprofit organizations, and neighborhood groups—have carried the region to where it is today. Pittsburgh and the Appalachians are perched at a crucial crossroads with sufficient natural and cultural resources to reinvent themselves yet again in creative and thoughtful ways.

References

Bollens, J. C., and H. J. Schmandt. 1965. *The Metropolis: Its People, Politics, and Economic Life.* New York and London: Harper and Row.

Hadden, J. K., and E. F. Borgatta. 1965. *American Cities: Their Social Characteristics.* Chicago: Rand McNally and Company.

Hays, S. P. 2003. Beyond Celebration: Pittsburgh and Its Region in the Environmental Era—Notes by a Participant Observer. In *Devastation and Renewal: An Environmental History of Pittsburgh,* ed. J. A. Tarr, 193–215. Pittsburgh: University of Pittsburgh Press.

Levy, J. M. 1997. *Contemporary Urban Planning.* 4th ed. Upper Saddle River, NJ: Prentice Hall.

Loeks, C. D. 1997. Planning for Metropolitan Regions. In Levy 1997, 286–98.

Schneider, J., and I. Susser. 2003. *Wounded Cities.* New York: Berg

Shropshire, Corilyn. 2005. Google Coming Because Local Talent Likes It Here. *Pittsburgh Post-Gazette,* December 16.

INDEX